VISIONS AND VOCATIONS

VISIONS AND VOCATIONS

The Catholic Women Speak Network
Edited by Tina Beattie and Diana Culbertson

Paulist Press
New York / Mahwah, NJ

Cover image: background texture photo by nopparatz/depositphotos.com
Cover design by Sharyn Banks
Book design by Lynn Else

Library of Congress Control Number: 2018948413

ISBN 978-0-8091-5416-6 (paperback)
ISBN 978-1-58768-793-8 (e-book)

Published by Paulist Press
997 Macarthur Boulevard
Mahwah, New Jersey 07430

www.paulistpress.com

Printed and bound in the
United States of America

Contents

CONTENTS

Contents

CONTENTS

Contents

CONTENTS

Contents

Foreword

Am I Catholic Enough?

Catholic Women Speak (CWS)[1] *works in partnership with Voices of Faith (VoF)*[2] *in our shared endeavors to enhance the representation and participation of women in the Catholic Church. CWS operates primarily through social media to create spaces for theological education, awareness raising, dialogue, and pastoral support among women, while VoF focuses on the promotion of women's leadership. Several of the essays in this book originated as talks given at International Women's Day events in Rome organized by VoF. Here, Gayatri Lobo Gajiwala writes on behalf of VoF to welcome the publication of this book.*

Am I Catholic? Among my twentysomething friends I would probably shrug and say, "My mom's Catholic and my dad's Hindu, but I'm not particularly religious." Why is it so important for me to make that distinction? And why is it that more and more young people I know make it a point to publicly distance themselves from any organized religion into which they are born?

Partly, perhaps, because to us the word *religious* carries with it the yoke of intellectual servility, and we are the generation born in an age of information; how can we possibly follow blindly, no questions asked? The other reason that comes to mind is that we find it hard to sit quietly and let hate, prejudice, bigotry, and cruelty occur simply because this is the way things have always been. We may not go to Mass, but instead we volunteer our time, stage protests, rally people across the world through a single hashtag, and call out racism and sexism in the workplace, not because we are young and stupid, but because we are young and hopeful, and determined not to sit on the sidelines and let the world happen to us.

And that, when you think about it, is the heart of it. Are we leaving the Church, or are we living the Church? What does it really mean to be Catholic today?

This book sets out to explore that question in the context of women's lives, offering layered and nuanced perspectives of how women approach their relationship with God, religion, and living the gospel in today's world. I know that I struggled with my own identity as a baptized Catholic, as did most of my friends, feeling rejected by the Church for being too gay, or too opinionated, or too loud, and too full of questions that nobody wanted to answer. I rarely received communion, never feeling Catholic enough. It was easier to reject a church that clearly did not want me.

And then I found myself speaking at the Voices of Faith event on International Women's Day in Rome, not once but twice. I returned the second time, not just because the women I met there—strong, driven, exceptional—gave me role models I had never previously considered, but also because they shared a vision for the future of the Church I wanted to believe in. That change was possible, worth fighting for, and they were warriors who, unlike me, had not given up. The world around me was finally listening to long-silenced voices. And here, in the midst of these inspiring women, I realized, as a young, Catholic woman, I had something to say.

When Pope Francis announced that the theme for the 2018 Synod of Bishops would be "Young People, the Faith and Vocational Discernment," welcoming our direct involvement, I felt relief. Were we finally being welcomed back into the fold? And then I read the Church's online questionnaire aimed at young people. Many questions had no space for the diverse answers I knew my friends and I had. How good would the Church be at reading between the lines? I wondered.

As you read the wonderful, poignant words of *Vision and Vocations: The Catholic Women Speak Network*, you will never feel the need to read between the carefully crafted lines of women who have long ago been subdued into speaking in subtleties, never giving offense. Instead, you will hear the strong and spirited voices of women who have not given up. You will find courage and clarity, and above all, hope, in the stories of today's women who are not afraid to ask for what we deserve. And perhaps, through their eyes, you will discover, like I did, what it means to feel Catholic again.

Gaya Lobo Gajiwala (29)
Voices of Faith Alumna 2016 and 2018
Mumbai, India

Notes

1. See Catholic Women Speak at https://catholicwomen speak.com/.

2. See Voices of Faith at https://voicesoffaith.org/.

Abbreviations Used in References to Church Documents

(These are all available to download from the Vatican website: http://w2.vatican.va/content/vatican/en.html.)

AA   Pope Paul VI, "Decree on the Apostolate of the Laity" (*Apostolicam Actuositatem*), November 18, 1965.

AL   Pope Francis, "Post-Synodal Apostolic Exhortation on Love in the Family" (*Amoris Laetitia*), March 19, 2016.

CCC   *Catechism of the Catholic Church*, Libreria Editrice Vaticana, Città del Vaticano, 1993.

CL   Pope John Paul II, "Post-Synodal Apostolic Exhortation on the Vocation and the Mission of the Lay Faithful in the Church and the World" (*Christifideles Laici*), December 30, 1988.

EG   Pope Francis, "Apostolic Exhortation on the Proclamation of the Gospel in Today's World" (*Evangelii Gaudium*), November 24, 2013.

GS   Pope Paul VI, "Pastoral Constitution on the Church in the Modern World" (*Gaudium et Spes*), December 7, 1965.

IS   Sacred Congregation for the Doctrine of the Faith, "On the Question of Admission of Women to the

Ministerial Priesthood" (*Inter Insigniores*), October 15, 1976.

LS   Pope Francis, "Encyclical Letter on Care for our Common Home" (*Laudato Si'*), May 24, 2015.

LG   Pope Paul VI, "Dogmatic Constitution on the Church" (*Lumen Gentium*), November 21, 1964.

MD   Pope John Paul II, "Apostolic Letter on the Dignity and Vocation of Women" (*Mulieris Dignitatem*), August 15, 1988.

MQ   Pope Paul VI, "Apostolic Letter Given Motu Proprio: On First Tonsure, Minor Orders, and the Subdiaconate" (*Ministeria Quaedam*), August 15, 1972.

NA   Pope Paul VI, "Declaration on the Relation of the Church to Non-Christian Religions" (*Nostra Aetate*), October 28, 1965.

PH   Sacred Congregation for the Doctrine of the Faith, "Declaration on Certain Questions Concerning Sexual Ethics" (*Persona Humana*), December 29, 1975.

Introduction

Women's Cultures, Women's Callings

Tina Beattie

The following are reviews of our first synod book, *Catholic Women Speak: Bringing Our Gifts to the Table* (Mahwah, NJ: Paulist Press, 2015):

> *This is not a series of essays that trashes the past or disdains any core doctrine. But it does ask whether we adequately name present realities.* (Bishop Timothy Doherty)[1]

> *These essays bring the bishops one step closer to the pastoral encounter that Pope Francis repeatedly emphasizes. Yet the relevance of the book extends beyond bishops. It is an aid for any person who wants to explore the experiences, joys and struggles of women in the church* (Luke Hansen, SJ).[2]

Catholic Women Speak is a global network of more than one thousand Catholic women, dedicated to forming supportive networks for the promotion of women's voices and vocations within the Church through dialogue, theological education, and awareness raising. Our members represent a broad spectrum of views, and we do not campaign on any single issue. Our aim is to create a forum for Catholic women to speak and be heard in a way that reflects our full human dignity and equality and our rich cultural, theological, and demographic diversity, and that sees our many differences as a gift to be celebrated and not as a problem to be overcome.

The absence of women's perspectives from Catholic teaching and leadership is becoming increasingly problematic in a world in which the struggle for gender equality is a central focus of public and domestic life across cultures and institutions. In her opening address at the Voices of Faith celebration on International Women's Day in Rome on March 8, 2018, Mary McAleese, former President of Ireland, asked the audience to imagine a scenario in which "Pope Francis calls a synod on Women and 350 male celibates advise the Pope on what women really want." She went on to ask, "How long can the hierarchy sustain the credibility of a God who wants things this way, who wants a Church where women are invisible and voiceless in leadership and decision-making?"[3]

Speaking of Faith

This is the second collection of women's writings published by Catholic Women Speak to coincide with a Synod of Bishops.[4] Our first book, *Catholic Women Speak: Bringing Our Gifts to the Table*, was distributed by the Vatican publishers *Libreria Editrice Vaticana* in the Synod Hall during the October 2015 Synod on the Family, and we remain deeply grateful for their assistance. More than three hundred copies of the book were given away, but not a single synod participant ever acknowledged that he had received it, let alone read it and learned from it. Nevertheless, we persist because we believe that ultimately the Church's survival depends upon women—not only as bearers of children for the Church of the future (a role that is more than adequately recognized already), but as bearers of visions and vocations that have yet to find space to flourish and grow in the sacramental, ethical, and social expressions of our Catholic faith.

Contributors to this book were invited to explore the 2018 Synod theme of "Young People, Faith, and Vocational Discernment" from a wide range of perspectives, informed by their own cultural, theological, and personal insights. Their stories show that women are a vibrant, varied, and dynamic life force in the Church today—irreducibly diverse, united by faith in Christ and participation in the sacramental life of the Church, but representing a lavish fecundity of cultures, contexts, and experiences.

All the women writing here remain deeply committed to and inspired by their Catholic faith, even those who, for various reasons, are no longer practicing Catholics. Catholicism is one expression of faith among many, but for the women in this book it is the interpretative lens through which they seek to understand and give meaning to their lives. Those whose vocations and identities are affirmed by the teachings and pastors of the Church express joy and fulfilment in their Catholic faith, even as they acknowledge the challenges they face. Those who feel that their vocations are denied or the insights and gifts they offer are rejected find it a more frustrating and dispiriting struggle.

Vocational discernment is a lifelong process, which is why contributors range from teenagers to women in their eighties, from young women just beginning to explore their vocations as they look to the future, to others who look back on a lifetime of learning and maturing. All are women who, like Mary of Nazareth, are willing to defy the conventions and expectations of those around them in order to hear and respond to God's call, even when that means setting out upon a rocky path of faith that winds through unfamiliar and difficult terrain. Contributor Jeannine Pitas writes, "Like those ancient Israelites who followed Moses through the wilderness for forty years, we humans traverse a wild landscape with unclear paths and no adequate map (and certainly no GPS). But as scary as this may seem, it is also a thrilling adventure."[5]

For many of the contributors, the life of faith is indeed a thrilling adventure, terrifying sometimes in its risks and challenges, ecstatic in its epiphanies of joy. For others, it is a determined struggle in the face of almost insurmountable obstacles and setbacks. Here, "feminine genius" is redefined as courage, persistence, humor, defiance, passion, hope, strength, heartbreak, and dedication—a genius that is sometimes vibrant with the erotic intensity of life in all its fullness, and sometimes desolate in its forsakenness and sorrow. This is a genius for living that belongs not to the feminine but to the human who is fully alive with the glory of God, to paraphrase Irenaeus. Christ promises that he has come so that we "may have life, and have it abundantly" (John 10:10). The women writing here ask what it means to have abundant life in Christ, and tell of how, in their different contexts, the institutions and teachings of the Catholic faith have both helped and hindered them in their capacity to receive this gift.

Women in History and Culture

In a remarkable letter addressed to the world's women on the occasion of the Fourth World Conference on Women in Beijing in 1995, Pope John Paul II observed that women "have often been relegated to the margins of society and even reduced to servitude....And if objective blame, especially in particular historical contexts, has belonged to not just a few members of the Church, for this I am truly sorry."[6] He went on to acknowledge that, while women have contributed to human history as much as men have, "very little of women's achievements in history can be registered by the science of history. But even though time may have buried the documentary evidence of those achievements, their beneficent influence can be felt as a force which has shaped the lives of successive generations, right up to our own."[7]

This prophetic and visionary letter was written nearly a quarter of a century ago, but in the intervening decades, the Church has become entrenched in the absolutism of some of its teachings, particularly with regard to issues of sexuality and procreation and, for some, the denial of any possibility of women's ordination. This has led to the stifling of theological debate and a deficit in pastoral care around some of the issues that most profoundly affect women's lives.

Pope Francis has brought hope and inspiration to millions with his call for a "revolution of tenderness,"[8] and in his living witness to a bold, joyful, and risk-taking faith. His Post-Synodal Apostolic Exhortation *Amoris Laetitia* does much to break the stranglehold of a heartless and punitive doctrinal absolutism in favor of a more pastorally responsive and compassionate Church. Yet, as the girls of the Ursuline High School point out in their letter to Pope Francis, *Amoris Laetitia* still fails to give sufficient acknowledgment to the many ways in which young women today aspire to be more than mothers:

> We aspire to be lawyers, nurses, teachers, musicians, athletes, engineers, doctors and some of us feel called to have a family as well. While motherhood is a really wonderful aspect of being a

woman, it is just one aspect, not the only one. In a changing society, it is important to change the ways that we as a Church engage with young people and women.[9]

We wonder how much time and attention will be given at the 2018 Synod to discussing the vocations of women and girls, and what pastoral responses might emerge in order to provide effective support and encouragement to the process of vocational discernment in the face of these young women's aspirations and visions.

Pope Francis writes that "the different peoples among whom the Gospel has been inculturated are active collective subjects or agents of evangelization. This is because each people is the creator of their own culture and the protagonist of their own history" (*EG* 122). All cultures include cultures of women, yet women are only now being recognized as "active collective subjects" and "agents of evangelization." Recent popes have acknowledged the need to involve women more fully as active subjects and agents of change in the Church, yet the Catholic Church lags far behind secular society in responding to this challenge. The papal rhetoric of inclusion has yet to be matched by effective action, so that Catholic women and girls face many conflicts as they seek to reconcile the rapidly changing opportunities and demands of modern life with traditional cultures and Catholic teachings. As Revai Elizabeth Mudzimu observes, referring to Zimbabwean culture, "Young Catholic women and girls experience a threefold ideological pressure from their culture, modernity and Catholic teaching."[10]

Women's vocations belong within a vast array of cultural contexts with different concepts of gender, but few cultures retain shared meanings and values nurtured in the matrix of women's experiences and capable of responding to the

challenges of modernity. Women around the world are beginning to realize that the cultural and vocational resources
available to them have not emerged from the acquired wisdom of women themselves. Rather, they are all too often
masculine projections that cast the female in a shadowy
realm of subordinate otherness, closed off from access to
much that is essential for human freedom and flourishing.
Gertrude Yema Jusufu's story is still all too common for millions of girls and women born into cultures devastated by
poverty, violence, and patriarchy. Writing in the context of
Sierra Leone, Jusufu observes, "My culture does not consider it important for girls to have educational opportunities,
but I always had a deep desire to study."[11] Describing a life
marked by traumatizing experiences of sexual abuse, war,
and starvation, Jusufu concludes, "I am a woman who has
never given up. In some way, I know God is present in my
life. To all that has been, I bid farewell. For the future, I can
only hope for a path that leads to life."[12]

These essays and reflections offer an insight into the
many ways in which women pursue this quest for "a path
that leads to life" in different contexts. Carolina del Río Mena
writes, "To promote liberating changes in the ways we view
feminine subjectivity is not an easy task when there is a complex and patriarchal normative/symbolic system in place."[13]
Gayatri Gajiwala asks her mother, Astrid, "When you are
taught your whole life that your identity does not matter, how
do you expect women to fight for anything that they believe
is important to them?"[14] Like the strangers, the fatherless, and
the widows of ancient times, women must gather what has
been forgotten and abandoned in the harvesting of history in
order to discover stories of inspiration capable of nurturing
their Christian vocation to fullness of life.[15]

Sara Parvis's essay shows that this is by no means a
fruitless quest.[16] Women today are discovering in the stories

of biblical women and women saints, mystics, and visionaries a rich source of inspiration. Many contributors express gratitude for the examples of mothers, grandmothers, and aunts. Their stories affirm Pope Francis's description in *Evangelii Gaudium* of the mutual enhancement that can result when Catholicism and cultures encounter one another and become incarnate in the lives of the faithful, even though this often entails "staying in and struggling on."[17]

Some contributors, however, expose the ways in which dysfunctional Catholic institutions can deform the cultures within which they operate. Colleen Hennessy describes how the "intertwined" relationship between the Catholic Church and the Irish state is unravelling as growing numbers of Irish people leave the Church because they feel betrayed by Catholic institutions.[18] Cettina Militello draws on forty years of teaching theology to seminarians to offer an unflinching critique of seminary culture.[19] Her essay is a reminder that cultures of men, including priestly cultures, are just as affected by the dramatic changes taking place in society as cultures of women, for men, too, are having to ask searching questions about their masculine identities and vocations.

Vocations and Relationships: Maternity, Sexuality, and Difference

Whether as mothers or as daughters, for many women the maternal relationship is one of life's most intense and complex challenges, shot through as it is with love and pain, hope and frustration, yearning and sorrow. The women who tell their stories here introduce a visceral reality into the abstract ideas that inform Church teaching on motherhood. Eschewing romantic and often sanitizing stereotypes, they describe the vocation to mothering as a lifelong struggle to nurture hope and vitality in the face of the sometimes devastating demands of maternal love. Others write as daughters who remember their mothers as role models and sources of wisdom, or sometimes as obstacles on their path to life.

Yet, as del Río points out, "Women do not satisfy their sexual needs and libido by being mothers; rather, they do so through sexual relationships and pleasure." This means recognizing that the body is, in del Río's words, "the epiphany of a person…a living word, open, explicit, inevitable. It is the word that reveals the deep, real, true 'I am' of each of us."[20] This is as true of those living celibate lives as it is of those who are sexually active. Madeleine Fredell, a Swedish Dominican sister, writes, "The vow of celibacy is of course about living a celibate life but equally about accepting our sexuality and sexual orientation. Each sister must come to grips with herself, with her body and how it functions."[21]

For many women, questions of sexual embodiment and desire are among the most challenging and elusive areas of personal discovery and growth. As Ruth Hunt observes, "Female sexuality, whether it's hetero or homo, is always passive, because we live in a patriarchal society. So for a woman in any context to assert her views, whether that's about something to do with pleasure, or about whether she wants children, or whether she wants sex, is quite difficult."[22]

Along with changing paradigms of heterosexual love and identities, there is growing recognition of the capacity of same-sex relationships to express the mutuality, commitment, and intimacy of sexual love. Church teaching has yet to fully acknowledge this, and the continuing refusal to accommodate faithful sexual love between same-sex partners can have a devastating impact on homosexual persons. Nontando Hadebe, writing in the context of African cultures within and outside of South Africa, argues that "the language of depravity and disorder" used by the Catechism to describe homosexual acts "is in itself violent"[23] and risks contributing toward the idea that "being homosexual is not only 'un-African' but 'un-Christian.'"[24] In a conversation with Tina Beattie, Ruth Hunt and Jeannine Gramick describe how their Catholic faith inspires them to raise awareness and to campaign on LGBTQI issues.[25]

The students of the Ursuline High School are evidence of the extent to which young Catholics have progressed far beyond official Church teaching in their attitudes toward homosexuality. They tell Pope Francis,

> Many of us find it hard to conform to the teachings of the Catholic Church which, although strongly preaching equality of all, subtly encourages a divide among those of different sexualities and genders. LGBT Catholic teens feel trapped within the walls set by this divide, causing some of us... to feel disconnected from our faith.[26]

These young Catholic women seek a Church that affirms and welcomes the full humanity of all, whatever their gender or sexual orientation. This includes women like Samantha Tillman, who tells her story and shares what it means to say, "I am a Catholic transgender woman."[27]

Amid these realities of incarnate life and the many different ways of being and belonging, questions of mental and physical disability are becoming increasingly significant with regard to theology and pastoral practice. As Cristina Gangemi argues, these also have a gendered aspect, for women who are intellectually disabled are often doubly marginalized in the Church. Gangemi points out that the Church's emphasis on marriage and motherhood as vocations for which women are uniquely gifted can leave intellectually disabled women feeling "excluded, lonely and isolated."[28] The emerging field of disability theology addresses some of these issues, but it remains true that, if there are limited opportunities for some women in the Church, "there is no role for women who are intellectually disabled."[29] Giulia Galeotti also explores issues to do with disability and faith when she describes how much she has benefited from working with the Faith and Light movement.[30]

Johanna Greeve offers a deeply personal insight into the devastating effects of mental disability when she describes how a lifetime of mental illness and repeated bouts of severe depression almost led her to undergo voluntary euthanasia at the Swiss clinic, Dignitas. She tells of how the support of her parents, the pastoral care of her parish priest, and the ministrations of an attentive psychiatrist helped her to arrive at a place where "I dared to talk about 'happiness' for the first time."[31] For such women, the growing awareness of intellectual disability and mental illness being promoted by Gangemi, Galeotti, and others is surely a sign of women responding to a vocation to hear and attend to some of the most marginalized people in the Church.

Women's Vocations: The Backbone of the Church

Amid these sometimes dramatic stories of vocation, conversion, and transformation, this book includes many reflections on ordinary lives that together offer an insight into the extent to which women's vocations are the backbone of the Church. In chaplaincies and parishes, Catholic women from all walks of life quietly minister to others, their presences often hidden, their efforts unnoticed. Time and again, contributors describe how their ability to fulfill these pastoral vocations is dependent upon the support of the hierarchy. While some receive positive support from Church authorities, others have found their endeavors mocked or thwarted.

There are a number of contributions from women with vocations to religious life, and others who—notwithstanding the Church's prohibition—experience a vocation to ordination. In a heartfelt piece on the nature of her vocation, Melissa Carnall writes of how she feels called to both religious life and priesthood:

> I am called to be both Sister and priest, like my male friends in religious communities, who are called to be Brother and priest. The only difference is that I cannot answer my call in a straightforward way as they can because I am a woman. It hurts.

That is a refrain running through several of the stories in this book. "I cannot because I am a woman, and it hurts."

Pope Francis has reiterated the teaching of his predecessors, that the question of women's priesthood has been settled and the answer is no. "That is closed, that door," he told a news conference.[32] Yet, in *Evangelii Gaudium*, he offers an image of a Church whose doors are always open:

> The Church is called to be the house of the Father, with doors always wide open. One concrete sign of such openness is that our church doors should always be open, so that if someone, moved by the Spirit, comes there looking for God, he or she will not find a closed door. (*EG* 47)

Despite his insistence that women cannot be ordained, Pope Francis has gone some way toward lifting the prohibition on discussing the issue, which, under Popes John Paul II and Benedict XVI, became one of the litmus tests of Catholic orthodoxy. His decision to establish a commission to investigate the question of women deacons necessarily opens up the question of ordination, because the diaconate is an ordained ministry.[33]

Called to Care for Creation

Finally, the theme of environmental awareness and respect for God's creation is implicit in many of the contributions. Fredell writes of the centrality of wonder and the beauty of nature to religious life.[34] Hadebe refers to the relationality of all created beings affirmed in Pope Francis's encyclical on the environment, *Laudato Si'*.[35] Two contributors here—Mary Colwell and Melanie Newbould—tell of how they feel called to respond to the call to care for creation in their lifestyles and vocations.[36] As the vision of that magnificent encyclical filters through the Church, we might hope that vast numbers of Catholics throughout the world will hear and respond to that call as an intrinsic dimension of what it means to be Catholic.

Laudato Si' is an invitation not just to the universal Church but to all humankind to recognize that our vocation to become fully human calls us to a new relationship with one another and with all God's creatures. Here, too, women have much to offer, if we are invited into partnership and solidarity to respond to what might be God's last and greatest call to humankind.

The lack of a gendered perspective in *Laudato Si'* is another sign that the institutional Church has not yet begun to engage with the realities of women's lives or to recognize the gifts they bring and the struggles they endure. It is disturbing that an encyclical that rightly shows deep concern for the suffering and abuse of Mother Earth and for the plight of the world's threatened species and poorest communities has nothing to say about the suffering of more than a quarter of a million of the world's poorest women who die in causes relating to childbirth every year. There is much work to be done if "Mother Earth" is not to become yet another romantic fiction drawing women ever more deeply into ideas divorced from reality, and draining away the sacramental vitality and vision we need to be cocreators with God in the healing of the earth and its suffering species.

God speaks as a woman in labor in the Book of Isaiah:

> For a long time I have held my peace,
>   I have kept still and restrained myself;
> now I will cry out like a woman in labor,
>   I will gasp and pant. (Isa 42:14)

The women in this book are in labor with God as we struggle to bring to birth new vocations and visions—as mothers and/or daughters, as single, married, divorced, gay, trans, religious, young, old, in sickness and in health, from many cultures and communities and walks of life. We have stories to tell, visions to inspire, and vocations to share.

Notes

1. Bishop Timothy Doherty, "Book: Catholic Women Speak," *Catholic Moment*, Diocese of Lafayette-in-Indiana, February 5, 2017, http://www.thecatholicmoment.org/bishop/2017/column020517.html.

2. Luke Hansen, "Bringing Doctrine to Life," *America: The Jesuit Review*, November 28, 2016, https://www.americamagazine.org/faith/2016/11/17/bringing-doctrine-life.

3. Mary McAleese, "The Time Is Now for Change in the Catholic Church."

4. To read about the first book, see Tina Beattie, "A Place at the Table: The Story of 'Catholic Women Speak,'" *Commonweal*, March 29, 2016, https://www.commonwealmagazine.org/place-table. To find out more about Catholic Women Speak, please visit our website: http://catholicwomenspeak.com/.

5. Jeannine M. Pitas, "Vocation: An Ongoing Journey."

6. Pope John Paul II, "Letter to Women," June 29, 1995, 3, https://w2.vatican.va/content/john-paul-ii/en/letters/1995/documents/hf_jp-ii_let_29061995_women.html.

7. John Paul II, "Letter to Women," 3.

8. Pope Francis, TED2017, April 25, 2017, https://youtu.be/36zrJfAFcuc.

9. The Ursuline High School, Wimbledon, "A Letter to Pope Francis."

10. Revai Elizabeth Mudzimu, "Motherhood as Mirage: The Role of the Catholic Church and African Culture in Shaping Zimbabwean Girls' Vocations."

11. Gertrude Yema Jusufa, "My Story: Hoping for a Path That Leads to Life."

12. Jusufa, "My Story."

13. Carolina del Río, "Conversion and a New Consciousness: The Challenge of Women's Equality for Sexuality, Society, and Church."

14. Gayatri and Astrid Lobo Gajiwala, "'Feminine Genius' and the Role of Women: An Indian Daughter and Mother in Conversation."

15. See Deuteronomy 24:19: "When you reap your harvest in your field and forget a sheaf in the field, you shall not go back to get it; it shall be left for the alien, the orphan, and the widow, so that the LORD your God may bless you in all your undertakings."

16. Sara Parvis, "What Young Catholic Women Should Hear."

17. Irim Sarwar, "Staying In, Struggling On: A Woman's Pilgrimage from Islam to Catholicism."

18. Colleen Hennessy, "Irish Women and a Church in Crisis."

19. Cettina Militello, "Seminaries and Priestly Formation: A Woman Theologian Reflects."

20. Del Río, "Conversion and a New Consciousness."

21. Madeleine Fredell, "From Knowledge and Power to Wisdom and Authority: Religious Vocation in the Life of the Church."

22. Ruth Hunt, in Tina Beattie, "Staying In and Reaching Out: Interview with Ruth Hunt (Stonewall, UK) and Jeannine Gramick (New Ways Ministry, USA)."

23. Nontando Hadebe, "Whose Life Matters? Violence Against Lesbians and the Politics of Life in the Church."

24. Hadebe, "Whose Life Matters?"

25. Beattie, "Staying In and Reaching Out."

26. The Ursuline High School, Wimbledon, "Letter to Pope Francis."

27. Samantha Tillman, "Does God Bless Your Transsexual Heart?"

28. Cristina Gangemi, "A Space to Grow: The Church and Women Who Are Intellectually Disabled."

29. Gangemi, "A Space to Grow."

30. Giulia Galeotti, "A Church of Women: Memories, Frustrations, and Hopes on the Journey of Life."

31. Johanna Greeve, "Living in Extra Time: A Journey from Despair to Hope."

32. Hannah Brockhaus, "Pope Francis Reiterates a Strong 'No' to Women Priests," Catholic News Agency, November 1, 2016, https://www.catholicnewsagency.com/news/pope-francis-reiterates-a-strong-no-to-women-priests-71133.

33. See Tim Reidy and Gerard O'Connell, "Vatican Announces Commission on Women Deacons," *America: The Jesuit Review*, August 2, 2016, https://www.americamagazine.org/faith/2016/08/02/vatican-announces-commission-women-deacons.

34. Fredell, "From Knowledge and Power to Wisdom and Authority."

35. Hadebe, "Whose Life Matters?"

36. See Mary Colwell, "Faith and Nature: Would Jesus Weep for an Eider Duck?" and Melanie Newbould, "*Laudato Si'*, Veganism, and the Interconnectedness of All Things."

PART ONE

CHALLENGES AND CHANGES

Catholic Women in the Modern World

"And no one puts new wine into old wineskins; otherwise the new wine will burst the skins and will be spilled, and the skins will be destroyed. But new wine must be put into fresh wineskins."

(Luke 5:37–38)

The Time Is Now for Change in the Catholic Church

Mary McAleese

Keynote address at Voices of Faith International Women's Day Conference, "Why Women Matter," March 8, 2018, Jesuit Curia, Rome.[1]

> *The historical oppression of women has deprived the human race of untold resources. Recognition of the equality in dignity and fundamental rights of women and men, and guaranteeing access by all women to the full exercise of those rights will have far-reaching consequences and will liberate enormous reserves of intelligence and energy sorely needed in a world that is groaning for peace and justice.*[2]

The Israelites under Joshua's command circled Jericho's walls for seven days, blew trumpets, and shouted to make the walls fall down.[3] We don't have trumpets but we have voices, voices of faith, and we are here to shout, to bring down our Church's walls of misogyny. We have been circling these walls for fifty-five years since John XXIII's encyclical *Pacem in Terris* first pointed to the advancement of women as one of the most important "signs of the times":

19

They are demanding both in domestic and in public life the rights and duties which belong to them as human persons....The longstanding inferiority complex of certain classes because of their economic and social status, sex, or position in the State, and the corresponding superiority complex of other classes, is rapidly becoming a thing of the past. (*PT* 41–43)

At the Second Vatican Council, Archbishop Paul Hallinan of Atlanta warned the bishops to stop perpetuating "the secondary place accorded to women in the Church of the 20th century" and to avoid the Church being a "late-comer in [their] social, political and economic development."[4] The Council's decree *Apostolicam Actuositatem* said it was important that women "participate more widely…in the various fields of the Church's apostolate" (*AA* 9). The Council's pastoral constitution *Gaudium et Spes* said the elimination of discrimination based on gender was a priority (see *GS* 29). Paul VI even commissioned a study on women in Church and society, which reported in 1976.[5] Surely, we thought then, the postconciliar Church was on the way to full equality for its 600 million female members. And yes—it is true that since the Council, new roles and jobs have opened up to the laity, including women, but these have simply marginally increased the visibility of women in subordinate roles, including in the curia. They have added nothing to their decision-making power or their voice. Remarkably since the Council, roles that were specifically designated as suitable for the laity have been deliberately closed to women. The stable roles of acolyte and lector[6] and the permanent diaconate[7] have been opened only to laymen. Why? Both laymen and women can be temporary altar servers but bishops are allowed to ban females, and where they permit them in their dioceses, individual pastors can ban them in their parishes.[8] Why?

Back in 1976 we were told that the Church does not consider herself authorized to admit women to priestly ordination (*IS*). This has locked women out of any significant role in the Church's leadership and authority structure. Yet, in justice their very permanent exclusion from priesthood should have provoked the Church to find innovative ways of including women's voices as a right in the divinely instituted College of Bishops and the man-made entities such as the College of Cardinals, the Synod of Bishops, and episcopal conferences.

Just imagine the normative scenario: Pope Francis calls a Synod on Women and 350 male celibates advise the Pope on what women really want. That is how ludicrous our Church has become. How long can the hierarchy sustain the credibility of a God who wants things this way, who wants a Church in which women are invisible and voiceless in leadership and decision-making?

It was here in this very hall[9] in 1995 that Irish Jesuit theologian Fr. Gerry O'Hanlon put his finger on the underpinning systemic problem when he steered Decree 14 through the Jesuits' 34th General Congregation. It is a forgotten document, but today we will dust it down and use it to challenge a Jesuit pope, a reforming pope, to real, practical action on behalf of women in the Catholic Church.

Decree 14 says,

> We have been part of a civil and ecclesial tradition that has offended against women. And, like many men, we have a tendency to convince ourselves that there is no problem. However unwittingly, we have often contributed to a form of clericalism which has reinforced male domination with an ostensibly

divine sanction. By making this declaration we wish
to react personally and collectively, and do what we
can to change this regrettable situation.[10]

"The regrettable situation" arises because the Catholic
Church has long since been a primary global carrier of the
virus of misogyny. It has never sought a cure, though a cure
is freely available. Its name is "equality."

Down the two-thousand-year highway of Christian history came the ethereal divine beauty of the nativity, the cruel
sacrifice of the crucifixion, the hallelujah of the resurrection, and the rallying cry of the great commandment to love
one another. But down that same highway came man-made
toxins such as misogyny and homophobia, to say nothing
of anti-Semitism, with their legacy of damaged and wasted
lives and deeply embedded institutional dysfunction.

The laws and cultures of many nations and faith systems were also historically deeply patriarchal and excluding
of women—some still are—but today the Catholic Church
lags noticeably behind the world's advanced nations in the
elimination of discrimination against women. Worse still,
because it speaks from the "pulpit of the world," to quote
Ban Ki-moon,[11] its overt patriarchalism acts as a powerful
brake on dismantling the architecture of misogyny wherever
it is found. There is an irony here, for education has been
crucial to the advancement of women, and for many of us,
the education that liberated us was provided by the Church's
frontline workers, clerical and lay, who have done so much
to lift men and women out of poverty and powerlessness and
give them access to opportunity. Yet, paradoxically it is the
questioning voices of educated Catholic women and the men
who support them that the Church hierarchy simply cannot cope with and scorns rather than engaging in dialogue.
The Church that regularly criticizes the secular world for

its failure to deliver on human rights has almost no culture of critiquing itself, and it has a hostility to internal criticism that borders on institutional idolatry.

Today we challenge Pope Francis to develop a credible strategy for the inclusion of women as equals throughout the Church's root-and-branch infrastructure, including its decision-making. Failure to include women as equals has deprived the Church of fresh and innovative discernment; it has consigned it to recycled thinking among a hermetically sealed, cozy male clerical elite. It has kept Christ out and bigotry in. It has left the Church flapping about awkwardly on one wing when God gave it two. We are entitled to hold our Church leaders to account for this and other egregious abuses of institutional power.

At the start of his papacy, Pope Francis said, "We need to create still broader opportunities for a more incisive female presence in the Church" (*EG* 103)—words a Church scholar described as evidence of Francis's "magnanimity."[12] Let us be clear: women's right to equality in the Church should arise organically from divine justice, not ad hoc from papal benevolence.

Pope Francis described female theologians as the "strawberries on the cake."[13] He was wrong. Women are the leaven in the cake. They are primary handers-on of the faith to their children. In the Western world, the Church's cake is not rising, the baton of faith is dropping. Women are walking away from the Catholic Church in droves, for those who are expected to be key influencers in their children's faith formation have no opportunity to be key influencers in the formation of the Catholic faith. Just four months ago the Archbishop of Dublin, Diarmuid Martin, felt compelled to remark that "the low standing of women in the Catholic Church is the most significant reason for the feeling of alienation toward it in Ireland today."[14]

Pope Francis has said that "women are more important than men because the Church is a woman."[15] Why not ask women if they feel more important than men? I suspect many will answer that they experience the Church as a male bastion of patronizing platitudes.

John Paul II has written of the "mystery of women" (*MD* 31). Talk to us as equals and we will not be a mystery! Francis has said a "deeper theology of women"[16] is needed. God knows it would be hard to find a more shallow theology of women than the misogyny dressed up as theology[17] that the magisterium currently hides behind.

And all the time a deeper theology is staring us in the face. It does not require much digging to find it. Just look to Christ. John Paul II pointed out that

> we are heirs to a history which has conditioned us to a remarkable extent. In every time and place, this conditioning has been an obstacle to the progress of women....Transcending the established norms of his own culture, Jesus treated women with openness, respect, acceptance and tenderness....As we look to Christ...it is natural to ask ourselves: how much of his message has been heard and acted upon?[18]

Women are best qualified to answer that question, but we are left to talk among ourselves. No Church leader bothers to turn up because we do not matter to them.

Back in this hall in 1995, the Jesuit Congregation asked God for the grace of conversion from a patriarchal Church to a Church of equals, where women truly matter. Only such a Church is worthy of Christ. Only such a Church can credibly make Christ matter. The time for that Church is now. Pope Francis, the time for change is now.

Notes

1. See https://voicesoffaith.org/event/. We are grateful to Voices of Faith and to Mary McAleese for permission to publish this address.

2. Holy See Statement of Professor Mary Ann Glendon, Head of the Delegation of the Holy See to the Fourth World Conference on Women, Beijing, September 5, 1995, http://www.un.org/esa/gopher-data/conf/fwcw/conf/gov/950905214652.txt.

3. See Joshua 6:1–20.

4. See Fr. P. Jordan, OSB, NCWC News Rome correspondent, "Changes Proposed in Role of Women in the Church," posted October 12, 1965, https://vaticaniiat50.wordpress.com/2015/10/12/changes-proposed-in-role-of-women-in-the-church/.

5. See Edward J. Kilmartin, "Full Participation of Women in the Life of the Catholic Church," in *Sexism and Church Law*, ed. James A. Coriden (New York: Paulist Press, 1977), 109–35, at http://www.womenpriests.org/classic2/kilmarti.asp.

6. 1983 Code of Canon Law, can. 230 §1. Cf. Paul VI, *Ministeria Quaedam (MQ)*, nos. 2–4, 7: "Formerly called the minor orders [of acolyte and lector], they are henceforth to be called ministries. Ministries may be assigned to lay Christians; hence they are no longer to be considered as reserved to candidates for the sacrament of orders….In accordance with the ancient tradition of the Church, institution to the ministries of reader and acolyte is reserved to men."

7. 1983 Code of Canon Law, can. 1031 §2.

8. Congregation for Divine Worship and Discipline of the Sacraments, "Letter on Possible Admission of Girls, Adult Women and Women Religious to Serve alongside Boys as Servers in the Liturgy," July 27, 2001, https://adoremus.org/2007/12/31/Letter-on-Altar-Servers/.

9. McAleese was speaking in the Aula of the Jesuit Curia in Rome.

10. General Congregation 34 (1995), "Decree 14: Jesuits and the Situation of Women in Church and Civil Society," no. 9, at https://www.xavier.edu/jesuitresource/jesuit-a-z/Decree-14.cfm.

The decree was written with the help of, among others, two Irish laywomen, Cathy Molloy and Edel O'Kennedy. For the background to the decree, see Margot J. Heydt, "Solving the Mystery of Decree 14: Jesuits and the Situation of Women in Church and Civil Society," *Conversations On Jesuit Higher Education*, September 15, 2015, http://www.conversationsmagazine.org/web-features/2015/12/27/solving-the-mystery-of-decree-14-jesuits-and-the-situation-of-women-in-church-and-civil-society.

11. UN Secretary-General Ban Ki-moon's remarks to the UN General Assembly on the occasion of the visit by His Holiness Pope Francis, New York, September 25, 2015, http://www.un.org/press/en/2015/sgsm17110.doc.htm.

12. Phyllis Zagano, "What the Pope Really Said," *National Catholic Reporter*, September 25, 2013, https://www.ncronline.org/blogs/just-catholic/what-pope-really-said.

13. Pope Francis, "Address to Members of the International Theological Commission," December 5, 2014, https://w2.vatican.va/content/francesco/en/speeches/2014/december/documents/papa-francesco_20141205_commissione-teologica-internazionale.html. Cf. Hanna Roberts, "Women Theologians Are the 'Strawberry on the Cake', says Pope," *The Tablet*, December 11, 2014, http://www.thetablet.co.uk/news/1508/women-theologians-are-the-strawberry-on-the-cake-says-pope.

14. From a talk entitled "The Church in Dublin: Where Will It Be in 10 Years' Time?" at St. Mary's Church, Haddington Road, as reported in the *Irish Times*, November 16, 2017.

15. Response of Pope Francis to a question from a journalist: "Will we one day see women priests in the Catholic Church?" on papal plane returning to Rome from the United States, September 29, 2015. See https://www.ncronline.org/blogs/francis-chronicles/popes-quotes-theology-women.

16. Interview with journalists on board plane on way to Rio de Janeiro, July 22, 2013. Cf. John Allen, "The Pope on Homosexuals: 'Who Am I to Judge?'" *National Catholic Reporter*, July 29, 2013, https://www.ncronline.org/blogs/ncr-today/pope-homosexuals-who-am-i-judge.

17. See Manfred Hauke, *Women in the Priesthood: A Systematic Analysis in the Light of the Order of Creation and Redemption* (San Francisco: Ignatius Press, 1988).

18. Pope John Paul II, "Letter to Women," June 29, 1995, 3, https://w2.vatican.va/content/john-paul-ii/en/letters/1995/documents/hf_jp-ii_let_29061995_women.html.

Conversion and a New Consciousness

The Challenge of Women's Equality for Sexuality, Society, and Church[1]

Carolina del Río Mena
(trans. from Spanish by Jeannine M. Pitas)

The idea that Eve was the only culprit and Adam her innocent victim has permeated the Christian imagination. In theology, a certain interpretation of biblical texts about the creation of man and woman and their fall (Gen 1—3) has been decisive in the elaboration of religious discourse and in the assignation of gender roles according to an original plan, from the "beginning." Moreover, in other areas of knowledge, certain paradigms that established a biological grounding for gender roles were assumed. In those paradigms women are usually confined to a private, hidden realm. In modern Western societies, traditional gender roles have been inscribed in a particular dichotomous order of the public and the private realms. The cultural model of women has revolved around the rearing of children and domestic responsibilities, in accordance with personality features considered to be typically feminine: warmth, expressiveness, dependence, cooperation, and special abilities of interpersonal relationships, rather than in the domain of intellectual skills and power.[2]

The irruption and new positioning of women in society has shattered these paradigms, and it is now necessary to revise them. Since the radical feminist movements of the 1960s, women have understood with increasing clarity that sexuality is not merely the human condition, but, as Anthony Giddens affirms, "a terrain of fundamental political struggle and also a medium of emancipation."[3] This political struggle also occurs in the church and in theology. Catholic women of the twenty-first century have moved quite far from the image of the "angel in the home" of previous decades. They denounce those discourses and the creation of meanings that imply power relations and hierarchical structures, not only in society and the Church, but also in interpersonal relationships—particularly marriage.

To promote liberating changes in the ways we view feminine subjectivity is not an easy task when there is a complex and patriarchal normative/symbolic system. In the case of sexuality alone, there are deep imbalances and chasms between the norms and mechanisms of subordination, in which women are socialized from childhood, and the deep experience, barely verbalized and systematically ignored, of internal rupture that they experience when they cannot completely internalize these models. This rupture has perhaps been shown best in literature and film, maybe because fiction does not seem like a threat—after all, it is only fiction. As Cecilia Inés Luque observes,

> Given that sexuality is a constitutive element of female subjectivity that had been denied and made invisible under the model of the angel in the home....we can read novels as stories of resistance to the constricting limitations of this worldview,

as well as tales of women's awakening to the free, unashamed experience of their sexual appetites.[4]

The woman who sets out on the path of becoming conscious of gender, of her personal worth, of the need for symmetrical relationships with men and the reciprocity that might nourish these relationships, embarks on a one-way trip in which, according to the Spanish theologian and psychologist Mercedes Navarro, her personal, subjective consciousness—her self-concept—is greatly altered. As a result, her moral conscience (her internal norms of obligation and value) leads her to experience a deep sense of unease and disillusionment as she approaches a difficult crossroad. Feminist theology has dealt with this unease, relying on the experience of those same women to reevaluate patriarchal theological discourses and resignify them from the perspective of women's life experiences, so that these might be recognized and valued as legitimate.

In the religious and theological field, US theologian Elizabeth Johnson argues that the first and most necessary step in changing spirituality, moral values, doctrine, and praxis is a change in women's minds and hearts.[5] Johnson argues that "women's awakening to their own full human worth can be interpreted at the same time as a new experience of God, so that what is arguably occurring is a new event in the religious history of humankind."[6] Moreover, this awakening is accompanied by a "concomitant judgment about the positive moral value of female bodiliness, love of connectedness, and other characteristics that mark the historical lives of women in a specific way."[7]

For Johnson, this awakening requires a process that she describes as having three stages: contrast, confirmation, and conversion. The contrast stems from a woman's awareness of the imbalanced situation that she is experiencing. When women have the intuition that things can be different, they resist and struggle for change. The contrast occurs between a woman's new sense of self-worth and the milieu in which she finds herself. This sense of awareness allows women to realize that their situation can be improved and, furthermore, that such an improvement is good and desirable.

Confirmation is intimately linked to memory, narration, and solidarity among women. Johnson explains that the woman who contrasts her own self-worth and dignity with her cultural environment and furthermore shares this experience with other women is capable of beginning to knit close links of solidarity in which memory keeps the past at bay and narration propels her toward what will come and needs to be built. The confidence that guides a woman in this stage of the process is firmly anchored in the absolute mystery of God, whom she has discovered as a foundation and invigorating force of her feminine being.

Finally, the conversion itself, the culmination of the process that Johnson describes, can be understood in a very different way from conventional accounts of conversion:

> The category of conversion here receives a description somewhat different from that of classical theology....If pride be the primary block on the path to God, then indeed decentering the rapacious self is the work of grace. But the situation is quite different when this language is applied to persons already relegated to the margins of significance and excluded from the exercise of self-definition. For such persons, language of conversion as loss of self, turning from *amor sui*, functions in an ideological way to rob them of power, maintaining them in a subordinate position to the benefit of those who rule.[8]

This process of conversion provokes a new consciousness in women, and from there they discover situations they did not see earlier, which creates a sense of imbalance and discomfort. Revising old paradigms demands looking not only at women's experience, in which they become subjects of their own sexuality, but also at a new status for male-female relationships. When a couple is united by sexual love in a relationship of coresponsibility—of reciprocity rather than subordination—it becomes very difficult to maintain a discourse of male superiority that envisions man as the head and woman as the body.

It is also no longer possible to maintain maternal discourses regarding women—as if their lives and sexual interests were only motivated by procreation. Women do not satisfy their sexual needs and libido by being mothers; rather, they do so by being women in sexual relationships and through sexual pleasure. Christine Gudorf writes,

> The procreative act does not in itself stimulate pleasure sufficient to act as reinforcement for engaging in sex for the majority of women. If the placement of the clitoris in the female body reflects the divine will, then God wills that sex is not just oriented to procreation, but is at least as, if not more, oriented to pleasure as to procreation.[9]

Women's new awareness of their worth and dignity includes a new perception of their bodies. Corporality is the visible form through which we become present to the other and communicate. This presence is not only a spatial fact (as a table in front of us would be) but one of a personal order: the presence of another that demands to be recognized as its own personal "I." The body is the epiphany of a person: it is language, communication, a personal expressive speech that has social significance as exchange and encounter, as gift. The body is a living word, open, explicit, inescapable. It is the word that reveals the deep, real, true "I am" of each of us. The body is the place of encounter with God; it is the tent, the dwelling, through which we proceed into the world and return from the world. That is the reason why God became incarnate in a human body: because God wanted to manifest himself without excluding any aspect of our humanity. In the words of Carmen Bernabé, "Our female bodies, with their specifications and all that they have configured (relations, life) are called to fullness—which does not mean, as the ancients said, being transformed into male bodies. They are called to divine scope and reality."[10]

New Consciousness, New Relationships

Revisiting the rules of male-female relationships from the perspective of this new feminine consciousness would allow us to unmask masculine behaviors that for now remain in the shadows. The romantic love that came to be so valued in the twentieth century has had negative effects on many men and women because it is interlaced with complex mechanisms of power that often lead to situations in which women are rendered invisible or enmeshed in subtle (or not so subtle) forms of subordination, even at the hands of their own spouses. The unease that women experience in these situations cannot always be easily named. Mercedes Valdivieso writes, "You make a murmur that in time is no longer present, and I, in some way, recognize the signs of your language; intensity and complaint resound within me; I take on signs that were transmitted to us women and that we repeat without knowing how to break free of them. It is the language that contains the migraines of my own story, and yet it is the same language that might also tell a different story."[11]

Theologies written by women are careful in how they speak of love, not because women do not desire to love and be loved, but because traditionally love has been seen as the total giving of oneself. But this self-giving has not been treated with respect in terms of self-affirmation, reciprocal relationships, or women's search for fulfillment; rather, it has nourished relationships in which women play a passive, obedient, self-abnegating role. There is a certain conception of love that has favored the subordination of women, a certain anthropological model that exacerbates the "natural" order, promoting complementary relations in which woman is the weak, subordinate complement—instinctive and emotional, silent and private. If the glory of God is the fully alive man, it is also the fullness of women, and everything that works against them also works against the glory of God; it is not redemptive. As Giddens points out, romantic love is distorted in its relation to power. Giddens writes,

> For women dreams of romantic love have all too often led to grim domestic subjection. Confluent love presumes equality in emotional give and take, the more so the more any particular love tie approximates closely to the prototype of the pure relationship. Love here only develops to the degree to which intimacy does, to the degree to which each partner is prepared to reveal concerns and needs to the other and to be vulnerable to that other. The masked emotional dependence of men has inhibited their willingness, and their capacity, to be made thus vulnerable.[12]

The new consciousness of women, in short, not only implies a new self-awareness in the history of humanity, but also an awareness of their relation to men, particularly in their love relationships. This new relationship that women establish with their bodies, their sexuality, their desire and eroticism, inevitably results in men experiencing a sense of displacement.

In 2004, a report on Chile by the United Nations Development Program said that men are living a silent crisis because they have lost their compass, their role, their identity.[13] The domains that previously belonged exclusively to men are now the domains of women as well. The discourses that were useful to them, and their imaginaries and classifications of women, do not help them to relate to empowered women who have successfully risen in society and are not willing to move backward for promises of love or for anything else. Either men will open up to a process of awareness-raising and rethinking their masculinity, or the misunderstanding between men and women will be long and painful. As Giddens argues,

> Men are the laggards in the transitions now occurring—and in a certain sense have been so ever since the late eighteenth century. In Western culture at least, today is the first period in which men are finding themselves to be men, that is, as possessing a problematic "masculinity." In previous times, men have assumed that their activities constituted "history," whereas women existed almost out of time, doing the same as they had always done.[14]

In the field of sexuality and the crossing of borders between theology and gender, this becomes urgent.

It is important for women to legitimize their bodies and sexuality—their womanhood—in a Church that, led by a collective of celibate men, has become accustomed to viewing and treating women as if they were in a permanent childlike state as well as being a constant threat to their own celibate state and "order" of things. This is an error because women's experiences can open great horizons of freedom and humanization for theology and indeed for our entire ecclesial experience.

Notes

1. This essay is an excerpt from the article "Y Dios me hizo mujer" ("And God Made Me Woman") published in Yañez y Reyes, ed., *Sexualidad(es) y Evangelio* (*Sexualities and the Gospel*) (Santiago, Chile: Ediciones Universidad Alberto Hurtado, 2015).

2. Vanina Leschziner and Silvia Kuasnosky, "Género, sexualidad y afectividad. Modelos culturales dominantes e incipientes," in *Religión, Género y Sexualidad* (*Religion, Gender and Sexuality*), ed. Carlos Schikendantz (Córdoba, Argentina: EDUCC, 2004), 82.

3. Anthony Giddens, *The Transformation of Intimacy: Sexuality, Love and Eroticism in Modern Societies* (Cambridge: Polity Press, 1992), 181.

4. Cecilia Inés Luque, "La sexualidad de los ángeles...del hogar. Mujeres, *ethos* sexual y religión en las novelas del boom de la literatura de mujeres hispanoamericanas" ("The Sexuality of the Angels...of the Hearth. Women, Sexual *Ethos* and Religion in the Boom of Spanish American Women's Literature"), in Schikendantz, *Religión, Género y Sexualidad*, 32 (trans. Jeannine M. Pitas).

5. For more on the process of women's conversion, see Carolina del Río, "Dios también es mujer ¿o no?" ("God Is Also a Woman, Right?"), in *Iglesia en crisis. La irrupción de los laicos* (*The Church in Crisis: The Rise of the Laity*), ed. Carolina del Río and María Olga Delpiano (Santiago: Editorial Uqbar, 2011), 131–57.

6. Elizabeth A. Johnson, *She Who Is: The Mystery of God in Feminist Theological Discourse*, 25th anniv. ed. (New York: Crossroad, 2017), 64.

7. Johnson, *She Who Is*, 64.

8. Johnson, *She Who Is*, 66.

9. Christine Gudorf, *Body, Sex, and Pleasure: Reconstructing Christian Sexual Ethics* (Cleveland: Pilgrim Press, 1994), 65.

10. Carmen Bernabé, "Yo Soy la Resurrección" ("I Am the Resurrection"), in *Y Vosotras ¿Quién Decís Que Soy Yo? (And You Women? Who Do You Say That I Am?)*, ed. Isabel Gómez Acebo (Paris: Desclée de Brouwer, 2000), 296 (trans. Jeannine M. Pitas).

11. Mercedes Valdivieso, "Refracciones" ("Refractions"), in *María Luisa Bombal: Apreciaciones críticas (Maria Luisa Bombal: Critical Appreciations)*, ed. Marjorie Agosin, Elena Gascón-Vera, and Joy Renjilian-Burgy (Tempe, AZ: Bilingual Press, 1987), 257.

12. Giddens, *The Transformation of Intimacy*, 64.

13. See Programa de Naciones Unidas para el Desarrollo, *Nosotros los chilenos: un desafío cultural, Desarrollo Humano en Chile 2002*, part 5, chap. 3, 214–22.

14. Giddens, *The Transformation of Intimacy*, 61.

In Search of Eternal Life

Reading the Scriptures through Women's Eyes

Anne Arabome

"You search the scriptures because you think that in them you have eternal life."

(John 5:39)

How should women "search the scriptures" in their pursuit of "eternal life"? The Bible is a complex document that encompasses a world far removed from ours and yet is still relevant for creating ethical principles, social norms, practical guidelines, and doctrinal criteria in the life of the Christian community. It would be a fair assessment to say that, for the most part, the Bible was written by men for men, and several of them have used it to control the lives of women. Take, for example, as Carol Meyers points out, "the simple matter of personal names. The Hebrew Bible mentions a total of 1,426 names, of which 1,315 are those of men. Thus, only 111 women's names appear, about 9 percent of the total. The enormous gap between the number of women's and of men's names signals the male-centered concerns of the biblical literature."[1]

As I see it, part of the problem stems from the gender bias that underlies biblical narratives and is reflected in their male-centered authorship and perspectives. To imagine the feminine in God through texts written by men is a challenge. Besides, the tendency to relegate women to marginality and obscurity has scriptural precedence. Not a few preachers, pastors, and evangelists still refer to the Bible to advocate the subservience and subordination of women in church and society. Yet, reconstructing gender interaction in the biblical past in order to understand relationships in a contemporary context is a daunting exercise. So, how should women read the Bible? There is no simple answer, but by drawing on my experience as an African woman, I offer the following as critical principles or points of reference for approaching the Bible.

As women from diverse cultures and backgrounds, and considering our experiences of oppressive and marginalizing patriarchy both in theological scholarship and doctrinal disquisitions, the first methodological imperative is to adopt a critical stance vis-à-vis the Bible. To recall an African proverb, "Eneke the bird says that since men have learnt to shoot without missing, it has learnt to fly without perching." The fact that official biblical exegesis and hermeneutics continue to be skewed by patriarchal proclivities, no matter how subtle, should arouse a hermeneutical suspicion in women. We cannot take its content at face value. Over the centuries, too many men have appealed to Scripture to define the place of women in church and society on issues as diverse as marriage, property rights, human dignity, maternity, and social relationships. Like Eneke the bird, women must learn to evade this trap and develop their own epistemological and hermeneutical resources for reading, understanding, and applying biblical data to their lived reality.

Women in Africa and elsewhere must look to the depths of wisdom available to them in various sources, including wholesome cultural practices in which women had important and eminent roles and positions in society, albeit patriarchal elements tried to eliminate those roles by their domination and control. In this sense, the Bible can be a powerful tool if wielded methodically with wisdom, courage, and tenacity in the quest for human flourishing for women and men. As Kwok Pui-lan reminds us,

> Third World women and minority women focus on the multiple oppression of women in the Bible because these stories speak to their reality and shed light on their existence, but their concern is not just limited to the texts on women or on marginalized women in particular. They seek to use these specific texts to uncover the interlocking oppression of racism, classism, and sexism in the past and in the present, thereby helping all of us to liberate ourselves from bondage.[2]

Second, like theology, Scripture is a mine of symbolic creation, production, and transmission of meaning shaped by contexts and surrounding cultures. Such contexts and cultures carry entrenched biases that have been the particular focus of gender studies aimed at deconstructing their distorted ideological foundations. Symbols and meanings are born in time and space, not ordained by the gods. Where male symbols have proliferated and dominated theology and Christianity, other symbols can be created, particularly those that honor the diversity and plurality of human experience and are inclusive in promoting human dignity and flourishing. Symbols are meant for human beings, not the other way around.

In light of this, for women, reading the Bible entails deconstructing gender-biased theological and ethical constructs in order to discover and construct a holistic and inclusive interpretative framework. I envisage the outcome of such an enterprise as freeing and emancipating for women and men, especially from the shackles of gender-biased analyses and perspectives.

Finally, it bears repeating that from Genesis to Revelation the Bible and its interpretation have been mainly the preserve of men. We need not become biblical or theological scholars to see the multiple evidence of this. As Teresa Okure poignantly reminds us, "The Bible is a patriarchal book not only because it was written by men (and for the most part for men), but because over the centuries it has been interpreted almost exclusively by men."[3] This "one-sided interpretation" overlooks the truth of reality as a composite of female and male as well as their gendered perceptions of reality. Women's quest to correct this imbalance and the impoverishment of Scripture represents a significant contribution to theological scholarship and the creation of a society and a Church fashioned in the image and likeness of a just God.

Notes

1. Carol L. Meyers, "Everyday Life: Women in the Period of the Hebrew Bible," in *The Women's Bible Commentary*, ed. Carol A. Newsom and Sharon H. Ringe (London: SPCK, 1992), 251–52.

2. Kwok Pui-lan, "Racism and Ethnocentrism in Feminist Biblical Interpretation," in *Searching the Scriptures*, ed. Elisabeth Schüssler Fiorenza (New York: Crossroad, 1993), 113.

3. Teresa Okure, "Women in the Bible," in *With Passion and Compassion: Third World Women Doing Theology*, ed. Virginia Fabella and Mercy Amba Oduyoye (Maryknoll NY: Orbis Books, 1988), 55–56.

Irish Women and a Church in Crisis

Colleen Hennessy

I recently attended a packed funeral Mass in Boston to celebrate the life of a cousin who had died at sixty-two from cancer. She was raised in an Irish American Catholic family, attended Catholic school, and, like most women in my extended family, she had turned away from the institution of Catholicism decades earlier. When the cancer became untreatable, she reached out to a hospital chaplain and found a renewed faith that gave her a sense of peace while dying. She was always a Catholic, but in the end, she had to find a way to live with her faith, despite her alienation from the Catholic clergy, institutions, and hierarchy. That is a critical issue for Catholicism.

The parish priest celebrating the Mass spoke of my cousin's faith, but something was missing. Her husband's eulogy soared with love. He saw her Catholic faith in her love for her family, in her work as a special education teacher in Boston for almost thirty years, in her love for her neighbors and for the women whose friendships she had nurtured through marriages, children, sickness, and grief.

Irish American parishes in the United States are struggling with a decline in membership. The parishes in which these families' ancestors worshipped in Ireland are in trouble too. The pews, parish councils, and altars are filled with people over sixty. Fifty-seven percent of priests in the Dublin archdiocese are over sixty years old. St. Patrick's Seminary in Maynooth, once the largest seminary in the world, enrolled only six first-year seminarians in 2017.

I am a Catholic American who lived in Ireland for ten years. I was confirmed, married, and had my children in Ireland. I am amazed at how Catholicism remains intertwined with the Irish state, education, health care, and community in such a way that the Church has been able to control people's lives for generations. Most Irish people remain Catholic in name and culture, but the latest census results from 2016 show a continued decline in the population who identify as Catholic[1] and a corresponding increase in the number with no religion, which grew by 73.6 percent since 2011. Just as telling is the growing movement for the separation of health care,[2] law,[3] and education[4] from control by the Catholic institutions that have betrayed their communities.

Irish women were betrayed in the worst way. Catholic priests, bishops, nuns, and cardinals abused and neglected their children and babies. They shamed women for sexual and reproductive behavior over which the women themselves had little control. They stole the joy of motherhood and betrayed women's loyalty by failing to protect their families.

Women today, myself included, struggle to reconcile their Catholicism with their identity as women, mothers, professionals, and activists. My expertise is in community development and social inclusion. I decided to conduct a survey by way of an online questionnaire as to why the Church is failing to engage with Irish women and retain their loyalty. I received 189 responses from women. While this result cannot claim to be a representative sample, it does offer an insight into how some Irish women define their relationship with Catholicism.

I asked twenty questions about their relationship with the Catholic Church and its role in Irish society. The questions were a combination of closed and open-ended questions. While 98.2 percent of the respondents were baptized Catholics, less than half had baptized their own children or intended to baptize future children. Only 27 percent affirmatively identified as Catholic now, while the rest either did not identify as Catholic or were unsure about their Catholic identity.

When the women were asked to explain their attitudes toward baptism and the other sacraments, responses were age dependent. Younger women (aged fifteen to forty-four) expressed little interest in the sacraments for themselves or for their children, while the vast majority of older women said they supported baptism and participated in the sacraments in order to ensure access to schools and avoid exclusion in the community.

Nearly all the respondents thought that gender equality is an important issue professionally and personally. Only 6 percent thought that the Catholic Church as an institution values women today, and a further 15 percent said that it sometimes values women. Perhaps more importantly, only 2 percent replied that they do believe that Catholicism values women in its teaching and principles. I believe this is the crux of the membership crisis in Ireland.

Most respondents believed it was impossible to be a Catholic and a feminist, and all reported that news about the Church made them angry on a regular basis (daily and weekly). Their advice to young women was focused on the importance of personal conscience, and many warned that participating in the rituals of the Catholic Church would damage young women's self-esteem.

One respondent wrote, "For many years, I was asked to be a reader in the church. I was also asked on a number of occasions for a reference for male deacons. I find both requests insulting and demeaning considering that women have no role whatsoever in the institution, and there appears to be no vision for this. The fact that it does not matter to the institution is the biggest insult. My daughters' generations will not accept this."

The Association of Catholic Priests (ACP) in Ireland has recently taken a halting first step to address the crisis precipitated by the alienation and exodus of women from the Church. It has asked every diocese to refrain from creating a permanent male diaconate until the Vatican commission on women in the diaconate set up by Pope Francis shares its findings. In a statement issued on August 11, 2017, the ACP explained,

> We believe that proceeding with the introduction of a male permanent diaconate at this time, and thereby adding another male clerical layer to ministry, is insensitive, disrespectful of women, and counter-productive at this present critical time.[5]

The ACP statement shows sensitivity to the current level of disrespect felt by Irish Catholic women. However, the need to integrate women more fully into Catholic institutions also relates to another looming crisis, which is the growing shortage of parish priests in Ireland.[6] I believe this could be an opportunity rather than a threat for the Church today. The parish priest should ensure that all the faithful in his parish are nourished through the celebration of sacraments, and therefore he has a responsibility to ensure that women feel welcomed and respected as equals in his parish. Irish priests do not need to wait for the Vatican commission findings to do this. They could start now by engaging with women and seeking to understand and respond to their concerns.

Catholic institutions and clergy need to develop parishes as places that strengthen individual faith through communal beliefs and practices. They need to approach this through community development principles of increasing the participation and inclusion of the most marginalized of their members. The tools are simple but the trust between women and clergy will only be built through humility and respect. The process of asking about, listening to, and acknowledging women's experiences and understanding of parish politics could be as important as any resulting change in policy.

Notes

1. Central Statistics Office, 2016 Census, chap. 8, "Religion," accessed July 2, 2018, http://www.cso.ie/en/media/csoie/releasespublications/documents/population/2017/Chapter_8_Religion.pdf.

2. See Sarah MacDonald, "Confusion Arises over Using Sisters' Land for Irish National Maternity Hospital," Global Sisters Report, May 22, 2017, http://globalsistersreport.org/news/trends/confusion-arises-over-using-sisters-land-irish-national-maternity-hospital-46811.

3. For example, in 2015, the Irish voted in a referendum to legalize same-sex marriage, and in 2018, they voted in a referendum to liberalize Ireland's strict abortion laws.

4. In a 2017 survey, 72 percent of parents surveyed agreed that law should be changed so baptism cannot be an admission requirement for state-funded schools. See https://www.equateireland.ie/educationandresearch (accessed July 2, 2018).

5. Association of Catholic Priests Statement on the Permanent Diaconate, August 11, 2017, https://www.associationofcatholicpriests.ie/2017/08/association-of-catholic-priests-statement-on-the-permanent-diaconate/.

6. See "Lack of Priests in Irish Catholic Church: The Problem Is Becoming More Acute," *The Irish Times*, Tuesday, August 25, 2015, https://www.irishtimes.com/opinion/editorial/lack-of-priests-in-irish-catholic-church-the-problem-is-becoming-more-acute-1.2327089.

Standing on the Threshold

Where Do Women Belong in the Community of Disciples?

Jennifer Reek

In *Lumen Gentium*, Vatican II's Constitution on the Church, there is a statement that "all men [*homines*] are called to this [eucharistic] union with Christ, who is the light of the world, from whom we go forth, through whom we live, and toward whom our journey leads us" (*LG* 3). The language is not inclusive in this 1960s text on the Church, but the message is remarkably so: *all* are called. The Church in *Lumen Gentium* is pastoral, positive, a pilgrim Church made up of the "people of God" (*LG* chap. 2). In the first session of the Council, Pope John XXIII referred to the Church as "loving mother of all, benign, patient, full of mercy and goodness."[1]

This was the image of Church that attracted me when I became Catholic almost twenty years ago, yet now I feel ambivalent about what I was once so sure was my spiritual home. It is as if I were standing on the threshold of that home, unable to imagine myself either fully inside or out. I know from anecdotal evidence and from narratives of women's alienation from institutional churches that I am not alone. The 1994 book *Defecting in Place: Women Claiming Responsibility for Their Own Spiritual Lives* surveyed seven thousand American women. "I have one foot in and one foot out," wrote one middle-aged Sister. "I feel freer that way. I participate only when I can do so authentically."[2] Like many of the women surveyed, I now find my consolation in women's groups, such as the Catholic Women Speak Network, that are struggling with the question of how to respond to Christ's call to discipleship in a context in which one's suitability for some of the roles that are implied in the term *full discipleship* is determined solely by gender.

I, too, have claimed responsibility for my own spiritual life, and I have tried to discern my calling. I am challenged by the question of how girls and young women might discern a vocation in a Church in which they are marginalized. I want to share here three examples of female exclusion and what they have taught me about this question: my mother's departure from the Church as a young woman, a girl made "invisible" in a public church gathering, and women denied participation in a holy ritual.

My Mother, the Seeker: My maternal ancestors were Irish and Irish American Catholic, but my mother left the Church, or, rather, it left her. When she was a teenager, she married a man she did not love so that she could escape an unhappy home. The marriage was miserable and brief and ended in divorce. She married my father not long after. They stayed together for the rest of her life—fifty-nine years, but the Church she loved told her she was an adulteress and could no longer receive communion.

Ironically, that was a gift to her, for she became a seeker of spiritual sustenance elsewhere. She raised my brother and me in the Episcopalian Church in New York and Virginia. After we moved away, she must have grown restless. She practiced transcendental meditation and joined the School of Practical Philosophy in New York. My father followed wherever she led. They went to a Quaker Meeting House on Long Island, then to a Unitarian Church in Virginia, and, finally, to an odd little congregation in an old movie theater in Palm Beach led by a minister who was a former dermatologist.

My mother became a model for my own spiritual journey, although it took me years to recognize it. She never stopped seeking, for she knew she was called "into his marvelous light" (1 Pet 2:9), despite intimations to the contrary from male clerics. When I feel spiritually homeless, thoughts of her console me and strengthen my resolve.

Girl Invisible: One "vocation Sunday" after Mass, the pastor of my church in Washington addressed a family of parents, two boys, and a girl, sitting in the front pew. The girl was about eight years old. The priest spoke of vocation to the priesthood, of the importance of the influence of the parents on the boys' lives, of the great gift to the Church if one day they were called to serve. The girl was not acknowledged. For the priest, and perhaps others in the congregation, it was as if she were not there. How can girls discern a vocation when they are unseen, unacknowledged, unheard? Those around them must speak up and stand up for them. I am ashamed I did not do so, but that was perhaps a turning point—the start of my gradual turning away. That little girl and others like her led me to make up for the lapse by finding my own voice and encouraging other women to find theirs.

Women Unwashed: A few years after the incident of the "invisible" girl, I attended a Holy Thursday Mass at a cathedral. As I discovered later, women were not allowed to participate in the foot washing ritual. The presiding cardinal was against it. As the ritual began, twelve young white Catholic men walked into the sanctuary and took their seats. The Cardinal knelt in front of each and washed their feet. A woman friend and I were appalled and hurt. In a Church where so much meaning is discovered and expressed in symbols, this exclusion told us that we were not truly disciples, not among those Jesus loved as "his own...to the end" (John 13:1). I have encountered many other Catholic women who find it particularly painful to be excluded from this ritual. And now we have the example of Pope Francis on Holy Thursday washing the feet of women, Muslims, prisoners, refugees—those who have been outcasts brought over the threshold.

What might my stories offer to girls and young women seeking to understand their faith and discern their vocations? *My Mother, the Seeker* shows the importance of allowing oneself to be drawn toward "the light of the world," restlessly seeking that light even if one finds no settled place of belonging. *Girl Invisible* tells us to work continuously toward creating visible, sacramental roles for women in the Church. *Women Unwashed* reveals the need for creating spiritual communities of women where we might find solace and space in which to know our full discipleship. The stories tell us that we journey together, that *all* are called.

Notes

1. Pope John XXIII, "Pope John's Opening Speech to the Council," in *The Documents of Vatican II*, ed. Walter M. Abbott (New York: The America Press, 1966), 716.

2. Miriam Therese Winter, Adair T. Lummis, and Alison Stokes, eds., *Defecting in Place: Women Claiming Responsibility for Their Own Spiritual Lives* (New York: Crossroad, 1995), 85.

What Young Catholic Women Should Hear

Sara Parvis

In April 2017, thousands of young Christian women shared their experiences of misogyny on Twitter. They were responding to a tweet by Sarah Bessey, a Canadian theologian, writer, and pastor, who had been reflecting on the question—familiar to feminists—of why women are discouraged from being ambitious, whereas for men ambition is considered a virtue. Bessey tweeted under #ThingsOnlyChristianWomenHear: "Ambition isn't godly."

Thousands of young Christian women from various denominations started using #ThingsOnlyChristianWomenHear to tweet their own experiences of misogyny and abuse. They spoke of a culture that condones rape, sexual assault, sexual harassment, and the blaming and shaming of young women for things done to them by men. As the #MeToo campaign has shown, these experiences are common to women from all social contexts and walks of life, but many of the experiences tweeted by Christian women included the poisonous twist that the young women were blamed or shamed or manipulated into minimizing their own sexual mistreatment on speciously Christian grounds.

Comments posted under #ThingsOnlyChristianWomenHear included the following:

- "'The most loving thing would be for you two to get married': said to me by the mother of my rapist."
- "Don't talk about what the pastor did to you. It's hard for him."
- (During counseling) "I'm sure your rapist feels awful about what he did to you. Let's pray for him."
- "You shouldn't tempt the brothers by showing your curves. They can't help themselves."

In response to these and many similar posts, another hashtag was launched, #ThingsChristianWomenShouldHear, this time to promote a more positive exchange. Many of those posting here were clearly older, theologically educated women, trying to respond to the pain being expressed by the younger women. They included many along the lines of "You are in the image of God," "Your gifts are valued and wanted," and simply "Galatians 3:28." One comment posted under #ThingsChristianWomenShouldHear that I found particularly interesting was this: "We apologize for contorting the Trinity to bolster the 'biblical manhood and womanhood' movement."

What things should young Catholic women hear if we are to assure them they are respected, valued, and wanted in the Church? Here are three humble but ambitious suggestions from an older, theologically educated woman.

1. God, qua God, is not male.

Divinity in its own essence has no sex: on this the ancient and medieval theologians of the Church are agreed. The term *divinity*, like the term *Trinity*, is feminine in both Greek and Latin while the term *God* is masculine, but no significance should be attached to this. Catholics do not believe in pairs of male and female gods, as the ancient Gnostics do, but in the One Who Is, the Living One.

Jesus taught us to call God our Father and to make disciples of all the nations, baptizing them in the name of the Father, the Son, and the Holy Spirit. We cannot, therefore, simply replace these by other titles such as "Creator, Redeemer, and Sanctifier," particularly in the sacrament of baptism itself. But we can note, and indeed insist, that these names do not map on to masculinity in the divine nature. The theology of God in the Hebrew Bible, which does not use "Father" as a common designation for God, encourages us to look for other reasons why Jesus calls God "Father." There is not room here to explore the many different views expressed on this point throughout the early Christian period and afterward, but the role of the father in Roman society—on which the theology of Irenaeus, for example, draws heavily—offers an important insight. It interprets God's fatherly love for us in terms of a choice rather than a necessity. The Roman father had the power of life or death over his whole household. A child was only recognized and allowed to live when its father picked it up; otherwise it was thrown out to die and to be eaten by animals, or to be reared by slave traders or child prostitution gangs. God is the Father who chooses all his children and intends and works for their lasting good. But God is also the mother who bore us, nurtures us, and teaches us. And God in God's essence is beyond these images.

When we turn to Jesus himself, we need to be careful to distinguish, as far as his human attributes are concerned (of which maleness is one), between the Eternal Word and the human nature that Word took on in the incarnation. The Eternal Word is called by both masculine and feminine names, Son and Wisdom (*Sophia*), and, being true God, is neither male nor female, though both images are used in

Scripture and so may properly be used in prayer. Jesus's human nature is male, just as Mary, the first and greatest Christian, is female. But both are models for all of us, not Jesus for men and Mary for women. Women and men should all imitate Jesus insofar as we can; men and women should all imitate Mary. There is no one other than Christ by whom any of us is saved; there is no one other than Mary who is able to show us wholly perfect discipleship.

The Holy Spirit is feminine in Hebrew, Syriac, and other Semitic languages, neuter in Greek, and masculine in Latin. Some of the qualities of the Spirit might seem feminine (melting, moistening, comforting), others masculine (acting as advocate for us, teaching us boldness). But once again, we must not confuse images we might find comforting and helpful in prayer with the essence of God, who has no sex.

Young Catholic women (and indeed young Catholic men) need to be clear on these points. We are not involved in some kind of Gnostic mythology that revolves around eternal sex. Jesus is not your boyfriend. Mary is not an icon of submission. Women and men are equally called, and if we are saved, we are equally saved, because all of us have been individually bought at the infinite price of the infinite love of the infinite God. The Trinity calls us to eternal life. Mary, assumed body and soul into heaven, has marked out the way and shows forth the complete redemption we are all called to. There is nothing either men or women can aspire to that is better than what she has achieved by the grace of Christ.

2. Women are, and always have been, part of the Magisterium.

The essential role of women in the teaching office of the Church was made visible most clearly by Jesus himself, when he chose women to be the first witnesses and preachers of the resurrection, without whom the gospel would have died in the first generation. He gave many other signs also of their importance as theological agents in his mission. He chose to begin his public ministry, which would end in his death, at the request of his mother (John 2:1–11). He allowed himself to be theologically corrected by the Canaanite woman, no doubt as a sign to his followers (Matt 15:21–28). He allowed Mary of Bethany to sit at his feet as his disciple (Luke 10:39), and either her or another woman to anoint him (Mark 14:3–9), calling for what she had done to be told everywhere the gospel is preached, in memory of her. He discussed the theology of baptism with the Samaritan woman at the well (John 4:7–27) and the theology of the resurrection with Martha, who recognized him as the Son of God from his words (John 11:21–27). He called Mary of Magdala by her name and sent her to preach to his brothers (John 20:11–18).

Some theological authority had already been given to certain women in Old Testament times. Deborah judged Israel (Judg 4—5); Hannah corrected the priest Eli (1 Sam 1); Lemuel's mother instructed him in how to be a good and just ruler (Prov 31).

In the early Church, women were crucial to the spread of Christianity, as can be seen both from the Acts of the Apostles and from the Letters of St. Paul. Early in the second century, we find Hermas asking Grapte to study his book *The Shepherd* with the women of the Roman Church. Later in the second century, we find women martyrs teaching and sustaining their fellow Christians. St. Blandina served as the image of Christ to her fellow martyrs at Lyon when they looked on her stretched out as though on a cross, and she urged them on in their faith. St. Perpetua shared her visions with her fellow prisoners for Christ. She was the first to teach that God responds to those who pray for the dead and grants them refreshment in answer to those prayers. St. Augustine, after years of resisting his mother, St. Monica, acknowledged how important she had been in his formation, not only in childhood but in adulthood as well. St. Gregory of Nyssa also acknowledged his debt to his sister St. Macrina as his great spiritual teacher.

In recent decades, four women from the medieval and early modern periods have been designated doctors of the Universal Church. Pope Paul VI so designated Sts. Catherine of Siena and Teresa of Avila, and Popes John Paul II and Benedict XVI added Sts. Thérèse of Lisieux and Hildegard of Bingen. This ipso facto shows that 1 Timothy 2:12 ("I permit no woman to teach or to have authority over a man") cannot be understood as meaning that women cannot contribute to the Church's discernment of Catholic teaching.

But are we yet ready to allow women to contribute to the magisterium in a systematic way? There is a crying need for it. Current magisterial teaching and practice on women lacks logic: men and women are deemed to be fundamentally different, but men are in sole charge of developing and policing Church teachings about women. This may have made sense in societies in which women had no education, or where women were not deemed capable of thinking systematically, but in modern societies in which women do at least as well as men in tertiary education, and many have doctorates in philosophy, theology, law, medicine, and other relevant subjects, such assumptions can no longer apply. Women often have different interests and different insights from men, however; they see and hear different things, and in particular, not surprisingly, they are much more alive to women's history and to philosophical and theological problems that are specific to women. Currently, only those insights that recommend themselves to celibate men are likely to be considered by the teaching office of the Church.

Without laboring the point, it is hard to imagine that women, or even fathers of families, would have taken so long to see why showing mercy to child-molesting clergy should not be regarded as more important than protecting children.

Having women deacons, and eventually women cardinals, would seem an obvious way of allowing women to be systematically included in the teaching office of the Church, at both diocesan and curial levels. Furthermore, in order to have a magisterium that has the capacity to address the theological concerns of women systematically, women should be included as a norm in the process of selecting episcopal candidates. Currently, when potential episcopal candidates are vetted, they are asked if they accept that women cannot be priests. Without discussing the rights and wrongs of this, the question risks excluding those candidates most likely to see women as their equals. This is not to say that bishops chosen under this system are necessarily misogynist, but it screens out one end of the spectrum of possible views of women, and risks a "misogynist drift" in the episcopacy in the future, with inevitable consequences for the episcopacy's ability to preside effectively over theological questions that mostly or wholly concern women. If the question about women priests is to remain, it should be complemented by a question about the candidate's ability to work with women in a team.

3. Language should be inclusive.

Languages vary in their gender usage, but certainly in English, young women do not generally describe themselves as "men" or "brothers," unless they are being ironic. They are very conscious of their difference from boys. I am involved in running our parish's Justice and Peace group. In preparation for the 2018 Synod, I thought I might order copies of *Docat*—a young person's guide to the Church's social teaching—for all the teenagers in the parish.[1] I thought I might also give copies to my nonpracticing nieces, in the hope of interesting them in the Church. On inspection, however, I realized that *Docat* uses exclusive language throughout, speaking always of "man," "men," and "brothers." This rendered what should have been a valuable catechetical and apologetic tool utterly useless. How can we expect teenage girls to take the Church's social teaching seriously when it does not appear to recognize their existence? When the Church insists upon sexual difference as essential to the nature of humanity and is so opposed to notions of gender fluidity, what sense does it make to call women "men" and "brothers" and then expect them to feel included in the Church and affirmed in their Christian womanhood?

Conclusion

Does the Church love and value young women and want them to continue as practicing Catholics at the heart of the Church? If so, it would be worth seeking more systematic ways of listening to them, understanding them, and speaking with them. I have outlined three aspects of theology, ecclesiology, and language that seem to me particularly urgent. But the most urgent thing young Catholic women need to hear is that the Church can be bothered to preach the good news (rather than a misogynist travesty of it) to them at all.

Notes

1. *Docat* is part of the *Youcat* series of books designed for young people. In the United Kingdom and Ireland, it is published by the Catholic Truth Society, see http://www.ctsbooks.org/Search ?searchTerm=YOUCAT.

PART TWO

DISCERNMENT AND DIVERSITY

Catholic Women in Cultures and Contexts

Jesus said to her, "Woman, believe me, the hour is coming when you will worship the Father neither on this mountain nor in Jerusalem....God is spirit, and those who worship him must worship in spirit and truth."

(John 4:21–24)

A Letter to Pope Francis—from Ten Young Catholic Women, Ages 14 to 17

Students of the Ursuline High School, Wimbledon

This letter was written as part of a study day at the University of Roehampton in London.

Dear Pope Francis,

As young women in the Church, we know that Catholicism is at the center of our lives. Our faith in Jesus Christ gives us our values: respect for all, compassion, wanting to change the world for the better, leadership, forgiveness, kindness, love, community, courage, peace. Our school motto is *SERVIAM* and we understand this to mean serving others and making a difference. We are so grateful that you are bringing issues of the equality and needs of the poor to everyone's notice, and the importance of caring for our world and environmental issues if we are to improve people's lives.

In response to your request for young people's views about the Church in our lives, we have considered the following statement from *Amoris Laetitia* and discussed in groups the issues that we think are important, and we have written down some of our responses as well:

The woman stands before the man as a mother, the subject of the new human life that is conceived and develops in her, and from her is born into the world. The weakening of this maternal presence with its feminine qualities poses a grave risk to our world. I certainly value feminism, but one that does not demand uniformity or negate motherhood. For the grandeur of women includes all the rights derived from their inalienable human dignity but also from their feminine genius, which is essential to society. Their specifically feminine abilities—motherhood in particular—also grant duties, because womanhood entails a specific mission in this world, a mission that society needs to protect and preserve for the good of all. (*AL* 173)

In this letter we summarize our discussions about the statement. We have directly quoted from some of the students' responses where we think this is the best way to show how we feel. We also share our views on femininity, sexuality, social media, and role models.

One of our group speaks for many of us when she says,

As our Pope you have inspired me greatly to uphold and respect the main values of Catholicism and to understand the way to be a good Catholic. At the same time I cannot ignore the prejudice formed against women in our societies.

As young women we feel it is our duty to raise the issues that are affecting us in our lives and that we feel are not given enough consideration by the Church. One member of our group wrote,

As a young woman in the Catholic Church, I have faith, but the Church does not enrich my sense of what it means to be a Catholic woman in the ways it could. Ideally, I believe the Church should be more outspoken in parishes about the roles of women beyond motherhood and about equality and women's leadership.

Missions, Motherhood, and "Feminine Genius"

We know that you recognize that women have ambitions outside the home, but we don't think this is properly acknowledged by the Church. We ALL have missions in our lives. We aspire to be lawyers, nurses, teachers, musicians, athletes, engineers, doctors, and some of us feel called to have a family as well. While motherhood is a really wonderful aspect of being a woman, it is just one aspect, not the only one. In a changing society, it is important to change the ways that we as a Church engage with young people and women.

We discussed what you say about the weakening of maternal presence and about "feminine genius." Initially "feminine genius" sounded complimentary, but then we asked ourselves what it really means. We think of the qualities it refers to that are supposedly inherent to womanhood, such as caring, nurturing, and receptivity. It is evident that there is a persistent reference to "motherhood" within Church teachings on vocations. We believe motherhood is really important, but for a number of reasons, focusing only on this does not relate to our ambitions as women or our experience of the world.

We believe using the phrase "feminine genius" puts a particular burden on women to be the "caring, nurturing" gender exclusively, yet there are no reasons why husbands and fathers cannot be these things also. We want to draw attention to the importance of a father in a child's life. Fatherhood is a central aspect of being a man—it takes two to make a baby. Carrying a child is unique but it is not the measure of a woman. Children need unconditional love and responsible guardians, a responsibility that does not depend on gender. A father who is not present in his children's lives is arguably as much at fault as a mother would be. Parents are equally responsible. What is the Church doing to tackle the problem of men leaving their families? We know that you do speak about fathers in *Amoris Laetitia*, but we think the Church should focus much more on the responsibilities of fatherhood.

One of our group described her experience and how it made her reflect on what it means to be a parent:

> *When I was twelve years old, my father left. It has taken these extreme circumstances for me to realize that "masculine genius" is also required in a family as well as "feminine genius." In an equal society, both parents ought to be equally responsible as parents for their children and equally engaged in activities outside parenthood, such as working, rather than women being restricted to a household environment. It is not right and just to say that only the mother has a responsibility and obligation to fulfill her duty as a parent and have motherhood as her only achievement. In Genesis 1:27, it says that "God created humankind in his own image"; I believe that this clearly refers to women and men. We are equals and consequently we should both have the whole life responsibility of parenting.*

Caring for young children is not a "feminine genius" but a human genius. Not all women are able to have children or are called to have children or have the opportunity to be mothers. What does this mean for them in the Church? Don't they have a mission if they are not expressing their "specifically feminine abilities" or carrying out their "specific mission in the world"?

We do not see a "weakening of this maternal presence" that you refer to. On the contrary, we see lots of young people like us being brought up by their mothers alone. We looked up the statistics: "Around 90 per cent of single parents are women; the proportion who are men has remained at around 10 per cent for over a decade. Single fathers are more than twice as likely to be widowed as single mothers."[1] In our experience, young people are often being really well brought up just by their mothers. We see no mothers walking away and abandoning their children.

Our Catholic mothers and grandmothers are our role models. Here is how one of our group described it:

> *I have felt more inspired by the inspirational Catholic women I know—particularly my grandmother and mother—than by what I hear in church on Sunday. They showed me what it means to be a strong woman and have given me the ideals and values I respect: caring, confidence, self-assurance, independence, and— through hard work and guidance—helping your family to flourish.*

Many mothers have been a role model for faith and womanhood in their faith and work, such as Margaret Mizen, who set up a charity in the memory of her son.[2] For all women who do not necessarily have these role models in their lives or the opportunities to meet such women, the Church speaking out more about their work will help. Praising women of faith for their achievement will help to support strong Catholic women in every community.

We believe women can work, lead, and be really good mothers. As one of our group said,

The women in my life all work outside the home as well as having a family.

Another said,

As a Catholic student I want to go in to science and pharmaceuticals but would also like to get married and have children; I can do both.

Somebody else wrote,

In the future, I aspire to become an engineer. I also want to have children. The human mind is capable of performing more than one task, more than parenting, more than one career. I have not heard of a mother who does not put her children first. Women are able to be more than just mothers because we ARE "genius."

All those who are able to care for children and bring them up in a loving and enriching environment with a high quality of life for them should be encouraged, whoever or whatever their gender, culture, background, ethnicity, or sexuality. These should not matter. A member of the group expressed well why we say this:

Growing up in London, we have been lucky enough to be surrounded by many different cultures, faiths, backgrounds, genders, and sexualities. In this environment it has become clear to me that the subject of becoming a parent and marriage is important to all of us. My neighbors are a good example. One couple is gay with children and has raised them to be fantastic, friendly, smart ethically, and sociable kids who are aiming for Oxford and Cambridge. I have neighbors who are young mothers taking care of their children on their own after the father has left them to their own devices without the role model of a father. I also know a newly wedded couple planning their first child.

Sexuality, Equality, and Gender

Equality: some see it as an opportunity, some see it as reality, and most of us still see it as unattainable. The Catholic Church teaches us that *everyone is made in God's image*, yet walls are built instead of bridges. We divide ourselves with regard to sexuality and gender, different roles for men and women are imposed on all people of the Church. We believe everyone is equal but different and this includes gender differences.

As young people living and studying in London, we are exposed to many different lifestyles and relationships. Here is what one of our group wrote:

Moving countries to live in new communities and cultures has allowed me to understand that all persons have the free will to decide their vocation, acknowledge their sexual orientation, and choose a way of life appropriate to their calling.

We live in the twenty-first century, when cultures have drastically developed and changed, and our views ought to become contemporary with regard to the issue of equality. This is possible while maintaining the traditional values of our Catholic faith. I believe that we, as a developed society, should and ought to be able to develop and introduce new concepts—within reason— without compromising Catholic views or being prejudiced or discriminatory against anyone, including women, because we are all made in the image of God and we were all given free will— informed by our faith—to do what we believe to be right.

In our generation, we are influenced and inspired by Catholic social teaching and our society to be open-minded to all our peers and accepting of everybody. Therefore, many of us find it hard to conform to the teachings of the Catholic Church, which, although it strongly preaches the equality of all, subtly encourages division among those of different sexualities and genders. LGBT Catholic teens feel trapped within the walls set by this division, causing some of us— because of the teachings that contradict our experience, our sense of our own existence—to feel disconnected from our faith. Which makes us wonder, do we exist in the eyes of God? Will my Church accept me? Individually, some of us believe God accepts everyone, but it seems as if the Church is saying something different. So what am I supposed to believe? Can I still go to church?

Young People and Social Media

One of our group described the difficulties we face because of social media:

> *Social media defines my worth and the worth of all young women. Our society gives such a narrow view of what a successful person is, what we look like, and how much money we are going to earn. This is not good, but my peers and I are growing up in a society where the number of likes we get on Instagram or Facebook is seen to make us the person we are. We are dissolved in this alternative reality that was created for the benefit of none, and distorts our view of society and the members within it. This horrible alternative world encourages immediate self-gratification and results in more self-obsessed young people; appearance is made to be everything. We need to do something about this. Young women—including myself— should be building themselves into magnificent, glorious people who can use their values to tackle the problems of the world, protecting our environment and improving the lives of others, as Pope Francis challenges us to do.*

Social media is a one-way route to mental health problems and suicidal thoughts for young people as it offers a false sense of reality completely flooded with photo editing, blemishing effects, and fake people. More and more women feel desperate because they lack a sense of belonging within society and have no way of reaching the online ideal of womanhood.

How can our Catholic faith help us? God is always there for us and with us. This is true, but in church on Sunday, there is no acknowledgment of the new technology and social media itself and the problems we are facing. None of us is aware of the Church raising or discussing current issues such as girls feeling worthless and empty within.

Mental health issues are an epidemic, so how can the Church help solve this problem? How can the Church understand and address the issues of mental health and give young women—through the teaching of the gospel—a sense of belonging and being loved and respected?

Our Voices: Making a Change

We have learned at church and in our religious education (RE) lessons that Mary Magdalene and Mary, mother of James, were the first witnesses to the resurrection, the first to tell the good news. Our RE teacher says they were the first evangelists. It is so important for the Church to offer female role models, to provide important jobs (not just motherhood) for women, and to hear the voices of women everywhere.

In our research we have learned that women perform two-thirds of the work but only earn 10 percent of the world's income. Two out of three people living in poverty are women.[3] Women must work to escape poverty for themselves and their children.

To tackle poverty, women need more education and more opportunity. Only very rich women can stay at home with their children. We do not know any women like this, and we are not living in poverty. The United Nations says that "women's equal participation [is] fundamental to democracy and justice."[4] Plan International UK says, "Educating girls helps break the cycle of poverty and inequality."[5] We passionately believe this.

Thank you for hearing our voices. We are grateful for your leadership and example. We hope that we have shared some of the experiences of being young Catholic women today. We pray for you and all in the Church who are working for a better world. Please include us in this work.

In love, faith, and hope,

Students from the Ursuline High School, Wimbledon

Notes

1. Gingerbread website, accessed July 2, 2018, https://gingerbread.org.uk/content/365/Statistics.

2. Jimmy Mizen, son of Margaret and Barry, was murdered on May 10, 2008, the day after his sixteenth birthday.

3. VSO website, accessed July 2, 2018, https://www.vsointernational.org/gender.

4. Michelle Bachelet, "Women's Equal Participation Fundamental to Democracy and Justice," Joint IPU/UN Women meeting, February 29, 2012, New York, http://www.unwomen.org/en/news/stories/2012/2/women-s-equal-participation-fundamental-to-democracy-and-justice.

5. Plan International UK, accessed July 2, 2018, https://plan-uk.org/about/our-work/education.

"Feminine Genius" and the Role of Women

An Indian Daughter and Mother in Conversation

Gayatri and Astrid Lobo Gajiwala[1]

GAYATRI: I read this tweet about how, when a financial institution asks for one's mother's maiden name as a security question, it is because that part of the mother's identity has been sufficiently erased from one's public history that it has become safe enough to be used as a password to access private information. To me, that makes it seem as though the only important thing in a woman's life is getting married and having children. Her life before marriage is completely erased.

ASTRID: For me the whole naming process is ambiguous. You use the word *maiden* as if it is specific to the woman, but you are really talking about a woman's father's name. It's a very patriarchal system, but I agree that changing one's surname is a subtle way of erasing a woman's life before marriage. Here in India it's more obvious because, particularly among Hindus, a woman is expected to change not just her surname but even her first name because once she gets married, she is supposed to be starting a new life in which her husband is supreme. She has to ask permission to visit her parental home. It's one of the reasons that girls are called *paraya dhan*—someone else's property—and women who suffer domestic violence do not return to their parental home.

GAYATRI: We raise women to think that their identity can be submerged. I was taught to adjust, adjust, compromise. It was never you, but all through growing up every time I said something mildly shocking or mildly rebellious, there were all of these aunties who would say to me either, "You will change when you grow up and get married, and you will stop thinking about all these things" or "How are you going to get married if you cannot compromise or adjust?" or "It is really important for a woman to adjust and compromise when she gets married."

When you are taught your whole life that your identity does not matter, how do you expect women to fight for anything that they believe is important to them? They have never learned to believe that anything is important to them. Even if it is important to them, it doesn't mean that it's important to the rest of the world, because the world doesn't think that they are important.

ASTRID: What came to my mind when you were talking is a concept that has become popular in the Church of late—"feminine genius." It's often used to describe the compassion of women and their ability to adjust and to bring peace. Listening to you, I'm wondering how much of that ability is based on strength and how much of it is based on vulnerability or maybe even powerlessness.

Is it possible to have a world of unity where both people can bring their strengths to the relationship or will this bring only conflict?

GAYATRI: I feel that is true of the friends I have now, who are both male and female—all feminists. They all believe that everybody is equally important and deserves equal opportunities. I realize that it is not about both being strong but about both being free to be strong and weak. So regardless of gender or sexual orientation, they are able to show their vulnerabilities and to bring in their strengths when it is important, and at the same time to adjust when it is important to adjust.

ASTRID: I like that word *vulnerabilities*. I totally agree with you, and that's why I have a problem with the phrase *feminine genius*. Is it "genius"? Are these qualities to which I referred earlier coming from a position of strength or from a position of powerlessness? Also, as you said, are these only "feminine" qualities or are they qualities that we also find in men and that we could nurture and develop in men too, so that we have a humanity that is more compassionate, more sensitive, more invested in creating life-giving relationships, in building peace?

GAYATRI: I find that word *nurture* fascinating, because it's almost always used exclusively for women. It's the most feminine quality that you can think of, and whether you're working in education or nursing or religion, whether you're a nun or whatever, it's this quality that's expected of women. This ability to nurture, the ability to put others' needs before one's own, the ability to take care of somebody else at a great cost to oneself and do it uncomplainingly, do it without the feeling that one's giving something up—I wonder when that will change—if ever.

ASTRID: I didn't use *nurture* in that sense. I used it more in terms of helping people to develop their capacities and capabilities, and I would not at all associate that with women only. I would expect a good leader, a good boss, irrespective of gender, to nurture these qualities in those for whom she or he is responsible.

Years ago we talked about the need for women to have jobs that were not confined to service-oriented, care-giving jobs. Today you find women in decision-making and policy-making jobs. In my own institution, the financial controller is a woman, and that is a very powerful position.

76

GAYATRI: But are they expected to bring that ability to nurture and adjust to the table as women? I notice in a lot of the women in management positions where I work that there's a softness that does not really come through with the men. They tone down criticism, even if it is constructive, but they offer it as suggestions. Rather than saying, "Don't do it like this, do it like that," they would say, "Do you think if you do it like this and not like that it would be better?" I often wonder when women are given positions of power, if they are expected to be *people* in positions of power or *women* in positions of power who bring these feminine qualities?

ASTRID: I wouldn't identify these as feminine qualities. If I were to look at myself in a leadership role, the question for me would be very simple: "What strategies should I use in order to get what I want done?" So if, on the one hand, the other person would be more likely to accept a proposal when I put it forward as a recommendation, I would do that without thinking, "Oh, it's the woman's way to do it." If, on the other hand, I thought that this particular situation needed somebody to give a very clear-cut order, I would do that. So I would not see that as feminine or masculine. I would just see it as a strategy to get the job done in the best possible way.

Notes

1. We are grateful to Voices of Faith for permission to use this conversation, which was first published on their website.

How a Visit to a Bookstore Changed My Life

Zuzanna Radzik[1]

I was raised in a practicing Catholic family in Poland, which is a predominantly Catholic country with a tiny Jewish community. I was never interested in joining Catholic youth groups, I did not grow up with traditional devotion to Mary, and pilgrimages held no appeal. Yet in the summer of 2000, I went on a young people's pilgrimage to the shrine of Our Lady of Częstochowa, attracted mainly by the socializing and the cool young Jesuits leading the group. As we were approaching the shrine, the preacher said we should think about what gifts we were bringing to Mary. In the heat of the moment I remember praying, "We both know I'm here by accident, but I have two hands, you could use me for something." As they say, be careful what you pray for.

In the months that followed, there were heated debates in Poland about Jewish/Christian history, prompted by the publication of the book *Neighbors* by Jan Tomasz Gross. The book described the murder by Poland's non-Jewish citizens of their Jewish neighbors during the German occupation. The controversy awakened in me a desire to learn more about the Christian-Jewish story. At the age of seventeen, I found myself sitting on the floor during a panel about Christian-Jewish relations (it was so crowded there were no seats left), and out of the blue I realized that this is exactly what I wanted to do with my life.

I spent the next couple of years exploring Judaism and Christian-Jewish issues. I was not the most studious teenager and I preferred having experiences to reading books, so I began hanging out in the synagogue and drinking tea with Holocaust survivors from the Warsaw ghetto. Before going to church and family lunch on Sundays, I would attend a class about *parshat hashavua*, which is a portion of the Jewish Scripture prescribed for reading in a particular week. I discovered the Christian Liturgy of the Hours because I envied my Jewish friend having his *siddur*, a prayer book with psalms and prayers to be said five times a day. I was fascinated by the new light Judaism shed on my Christianity.

I was a teenage Catholic girl who had become a regular visitor to the Jewish community in Warsaw, but one day, someone approached me in a cafeteria and said, "You are a Catholic, right? Do you know what Catholics think about the Jews?" Of course I knew. I had memorized the best quotes from *Nostra Aetate* and other Church documents, and I knew that Pope John Paul II had said that Jews are our older brothers in faith and that anti-Semitism is a sin. However, as I started to explain, the man interrupted me. "That's not what I mean," he said. "Go and look in the bookstore across the street. That's what Catholics really think about the Jews." Disturbed by this conversation, I went immediately to the church bookstore and contemplated its shelves in shock.

It was full of anti-Semitic literature: conspiracy theories, lists of Jews hidden among politicians, revisionist history. For months I kept going there and reading, to avoid supporting them by buying any of the books. After some inner wrangling, I approached the parish priest and asked if he was aware that the literature they were selling was against the Church's teaching. "I'm not going to be a censor," he said, speaking through an intercom. He explained that he was just renting out the space. Would he have used that excuse if they were selling pornography and not "just" hate and prejudice? My arguments failed to persuade him. He said, "God bless you!" and hung up. I stood sobbing in front of his closed door.

It took several months before I tried again. This time I approached the bishop's office and asked for a meeting. Eventually, after much to-ing and fro-ing, I managed to speak to the archbishop's chancellor. That was as far as things went. It felt like being slapped. Here I was, almost nineteen years old, allowed to buy alcohol, drive, and vote, but unable to get an appointment with my own bishop.

It was one of the worst conversations of my life. The chancellor dismissed the whole issue and refused to listen to my arguments. At one point he asked, "Why is a laywoman dealing with this issue and not a priest?" "Why not?" I thought, but said nothing. I knew they disciplined and punished priests who caused trouble by moving them to difficult or poor parishes. The lesson I learned that day was that laywomen are far more difficult to stop, which probably makes us more threatening.

That experience led me to question whether or not I should stay in the Catholic Church. I suddenly felt I was surrounded by hypocrites and no one was interested in hearing me out. The young idealistic Catholic girl in me had died, giving birth to an adult sceptic. I was angry, but anger is also a sign of commitment. So I stayed, helped by long conversations with an experienced lay Catholic activist who told me clearly, "This is the first time you have been disappointed, but it won't be the last. You need to get tougher."

The ultimate irony is that I pushed myself to study Catholic theology. I wanted to specialize in Christian-Jewish relations, having discovered how fractured they were. As for the bookstore, after many failed attempts and five years later, it finally closed.

That bookstore carved out my path in life. It determined my profession but also how I approach the reality of the Catholic Church. The bookstore experience became a metaphor for what it was like to find myself helpless before such a massive institution that tolerated breaking its own principals by giving a place to anti-Semitic teachings. It was about being undermined and ignored as a young woman, and I have to say that the degrees I have earned and the experiences I have had since are no remedy for that. There needs to be a change of culture in the Church if it is to fulfill the egalitarian vision of Galatians 3:28: "There is no longer Jew or Greek, there is no longer slave or free, there is no longer male and female; for all of you are one in Christ Jesus." Young people must be taken seriously, women must be listened to, and nobody should be ignored.

Still today I feel uncomfortable in the bishop's office, even when I am invited. Always ready to be rejected by the Church again, I keep my expectations low to avoid being hurt. I believe I have unique expertise to offer, but I no longer want to be treated as a usurper. I once offered to facilitate a group of priests who were learning about the Holocaust. I was told that I could act only as a translator, because they would reject a woman as an expert. Why should I try again? How many women have similar stories to tell? I see those women all around me. They may be the best in their field, but they are not good enough for leadership in the Catholic Church because those positions are for priests. I am with those women as they swallow the pain of rejection—again and again.

Why do we stay in the Church, despite being treated as second-class citizens? I stay because this is where I belong and I am nourished by Catholic tradition, theology, liturgy, and sacraments. I am at home. I do not want to go anywhere else. I am a Catholic, but one that cannot stand gender injustice in the global Church, or quiet acceptance of racism and anti-Semitism in the Church in Poland. I am not going to ask for forgiveness for my outrage. My questions to the priests, bishops, cardinals, and the pope is why are you not eagerly fighting with us? Why are you so often against us? Why do you ignore and disregard these realities?

Despite all the difficulties, we are here, in the Church—competent, engaged, prepared for work that is rarely given to us. Even if we are angry, our anger shows that we are committed and not giving up on the Church, and we trust that she will not give up on us and our vocations. We are ready to be included and involved at any time—and the time is now.

Notes

1. We are grateful to Voices of Faith for permission to publish this edited version of a talk given at the Voices of Faith event in Rome to celebrate International Women's Day on March 8, 2018. See https://voicesoffaith.org/zuzanna-radzik/. A video of the talk can be found at this link, accessed July 2, 2018: https://www.youtube.com/watch?v=tNtPq_0u7as.

A Church of Women

Memories, Frustrations, and Hopes on the Journey of Life

Giulia Galeotti

For Sara

Introduction: Sara Departs

It's a warm Saturday at the end of July. I'm at work when a photo appears on the screen of my phone: it's Sara, my nine-year-old niece, about to leave for Guide camp. She's wearing a green cap with yellow stripes, a blue shirt, and blue corduroy shorts, with a scarf around her neck and a backpack. A smile lights up her blue eyes.

So much binds me to this little girl. It moves me that she's about to embark on an adventure that used to be such a positive part of my own life. Among other things, my long years of being a Guide—from childhood to early adolescence—reconciled me with a Church that I had very nearly felt was not for me—a reconciliation that an adult encounter with Faith and Light (the international movement that brings together people with mental disabilities, their families, and their friends) later cemented.

A Little Girl's Doubts

A little girl is attending the funeral of her friend's grandmother. She keeps silent as one by one the priests go up to the altar—eight men to commemorate a woman who has died. For a long time, this scene would eat away at the mind of the child that I was. In my eyes it was a tangible image of the misogyny of the Church.

The ideas that I was picking up were not encouraging either: God was male, his Son was male, the popes and the priests were all male, so were the authors and the most important characters in the Scriptures. Yet, by contrast, the Mass was attended mostly by women.

Questions chased one another wildly around my mind: why was the Church, a feminine noun in Italian, ruled by male generals with an army of women? Why, if Jesus said that we are all children of God, did the voices of some children have more value than others? This Church seemed to me truly unfair. In primary school we had a wonderful teacher, Miss Tiné, an atheist who was very angry with the Catholic Church. Sometimes I was offended and reacted to her anticlericalism, but deep down I knew that she was right.

The Church of Women: The Guides

When my parents moved to a new parish, I joined a group of *Agesci* (the Italian Guides and Scouts Association). While other children went to lunch with their grandparents on Sundays wearing their smart clothes, I was running around in the woods, dirty and free, in creative and stimulating proximity to boys as well as girls. That would have been unthinkable with my classmates. I returned to school on Mondays convinced that my life was a cut above the rest. Meanwhile, during occasional gatherings with my extended family, I discovered that my cousins were members of Scout groups in which the sexes were separated (*Scout d'Europa*) and that they accepted this separation as the way it should be.

Only afterward did I discover the reason for these different approaches. Like so much else in the Church, even the Italian Scouts had been divided since the Second Vatican Council. On the one hand were those who remained faithful to tradition (my cousins and their *Scout d'Europa*), and on the other hand were those who wanted to open up to the fresh winds of the Council. When the Italian Associations of Scouts (*Asci*) and the Italian Association of Guides (*Agi*) decided to embark on a merger, *Agesci*, in 1974, one part of the movement kept its distance.

So I grew up living with activities, adventures, and prayer times led by young women, and I saw the world through their eyes. I began to understand that the message pronounced by priests was coming to life in the heads and in the hands of women who constituted the real Church. Of course, the women could not proclaim this Church from the altar, but the die had been cast.

Confirmation: Faith and Light

My journey with Faith and Light began when I went to university. The origins of the Faith and Light movement can be traced back to the summer of 1967, when a French couple, Camille and Gérand Proffit, were keen to take part in their parish pilgrimage to Lourdes, but their profoundly disabled sons, Thaddée and Loic, were not accepted. "Your sons will understand nothing about the pilgrimage, and their presence might disturb the other pilgrims," was the response of the parish priest. They decided to go alone, but when they reached Lourdes, they struggled to find a hotel willing to accept them. When they finally succeeded, the staff insisted that the family must eat their meals in the room so that the sight of Thaddée and Loic would not disturb the other guests.

This experience inspired them to organize a pilgrimage to Lourdes for people with mental disabilities. They were assisted by a French woman, Marie-Hélène Mathieu, who in 1963 had founded the *Office Chrétien des Personnes Handicapées* (O.C.H.) (Christian Office for Disabled People) in Paris. Over the years, Mathieu had had the opportunity to see for herself the loneliness of parents of children with mental disabilities, their anguish about the future, their feelings of guilt, and their suffering, which was increased by the knowledge that they were not even welcome in the Church. Mathieu helped to make the Lourdes pilgrimage for people with mental disabilities a reality, in collaboration with Jean Vanier, the founder of *L'Arche* (a community in which people with and without mental disabilities live together). This changed the very notion of pilgrimage: since then, Lourdes has welcomed people with mental disabilities.

Officially established in France in 1971, the Faith and Light movement arrived in Italy thanks to a remarkable woman whom I had the privilege of knowing well: Mariangela Bertolini (1933–2014). At her funeral, during the offertory, a fruit tree was carried up to the altar as testimony to a commitment that has not yet stopped bearing fruit. I was and am one of those fruits.

So my childhood intuition of a Church constituted by women working in the field found a better informed and more mature awareness. Women are an important connection between mental disability and the Church—above all, those mothers and sisters, nieces and friends who have suffered and struggled to ensure that people with mental disabilities have the right to be given a place in our churches.

Their full inclusion is still a long way off, but the journey has at least begun.

Conclusion: Sara Returns

Sara returned from her first Guide camp. My thousand questions have not yet had a response: she will tell me about it when she is ready. In the meantime, I am enjoying the beauty of seeing her at the beginning of her journey, when everything is still possible.

I hope that Sara grows up in a Church in which there is space for women's perspectives—a Church that is able to recognize the strength that is unleashed when everybody, male and female, clerical and lay, is treated as equal in value and equal in dignity.

Fire in My Heart

A Young Pakistani Woman Discovers Her Vocation

Mishal Francis

A loud banging! Somebody was violently knocking on our door.

It was August 14, 2001, the seventh anniversary of my grandfather's death, and our family had come from all over Pakistan to attend a remembrance Mass at our house.

"Mishi, will you get the door?" shouted Mamaji (mother) from the kitchen.

I rushed across the veranda to the door. I was a little annoyed. I had been comfortably settled beside my Nannoji's (grandmother's) armchair, resting on her knees and listening to her stories of my grandfather during his evangelizing days. He was very popular as the local catechist. He travelled all over Punjab before Partition and converted many families to Christianity. Later, he became a respected teacher in the senior seminary in Karachi, the largest city of Pakistan.

"Who is it?" I asked.

"Is this the engineer's house?" asked a deep voice that I did not recognize.

Before I could answer, they pushed the door open.

There were three armed men with pistols. They were shouting and swearing. They pulled out the telephone wires from their sockets. They had come to warn us to leave *their* country because we were Christians.

This horrifying experience is a snippet of my childhood in Pakistan. After this incident, we knew that our lives were in danger and so we made plans to flee the country.

We arrived in Scotland to start our lives anew in January 2003. I was fourteen. We were welcomed like angels, and we quickly settled into our local Catholic Church, where I became an altar server. My siblings and I went to the nearest Catholic school to begin our secondary education, but initially I found it hard to make friends. I was experiencing culture shock. Young people in Pakistan were hungry for good education and felt strongly about their faith, and I could not understand why so many of the students in my year had little interest in their faith or their education. Nevertheless, I became involved in extracurricular activities and joined the school choir and literary club, and soon I was thriving. I made new friends and was doing well in my studies. I went on to do a degree and then a master's in aeronautical engineering at the University of Glasgow with the aim of one day becoming an accomplished engineer like my father.

For my last year at university, I moved to California for five months to work on a research project. Once again, there was the difficulty of adjusting to a new culture, but I was excited to discover a young adult group called RISE. Joining that community of young adults like myself helped me to feel at home. During our discussions, I spoke of my Pakistani background. I was flourishing in my engineering studies, but there was a fire in my heart to speak about Christians in Pakistan. My family and I had found safety in a new land, but many Christians in Pakistan still endured religious persecution, and my love for the persecuted Church was intense and unwavering. I returned home, and after my graduation in 2012, I took a gap year to discern my career path before applying for graduate engineering jobs.

That year, my father was made redundant from his engineering job due to his deteriorating health. It felt as if we both found ourselves discerning our future careers at the same time. I spoke to him about how strongly I felt about Christians in Pakistan, and I found out that my parents had been quietly supporting Christian families and some widows in Pakistan for all these years. This was a turning point for me. I knew that the Holy Spirit was speaking to me in a powerful way that I could not ignore. Christ was calling me to a mission: to be a voice for the voiceless, his persecuted Church. That conversation with my father was the birth of Hope Human Development & Welfare Association (Hope HDWA). Our family established this charity in 2013 to support Christians in Pakistan who live in extreme conditions of poverty and persecution, and to provide education for children that encourages a harmonious and peaceful attitude toward others regardless of religious differences.

I worked as a volunteer for Hope HDWA and went around parishes, speaking to people about my experience as a Christian in Pakistan and encouraging them to pray and support the persecuted Church. I was discovering that I had good speaking skills and that my background and experiences struck a chord with other young adults who also had a hunger for spirituality. As there was nothing to offer in my local parish other than guitar and drama clubs, I established a young adult group, Imago Dei, in my local parish. Within a few months I was leading and spiritually guiding this group of twenty young members, as we explored Scripture and spirituality. I was recognizing my true vocation as a daughter of God: Christ was calling me to continue the work my grandfather had started, and I was being called to evangelize young people through Hope HDWA. However, there was still so much I desired to know about the Scriptures and my faith, so I applied to the University of Glasgow for another master's, this time in theology.

Studying theology encouraged me to change career paths. This was a leap of faith, leaving the known behind to discover the unknown and recognize the truth of my very being. In the words of Lao Tzu, "The journey of a thousand miles begins with one step."

The youth work in my local parish had been bearing much fruit and came to the attention of the bishop. I was offered a job as a youth development officer in the diocese, moving among parishes and establishing youth groups, providing them with an opportunity to deepen their faith through catechism and Bible study, through eucharistic adoration and prayer, and through developing a sense of community within their parishes.

Along with this work, I have been doing a part-time PhD in theology, and I am on the Board of Trustees of Hope HDWA. My passion for Christians in Pakistan and ministry to the youth of our Catholic Church is the witness of my own faith and love for Christ Jesus. My life's journey so far has also been my faith journey.

Life, Freedom, and Dignity

Reflections of a Black American Catholic

Leslye Colvin

The words were centered across a billboard over the image of a man's lifeless body. As I moved away, the words stayed with me: "He died for you." The church advertisement was an invitation to the region's Christian majority, to affirm a debt owed with an automatic response of "Amen." Instead, I found myself thinking, "He lived for us."

Indeed, he lived for us before dying! To enter the human experience, as Scripture states, he emptied himself to live among us, with us, and as one of us in the historical Jesus. His humility was shown long before his betrayal and crucifixion. By becoming human, he accepted an invitation to the joys and sorrows and laughter and tears of life. Within this context, death is inevitable. Accepting the first breath of life is to release the final breath imposed by death. Jesus's life was about much more than his death.

The marginalized can relate easily to the life of this man Jesus. He was conceived out of wedlock and born into a loving yet economically disadvantaged family in an oppressed land. A faithful Jewish man in the Roman empire, he was embraced and rejected by the chosen people to whom he belonged. He was well acquainted with the whispers and stares of those mired in dualism as he consciously embraced "the other" and the ritually unclean. He was one of a countless number to face a shameful, state-sanctioned execution. His death was not an isolated incident, but rather a part of his life. He loved us enough to live in the tension of this good and messy world.

When I listen to Mass readings of Moses leading his people from bondage to freedom, I hear it as an invitation to remember the bondage of my African ancestors and the continuing struggles of my people simply to have their dignity recognized in theory and in practice. As a child, Jesus learned of this journey from slavery to liberation and his people's continuing faith in God. In my own childhood, the song "Let My People Go" resonated as an ancient and modern call that was deeply personal.

As history shows, these struggles persist until a single event appears to become a catalyst for change. Those engaged in the struggle know well the tears and heartache borne along the margins, knowing that at some point God will answer not only our prayers but those of our ancestors whose trauma I cannot begin to grasp. In a single moment, their lives were forever changed as they were kidnapped as people and sent into slavery as cargo. To their posterity, they gifted an undying desire for freedom as affirmed generations later in the lyrics to the famous African American Gospel song, "Oh, Freedom": "Before I'd be a slave, I'll be buried in my grave. And go home to my Lord and be free."

Three generations of my family entered the Catholic Church in the racially segregated Alabama of the 1960s. As my paternal grandparents and aunt entered the church in Ozark, they were surprised to learn how God was leading my parents to make the same decision for their young family twenty miles away in Dothan. Both towns had many segregated churches of other denominations, but each had only one Catholic parish and they both welcomed us. However, it is important for me to acknowledge that our experience of welcome was not shared by all African American Catholics. As Fr. Bryan Massingale eloquently states in *Racial Justice and the Catholic Church*, racism "is a tragic brokenness in our society and church."[1] Growing up African American and Catholic in a Protestant region and an intensely racialized society presents its own unique challenges, but entering the Catholic Church momentarily moved us beyond constant segregation.

My siblings and I were raised in a house built by our father and other family members who were brick masons and carpenters. Together, our mother and father made it a safe and loving home. They attempted to shelter us from what they knew to be inevitable. From experience, I know the doctor's second and smaller waiting room with no windows and the adjacent examination room reserved for us. I know the child's curiosity aroused by going to the dentist with a toothache after calling the office only to be turned away upon arrival. I know the revulsion of seeing the unpatriotic flag of secessionists that was proudly waved at cross burnings and lynchings.

Even with regard to the parish, our protective parents would occasionally remind us that we were black. As a child, I could not grasp what they were trying to tell us. It may have been more apparent had our parish been more diverse. It is easy to embrace a few, but challenging to welcome a significant number. In high school, I became involved with a movement for young Catholics known as "Search for Christian Maturity," through which I met other African American Catholics of my age from larger cities. It was a transformative weekend to cross the racial divide by spending time together with each other and with God.

Three decades later, I enrolled in JustFaith, an intensive

program on the Church's social teachings. Through this experience, I gained the vocabulary to speak to the rich social justice tradition that I consider to be the heart of the gospel, the heart of Christ. JustFaith was a full-circle moment for me in that I saw my family's welcome into the Church as an acceptance of our God-given dignity.

Now that I am an adult, the rose-colored glasses of childhood have been removed. While my spiritual journey deepens my faith, experience exposes the institutional Church as another system that often perpetuates the injustices of society. The love of the Divine that we profess is too often negated by social divisions. The Church founded by Jesus Christ was never intended to be a dualistic law-and-order system dependent upon the dotting of all *i*'s and the crossing of all *t*'s. At a young age, we begin to teach children that Christ dwells in the tabernacle and in their hearts. It is not a matter of "either/or" but of "both-and." Similar is our belief in one God whom we encounter as three. Again, it is not a matter of "either/or" but of "both-and." We learn to live in the tension by experiencing the beauty of mystery found in this good and messy world.

For most of my life, I have been involved in some form of ministry within and beyond the walls of the parish. As neither a wife nor a mother, I have learned through decades of experience to move beyond my comfort zone and introversion to find my niche. Even when most gatherings are designed with spouses and parents in mind, the presence, the perspectives of single adults, the divorced, and the widowed of all ages are needed.

The only words I remember from my grandfather's funeral were spoken by the priest who had welcomed him into the church a quarter of a century earlier. "He was the freest man I have ever known," said the priest. Today, I continue to reflect upon how the life of this master brick mason who was orphaned at an early age symbolized freedom to this Irish priest.

As we move along the spiral that is our faith journey, spiritual maturity compels us to act when confronted with suffering generated by the denial of human dignity. Witnessing the suffering of today's marginalized and poor is an invitation to recall the suffering of Jesus, the man, as he, too, was subjected to unjust and oppressive systems. The mystery of faith did not begin or end on the cross. Rather, the life, death, and resurrection of Christ Jesus are woven into the hearts of his followers, charging them to simply love God and their neighbors. We live because he lives for us.

Notes

1. Bryan Massingale, *Racial Justice and the Catholic Church* (Maryknoll, NY: Orbis Books, 2010), xiii.

Confessions of a Jamaican "Flatalik"

Anna Kasafi Perkins

The Rastafarian faith is indigenous to Jamaica, where it emerged as a form of resistance to the colonial church and society. Rastafari (Rastas) refer to the non-Rastafarian world as "Babylon," a biblical name that for some conveys contempt and hostility.[1]

Catholics in Jamaica are in a minority, and it is not unusual to encounter claims such as "Catholics worship Mary!" "Catholics pray to Mary!" "The Pope is the Beast!" "Catholic is a White Man Church!" Sometimes the Church is dismissed as a place where "society people" and "tapanaris" (elites) gather, and accusations are made about the sexual orientation and activities of clerics. Reggae artists sing of "bu(r)ning fyah pon Rome" or call for the hanging of Pope Paul (a stock reference to all members of the papacy, owing to the Vatican's support for the Italian invasion of Ethiopia in the 1930s). Yet Catholic high schools enjoy widespread support in Jamaica, and many of the poor are taken care of by Catholic organizations. There are anecdotal stories about holy water disappearing from churches because of the power it is believed to possess, summed up in expressions such as "Faada a di bigis obia man" (Father is the most powerful Obeah man).

I grew up in the 1980s in a low-income community in the Parish of St. Andrew in the southeast of Jamaica. During our preparation for confirmation, some of us chose to wear small wooden crosses as a sign of our faith and our desire to help the poor. We were a strange minority among Adventists, Pentecostals, Revivalists, and others. A group of Rastamen in the community took every opportunity to taunt us with their Rasta skills at wordplay, calling us *kraasiz* (crosses), which was a reference to the crosses we wore but also a play upon the Jamaican word *kraasiz*, which is always in the plural and means "adversity, bad luck, evil, or trouble." So a person experiencing great adversity might exclaim, "*Unu si mi krazis!*" ("Do you see my crosses!") Taken literally, this is a reference to Christ's cross and to the gospel admonition to take up one's cross and follow Christ (Luke 9:23; Matt 16:24), but when used to refer to people, it is a form of insult. The Rastas also taunted us with the neologism *flatalik*, again a clever play on words and sounds—*Catholic* and *flatter*. In the Jamaican context, a "lik" is a hard strike that causes someone to "flatter" (fall to the ground and flutter/convulse). Essentially, they were taunting us for choosing the white man's church, the church of the oppressor. The history of the European Catholic Church and its sins against the African people has not been erased from the minds of many Jamaicans—despite the indigenization of the Jamaican Church and a theological anthropology that recognizes human dignity in all persons. How do we as Jamaican Catholics respond to this perception?

Chevannes and others dismiss this Rastafarian posturing as "ritualized aggression" with no real physical harm threatened. Chevannes describes it as "a sort of confrontation between the sacred and the profane at the level of the symbolic."[2] It is a shock tactic intended to wake us up and call us away from Babylon. (Many Christians engage in similar tactics to frighten people into converting.) However, as a teenager this treatment left me feeling threatened, cursed, disrespected, and shamed. It made me even more determined to hold on to my faith and learn more about it, which was perhaps one of the influences that led me to study theology.

Today, having chosen to lock my hair, wear little or no makeup, and dress reasonably modestly, I am addressed as "empress" by Rastamen and more "conscious" Jamaican men, who claim to honor a black woman who is "natural." Yet my experiences lead me to reflect on the shaming of women in both society and Church. I wrestle with questions of the female body, which is sexualized in popular culture and problematized in the sacred/ecclesial space.

There is lyrical violence in our culture, which uses words to do harm to others, especially women, whose body parts are used in the Jamaican language—as in many others—as curses or swear words. As an unmarried and childless woman, I am often unwittingly given the title of "maada," as Jamaican males valorize the mother figure and assume that women of a certain age have children. A woman in her reproductive years is measured and weighed for her attractiveness, her ability to satisfy a man's sexual needs, and her childbearing abilities. Our popular Jamaican music helps to reinforce these ideas among women as well as men.

As a Jamaican/Caribbean Catholic woman, I ask how the Church can challenge such cultural posturings when in subtle and not-so-subtle ways it is involved in the bodily shaming of women for being women—for being female bodies that menstruate and cannot stand *in persona Christi*. Women in more conservative churches often preach; preside at funerals, baptisms, and weddings; and lead Bible studies. Even as I enjoy their preaching style, I sometimes cringe at their literalist and often convoluted exegesis. Yet I marvel that they have managed to see beyond these literalist readings of Scripture and to offer their talents to their churches.

An African American colleague once described me as "a strange bird," being a single laywoman theologian in the Jamaican Catholic Church. Yes, I am a strange bird to whom the Catholic Church has given birth and has given room to grow. At the same time, my identity as Jamaican, woman, and Catholic means I must continue to play my part—to give a "flatalik" to all that dehumanizes God's people, especially those who are woman shaped.

Notes

1. For more information about Rastafarian beliefs and culture, see Barry Chevannes, *Rastafari: Roots and Ideology* (New York: Syracuse University Press, 1994).

2. Chevannes, *Rastafari*, 208–9.

Staying In, Struggling On

A Woman's Pilgrimage from Islam to Catholicism

Irim Sarwar

I was born and raised in Maryland, USA, near Washington, DC, the daughter of Pakistani Muslim parents who had been displaced during Partition. That harrowing experience meant that despite being lukewarm practitioners of Islam, they held tightly to their identities as Muslims, which had been the reason for their trauma. Therefore, it was essential to them that their children carry on the culture and religion they had seen so many others die for. Unfortunately for them, I was not that ideal child.

I was the child who had a dream about leaving my mother at the nearby Catholic Church, then told my father about it. I was the child who would devour copies of *Bible Stories* before they left the house to be put in my pediatrician mother's waiting room. In 1978, I was the child who rejoiced when John Paul I was elected and sobbed when he died. Oscar Romero and Denis Hurley were my first clerical crushes, causing a subsequent priest friend to observe wryly, "No wonder the rest of us have disappointed you."

One might think that this young fascination with the Catholic Church would have disappeared with the passing of time, against a background of study and Islamic Saturday school, while struggling with a deeply dysfunctional family and an uncle's sexual abuse. Instead, it turned out to be an early glimmer of my pilgrim path home.

My parents believed in God because they were told to, but even as a very young child, I could feel God brushing against my skin in all things—I'd even talk to dust particles as if they were sentient. That sense of an immanent God clashed with the Islamic concept of a God far above us who required submission.

That wasn't the only point of discord. I grew up in an immediate family that viewed other people as objects: to use and discard, to step over on the way up. At best, my parents' Islam was cultural, but it was far more often a means of control, especially over a girl who had the nerve to shout back at her raging father. Somehow, in the midst of it all, I had an unshakeable sense that "this isn't how you treat people," that you sacrifice yourself for what is greater than you are. Even before I had any clear idea of who Jesus was, I understood why he was on that cross. I felt that he was a kindred spirit.

Eventually the rift between Islam's theology and my intuitive faith became too great. In my adolescence, I lapsed, with all the requisite snark of a Generation Xer. I moved out after my mother juxtaposed *arranged* and *marriage* in one sentence. (I left a note on the fridge to tell them I'd left.) Only then did I feel safe enough to do something other than rebel.

In September 1992, I began teaching in an Orthodox Jewish School, with trepidation because of my Muslim background. I need not have worried. For four years, the sound of prayer punctuated the rhythm of the day; wonderful, warm staff invited me to their Seders, Purim services, and cantorial concerts; cheeky students patiently explained rabbinical commentary; shaking my head affectionately, I passed rabbis arguing in hallways, many of whom became good friends.

I became immersed in a religion that was grounded in daily life, one that was a way of being, not just an identity ritual or something to learn on a Saturday. To this day, this homegoy™ (my Jewish friend's term for her non-Jewish friends) can feel the rhythm of the Jewish liturgical calendar in her bones.

I joke that I nearly converted to Judaism, but bacon and shellfish got in the way. That's not quite true: it was that kindred spirit, Jesus, who did.

October 1992 brought the final step in my journey when I befriended Anni, whose parents took me in as if I were their long-lost daughter. Wrapped in their love, I learned that American Catholicism was as much about boisterous affection, fuzzy toilet seat covers, pictures of Our Lady and the pope, and "tuna casserole Friday" as it was about going to church. It was with Anni that I discovered the joy of Latin Mass in the Shrine of the Immaculate Conception's Crypt Church, where I was able to experience a sense of the sacraments as being heaven kissing our lives on earth, invisible love made visible.

When my mother was diagnosed with breast cancer in December 1993, I realized that I needed a spiritual community, somewhere to fall. I said to Anni, "If only I could become Catholic."

"You can," she said, noting that it was too late to join RCIA that year, but if I still felt the same the following September, I could begin then.

On Saturday, April 15, 1995, at the Easter Vigil Mass at St. Michael's Church, Mount Airy, Maryland, I was baptized by Fr. Michael Ruane and confirmed by Bishop Frank Murphy. Eighteen months later, I left the cozy world of being a eucharistic minister in my American parish church to come to Oxford to study for a master's degree in teaching, learning, and teacher development. I rejoiced when I stumbled upon a church that had a Latin Mass on Sundays. I had found a church that would be my new home. That turned out to be about as smooth a journey as travelling along a Himalayan mountain road!

English Catholicism's victim mentality jolted me, coming from the unselfconscious Catholicism I had known in America. Most of those who played the victim were not recusants, but converts whose ancestors had chosen personal survival over martyrdom. The reactionary right-wing baggage that accompanied the Latin (and later, the return of the Tridentine) Mass went from a trickle to a tsunami, leaving adrift those of us who were committed to Catholic social teaching yet loved a high liturgy. The rules that dictated that only men could be altar servers and eucharistic ministers excluded women from the sanctuary except as lectors. Any argument was met with a mocking rebuke: "You're just an angry feminist." Shades of my emotionally sadistic father were everywhere.

But like a butterfly beating its wings against a chrysalis, growth needs resistance, and the resonance with my father turned out to be a blessing. As an adult I had the resources to resist patriarchy, and this helped to heal the child who had struggled so hard to resist. Whether it was in my particular church, or more broadly with the growing neoconservatism encouraged by Pope John Paul II and Pope Benedict XVI, staying in and struggling on brought into focus what really mattered, stripping my faith back to the essentials: my relationship with God, my unshakeable faith in the events of Holy Week, my belief in the sacraments (particularly the Real Presence) as emanations of the holy into the mundane, my commitment to Catholic social teaching, the oneness of God's creation.

That faith keeps my feet on the pilgrim road, my conversion new every morning, my prayer one with Charles Wesley's:

Ready for all thy perfect will,
my acts of faith and love repeat;
till death thy endless mercies seal,
and make the sacrifice complete.

Everything Is a Process

Learning to Live, to Change, and to Grow

Clare Keogh

I am a young Australian woman, with Irish, Dutch, and English ancestry, currently studying for a master's degree in occupational therapy practice. I am both feminist and Catholic. Today the faith of my childhood has grown into something more complex and less definable, but it is still there. I have learned to appreciate the good things about being Catholic through my extended family and friends, and through a few well-informed priests—one in particular who was a friend of my family and showed me a faith that was not rigid and tradition bound but flexible, meeting young people where we are at rather than instructing or confronting us. I believe that Jesus's teachings and the teachings of those who follow him are still important for our lives today.

I have also been sickened by the child abuse scandals and the inequalities and hypocrisy of the institutional Church with its inflexible hierarchies and "top-down" solutions. Much church life is closed off to women, through structures that are still geared toward men. I think that there needs to be a rethink on how all the people of God—religious and lay, married and single, women and men—can contribute.

Stories and music are the building blocks of my life. A

voracious reader from a young age, I enjoy looking beyond the story and imagining more. This has become more important as I have grown up and engaged more critically with my faith. I have discovered a faith that asks me to engage and to think about the meaning behind the words we use and how that is influenced by our own contexts and the contexts of the authors. I begin to see what is worth respecting and what, perhaps, we need to think about more deeply—and change—if the Church is to keep being relevant and a source of good in people's lives.

For example, many spiritual advisors and lay motivational speakers present issues of human sexuality and relationships in either/or terms, in a way that inhibits young people like me from seeking guidance. I am not a logical puzzle to be solved with a formula, and I want to choose a path that feels right for me, rather than being forced to conform to a single "ideal." I believe that we should be striving for authenticity in all aspects of our lives—including gender and sexual preference. Jesus was harsher on those who discriminated and judged others and were hypocrites than he was concerned about people's sex lives.

We young women are often struggling with decisions such as whether or not to have sex before marriage, to partner with somebody who might not share our faith, to accept diverse sexualities, to marry or to choose some other form of partnership, but we are often confronted with what feel like starchy, out-of-date Church teachings. It would be more helpful if there was less emphasis on the sexual and more focus on the need for young women to develop a sense of our own agency, in order to decide when we are emotionally ready for the decisions that we face. That means being able to choose options that some disagree with, trying things out, and sometimes getting it wrong. Young Catholic women like me need an open-hearted approach that sets aside judgmental-sounding words for compassionate and active listening. Without that openness, with choices verbally blocked, it becomes harder to be fully open with ourselves and others, even when we want to be. We face a lonely path if our struggles are surrounded with secrecy for fear of disapproval and if we cannot trust those we turn to for guidance and help because we are afraid of being confronted with shame and disappointment.

In order to understand my own life choices, I have had to look into Church teachings anew, using other sources and doing a lot of personal reflection. For example, I believe that contraception should be an informed personal choice, and that IVF and other supported fertility treatments have benefits that outweigh the "playing with life" label that some religious people might attach to them. I believe that everyone has a right to life, including the unborn. I also believe that "God does not make junk," so aborting a fetus *just* because of a disability, or the circumstances of its conception (and/or designing a fetus specifically to edit out a disability "just because"), is *wrong*, but I think we need to talk about these things, and that we should be working on social reforms that prevent abortion by providing better options, while keeping it safe and legal.

Being a Catholic is, to me, about trying to grow toward authenticity in myself, in my relationships with others, and with the wider world. My faith gives me emotional support and spiritual guidance, and feminism has helped me to learn about relationships outside of the religious paradigm. Through this ongoing process, I have learned that my principles can change, with appropriate reflection and lived experience, and I am growing into who I want to be.

Does God Bless Your Transsexual Heart?

Samantha Tillman

A friend of mine once asked me for advice on men, with the justification, "You know what it's like to be a man." I don't know what it's like to be a man, but at the same time I don't know what it's like to be a woman. I only know what it's like to be me—Samantha—and I know that, for whatever reason, my body runs better on estrogen and my brain runs better when female pronouns are used to describe me.

I am transgender. I am Catholic. I am a Catholic transgender woman. I could explain what this means but, frankly, I am tired of explaining. I am tired of having to explain my body, and my genitals, as if people were entitled to me. I am tired of having to explain my faith and beliefs. I am tired of always defending the basic facts of my existence. Yes, I know what my body is, I know what my chromosomes are, and I am not deluded. And I know that I am a woman.

This was not always the case. I did not always claim the label of woman. It was something I thought I could never claim. After all, I did not—and still do not—know what it's like to be a woman. But you can only lie for so long. And dysphoria, the experience of discomfort in the gender we are assigned at birth that many trans people experience essentially made living as a man a lie. I am not, and in retrospect never was, a man.

So I claimed the label of woman. This was me; I wanted to yell, to scream at the top of my lungs. I thought I knew what it was like to be a woman, just as confidently as I knew that the Church rejected me. I had heard, sometimes from those that claimed to love me the most, or claimed to know most about the faith, that I was insane, possessed, a figure of the satanic. So, I thought, let me be evil. If I am a perversion of the image of God, let me be perverse. I turned my back on the faith and sought to live on my own. Maybe God made me a man, yes, but I knew I was a woman, so I would wrench God's creation to my own design and remake myself, glorious and monstrous. I would make this man's body into a woman's. A perverse reflection of a woman's, yes, maybe, but a woman's nonetheless. I could not lie. I was done with lies. I had no other choice.

I was wrong.

I did not find God again in church, or in the many good-natured, well-intentioned people who calmly informed me that, no, I was really a man, and that I should try to be the man God made me to be. I did not listen to the calls to repentance because they always included an added comment. "You are not a woman," they told me, in a thousand kind, cruel ways. "Your body is not a woman's body. Your body is a man's body." I did not listen to this lie. How could I? I did not find God in it, but rather in a punk rock song.

"Does God bless your transsexual heart?"

Laura Jane Grace, herself, like me, a trans woman, and the lead singer of the punk band *Against Me!* sings this in "True Trans Soul Rebel," a defiant, angry, and proud song. This is not what most would associate with God's action in the world, but, on my more contemplative days, I wonder if Grace's name is not a coincidence. In a very real way this song saved my life and brought me back to the faith.

When I was young, I was taught that my body was a man's body. I was taught that this was how God had created me. So I grew mad at God. How could an all-just, all-loving deity force me, who knew she was a woman, to live in a man's body? This was monstrous, so, in rebellion, I decided to become a monster. Let me take this man's body and remake it into a woman, in defiance of the Divine. Perhaps it is sin, but then I shall go proudly down to hell, where at least I can be me, Samantha, a woman.

I was wrong.

When I heard Laura Jane Grace sing this, a new thought opened in my mind. What if God hadn't made a mistake? Not in the sense that that very same phrase had been used against me, to imply that God had made me male, and I was mistaken for being so utterly convinced I was female. But what if God had made me the trans woman I am today?

Did God bless my transsexual heart? Like a seed, the thought grew inside me, pushing out the darkness and despair I had so proudly and desperately held onto until it became a garden of new light and life within, reaching up, as if to grab the sun itself. God had not made a mistake. How could a God who had made all things good make a mistake? God had made me exactly as I am, Samantha, a trans woman and, with that realization, a Catholic trans woman. I am not trapped in a man's body. This is my body, and I am not trapped in it. God made me as I am, a woman with a woman's body, even if that body is also trans. God did bless me, in the end.

I have been on hormone replacement therapy, a mix of estrogen and an antiandrogen, for six months now, and my body is changing rapidly. Day by day I see it. I am not becoming a woman, I always was one. Nor do I know what it is like to be a woman. There is no one way to be a woman. All I know is that I am me, and the hormones, and whatever other medical treatment may be necessary, are only revealing what I knew was there all along, hidden beneath lies I was forced to tell.

Some call it monstrous, yes, and, indeed, this process comes with many new oddities every day. There are new worries as well as joys. Will I be safe at any particular Mass? Which priests will condemn my very existence? Does this person see me as a woman, or, pardon the slur, just a man in a dress? Do I need to fear this Catholic? Will some scholar call me evil, instead of rejoicing in the strange, beautiful theology of transgender bodies, of changing bodies, and of bodies that society sometimes rejects as fundamentally wrong? But if I am monstrous, I am at peace with it, because I know I serve a God who creates and loves us all, even us monsters.

My Story

Hoping for a Path That Leads to Life

Gertrude Yema Jusufu

My culture does not consider it important for girls to have educational opportunities, but I always had a deep desire to study. Money for school fees was a problem: my mother and father were separated, and that made it very difficult to pay for my studies.

Before their separation, I was threatened twice with rape. When I brought tea to my aunt's husband one morning, he told me to sit on his lap. Of course I said, "No," but he grabbed my hands. I wrested my hands away and slapped him; I ran to Ya Yeabu, who lived downstairs. She told me never to serve him tea again.

The second time, I was approached by the son of the landlady. He offered me money to have sex with him and his two friends. Once again, I ran down to Ya Yeabu's small place and was saved from a horrible experience.

These experiences taught me to fear, but I was still bent on getting an education. A close friend paid my school fees initially, and then the principal of my school in Freetown, Fr. Jude Lynch, gave me a scholarship because he was aware of my intelligence. After that, I left Freetown—still traumatized by what had happened to me there—and I went to the town of Bonthe to live with my grandmother. It took me some time to regain my health and sanity.

After successfully completing secondary school, I returned to live with my mother in Freetown, where she was teaching. Despite having little money, I went to Teachers' College, where I was considered a student of distinction, which made my beloved mother proud. When I qualified, I was able to teach in the same school as her.

During this time, I experienced a call to join the School Sisters of Notre Dame, a community with sisters all over the world, which gave me many opportunities to learn about other cultures. I attended the order's novitiate in Ghana from 1991 to 1993, and after profession, I returned to Sierra Leone with another sister.

It was not long before the war came. The SSND provincial invited us to Rome for safety, and I enrolled for a course in acculturation. Sadly, our teacher died of the flu just two weeks into our studies. Perhaps attending his funeral was the greatest shock for me—in white man's land, nobody cried! How sad that seemed to me.

A few months later I was asked to go to the United States and teach in St. Louis, where I had another opportunity to experience white culture; I was surrounded by white sisters. In Sierra Leone, the novice mistress had told me to cut my hair to be a sister, but in the United States, I experienced the reverse message—they had a hair salon there!

During the day, I taught at a school in a low-income black community. When the children learned that I was from Africa, they asked me many questions. One black child asked if I was a monkey. He touched my skin and hugged me; somehow, he realized I was his sister.

After my experience in the United States, I went to Kenya at the suggestion of my superiors. I spent two years there teaching, working as a librarian, and running the school canteen. It wasn't easy to adapt to East Africa, although my acculturation studies helped. I was longing to continue my studies at Tangaza University College in Kenya, where the SSNDs were shareholders, but my congregation refused to let me study. Finally, I returned to Sierra Leone. At that point, I left religious life.

The war was still raging. All the neighbors came flooding to us for help. There was no food, no water, babies were crying—then a bomb fell in our compound. We picked up our things and ran to my father's home. When the battle came closer, we ran to the mosque for safety—safety that didn't exist. Many women were raped and killed on the spot. Pregnant women who were about to deliver would go into the bush to have their babies. Sometimes, rebels would slit open the mother's stomach, remove the fetus, and kill it; they would drink the blood as part of a ritual to make themselves stronger for battle.

After the third attack on the mosque, I was separated from my father and stayed at the pastoral center in Kenema, where we experienced the fourth attack. Bishop O'Riordan, the spiritual director there, was shot in the leg. We crossed the river in a small boat. When we looked back, we could see that the secondary school had been set on fire.

I met a nurse from Germany who was treating the wounded with jelly water, papaya leaves, and papaya seeds. With the assistance of the Catholic community, I helped to feed thousands of people out of what seemed like nothing, and when it was all over, I had nothing left.

All of us who were left came out of the bush. Like the early apostles, we lived together and shared everything. During this time, I reapplied to college. I was admitted, but I had no money! Fortunately, a priest I knew helped pay my fees, and I spent two years there making up for lost time.

Another rebel attack on Freetown meant that I once again had to escape with my mother and family. We were tired, hungry, and weak, but relieved simply to be alive. Those times were incredibly stressful for us all.

Just when I thought my troubles were over, the male vice principal at the school I was teaching at took a dislike to me and made false allegations against me. I returned to Freetown and worked with the Christian Brothers, and though I experienced some difficulties and was not involved in any decision-making, I survived.

After that I worked in Kenema for five years with Caritas and with two major organizations—UNHCR and Catholic Relief Services. My work included travelling on terrible roads to conduct monthly supervision visits. I fell off my bike many times and even broke a few bones.

In 2012, my beloved brother Elis Jusufu died. This was very painful for me, since I had taken care of him. I decided to take a break, so I went to Ghana and found a job with the SSNDs, but sadly my mother died later that same year, so I returned home.

Now, my blood sister and I are the only ones left here out of six children. Our lives are complicated and sometimes our struggles make me unhappy, but I am a woman who has never given up. In some way, I know God is present in my life. To all that has been, I bid farewell. For the future, I can only hope for a path that leads to life.

Living in Extra Time

A Journey from Despair to Hope

Johanna Greeve

In the middle of my tenth depression, I called my mother. It was one of those days when I lay on the couch, panting with stress.

"Mom, I can't take anymore," I said. It was silent for a moment.

"Do you want euthanasia?" my mother asked, realizing the shape I was in.

"Yes," I replied.

It's not that my parent wanted me dead, of course, but she had been witness to a life of suffering.

Not much later, my parents and I were sitting in the GP's waiting room. I had my declaration of intent with me.

"I am here because I don't want to live anymore," I informed the GP.

"We haven't seen our daughter smiling for two years," my mother said. Then, "Otherwise she will end her own life. Believe me, she's going to do it."

My father kept silent while my mother cried. I handed her the box of tissues that sat on the desk. My GP said she wanted to think about this for a week. We were outside again quickly.

During the following week, I contemplated and discussed my funeral. I wanted it to be modest: a funeral service in my parents' house. Some music, something religious. A German song from the ecumenical monastery of Taizé:

Gott, laß meine Gedanken sich sammeln zu dir Bei dir ist das Licht, du vergißt mich nicht. Bei dir ist die Hilfe, bei dir ist die Geduld. Ich verstehe deine Wege nicht, aber du weißt den Weg für mich.[1]

I was relieved that my family was standing beside me. However, something kept bothering my conscience, something in that Taizé song: "But you know the way for me." These words made me start to doubt my decision. In the end it appeared not to be the way for me to be six feet under.

When the GP declined my request after that week, I was sad. But now I am happy things played out that way.

For me there was hope, against all hope.

☙ • ❧

When I was only a toddler, I already felt something odd in my head. My brain felt like an overheated motor, and I was concerned about it, as young as I was. At the same time, I was clever enough to conclude that I was not lagging behind in the development that was expected of me. Unfortunately, I was too introverted to tell this to my parents.

School was an alienating place for me. I did not have the ability to comprehend other children, let alone adults. My brain worked overtime, and I suffered social stress as I was trying and only half succeeding to fit in.

What made matters worse was my difficulty in believing in God. (My parents did not go to church, but I went to a Protestant school.) That was bad, because I needed God as a fixed orientation point and as a source of consolation. But now it seemed that even the grown-ups doubted his existence! At five years old I solemnly made it my vocation to search for evidence of God until I had found it.

After secondary school I began studies, twice over, and both times I failed. I turned my day and night rhythm around and stopped tidying my room. I didn't realize that I was depressed. I felt guilty because of my behavior.

When I finally asked for professional help, the mental health organizations, not knowing how to label me, passed me on from one to another.

From that time on—I was twenty-three—I became a chronic psychiatric patient. I received treatment for depression, then resocializing therapy, and when I started to cut myself, I was labeled a borderliner and had behavioral therapy. I tried numerous medicines. In between, I was hospitalized so often that I lost count, and I went from one crisis to another.

In 2008, I asked for help with an anthroposophic psychiatrist. He suspected that I was psychotic and had me hospitalized immediately because for the past half year I had been presuming that I had seen the light. During my depressions I always sank deep. But now I had been launched into the sky from one hour to the next: I saw God. There it was! My God evidence! I was convinced I would never suffer again. I still don't know if I was seeing God or just being psychotic. Maybe both.

During my hospitalization the psychiatrist took me aside and said, "Diagnosis time!" I had been labeled with so many stickers in my life that this came as a surprise.

"I suspect you have an autism spectrum disorder. Depression and psychosis are secondary," he said.

Deep down I had suspected this myself. But it is common knowledge that autism is harder to detect in women, who are conditioned to be sociable at all costs and therefore show different symptoms.

A second opinion confirmed the autism, but the alleviating effects failed to happen at once. Another six hospitalizations followed. In 2012, I was struck with a severe psychosis that lasted half a year. After that I was totally fatigued. I became depressed for the umpteenth time and did not succeed in finding the right treatment, despite looking for it everywhere. It is hard for an autistic adult woman to find help.

That was the moment I took the phone and called my mom. Enough was enough.

When the GP declined euthanasia, I concentrated on suicide. I already knew how I was going to do it. My father even said that he wanted to stay with me, but my mother feared juridical consequences. I also wrote to a special clinic for euthanasia, and I explored the possibility of assisted suicide in Switzerland, by the Dignitas Foundation.

During those weeks, my longing to disappear battled fiercely with my fear of purgatory. Since my early twenties I had been frequenting a Catholic Church. I had seen such misery in my life that I did not feel like doing it over again in purgatory.

I emailed the parish priest. "I am about to end my life. Can I please talk to you?" I wrote.

I went to see him and he calmed me down. I knew, of course, what he would advise me.

"I won't do it," I thought after the conversation. "I will try one more treatment."

I ended up at a department for developmental disorders. At the intake with a psychologist I threw a cardboard tea cup across the room, because I had had enough of talking. At that moment a psychiatrist entered the room.

"I will take her under my care," she said.

She was the first psychiatrist who gave me a feeling of being human first and patient second. She took me ever so seriously and did not hesitate to go around protocols to help me to get better. She prescribed the most wonderful pills, for chronic use. Her method worked. One year ago I dared to talk about "happiness" for the first time.

Now I am so happy that I sometimes don't know how to handle it! I still have to get used to the feeling. For a long time I thought that paid work would make me happy. I suffered because of my marginalization (on top of the psychiatric problems), but now I am not pushing myself to do anything. I have accepted that I will never be able to earn my own income, and that I will never be able to have many social contacts; I am too sensitive to stimuli for that.

So now I am sort of a happy hermit. I only leave my house to do the groceries, or to go to Mass, or to visit my parents. I have one good friend who visits me regularly. I clean, I cook, I have a few hobbies, and I read *Donald Duck* magazine. I always say that I am living in extra time.

Notes

1. These are the words of a prayer written by Dietrich Bonhoeffer while he was in prison. "God, let my thoughts be gathered to you. With you there is light, you do not forget me. With you there is help, with you there is patience. I do not understand your ways, but you know the way for me."

A Space to Grow

The Church and Women Who Are Intellectually Disabled[1]

Cristina Gangemi

Disabled women, especially women who are intellectually disabled, face particular challenges when seeking to respond to and activate their own personal call to vocation within the "ecclesial community...where God's call is born, nourished and expressed."[2] Because of what I call a "hierarchy of ability" in the *sensus fidelium*, disabled people have been largely conspicuous by their absence within the active and participatory life of vocation in parish communities. This absence has resulted in an experience of lament for disabled women who are prevented from exercising their place of belonging.

In sharing my own journey of vocation with disabled people and through the lens of disability theology, I have come to understand how women might face a "double discrimination" within the ecclesial community. I suggest that the Church is enriched where the vocations of disabled women and men are recognized and enabled.

Language and Terminology

Disabling factors (physical, intellectual, and/or emotional) may be a part of a person's life, but all of the disabled are "persons first."[3] Negative language and the "setting up of physical, cultural, spiritual and attitudinal barriers"[4] disable people and prevent them from living fully. When these barriers are intellectual, requiring a person who is a creative and visual learner to engage exclusively in activities that are intellectually inaccessible to them (written words, complicated syntax, inaccessible semantics), the person is *intellectually disabled*; he or she is asked to learn outside of who he or she was born to be. Many people are told that they are people with "learning difficulties," but I wonder if it is more correct to say that they suffer from *teaching* difficulties. To this day, I have never met any person who could not learn. Sometimes, this learning involves *being with others*, or *knowing peace*. I have met many creative learners on the autistic spectrum who have been enabled to learn in this way.

My Own Story

Among the few memories that I have of my early years, one finds me sitting in my dining room, aged about seven, asking what life was all about. I thought to myself, "What will I do? How long will I live? How will I know what I have to do?" I recall a clear inner voice asking, "Will you work for me?" Surprised and a little scared, I went to my mother who was cooking in the kitchen. "Mum," I bellowed (I was a loud child),

"God just told me, he wants me for something." My mother, a busy woman of great faith, responded, "Don't be ridiculous, you could never be a nun, God wouldn't call *you* to be a nun." For her at that time, the only possible vocational role for a woman would be the call to a consecrated life. I remember experiencing a piercing sense of rejection and injustice.

As the years have passed, I have moved from working in the travel business to experiencing the vocation to motherhood and finally to living out what God asked of me as a child. I have benefited from some of the opportunities that have opened up for some women since my mother's comments in 1969. Over the past fifty years some women have lived through a monumental shift in society where feminist thinking has made powerful contributions to the world, to academia, and to the organized Church. I have noted opportunities for women to participate as catechists, lay ministers, advisers, and as academic theologians. However, such opportunities are only open to *some women* in the Church, for there is no role for women who are intellectually disabled.

A Theology of Disability: Whose Story Is Valued?

In 2013, the International Association of Catholic Bioethicists held a discussion on personhood and the place of people with intellectual disability in health care, in the Church and in the ongoing study of bioethics. The consensus statement that emerged from this gathering of over one hundred theologians, doctors, practitioners, and intellectually disabled people affirmed that "every human person has an intrinsic dignity and equal worth. These do not vary according to an individual's characteristics, abilities or level of quality of life."[5]

In 2016, a conference in Rome provided a space for men and women who have been disabled to share their stories and express their own personal call to vocation. The conference produced a theological statement and charter for the Church, calling it to provide a stark contrast "to cultures in which persons with disabilities and their families are all too often neglected, isolated, excluded and/or relegated to the margins of social or community life."[6] The delegates expressed how they wished the Church would "treat me like you do everyone else'" and that they had "so much to offer, receive it!"[7] These cries for recognition and value form a lament from men and women who wish to take their place and live out their call to vocation. This lament expresses the desire for baptized members of the Church to belong and to show that their stories contribute to the life and mission of the people of God. They have a place and a vocation to live, too.

Disability theology has forged a way forward for the Church to encounter the lives, stories, and desires of people with disability, but the faith stories of intellectually disabled women have not yet been taken into account. This lack creates barriers that exclude intellectually disabled women in the Church. Other than the story of the unique community of the Little Sisters of the Lamb of God, where women with and without Down syndrome live out their vocation as consecrated religious sisters,[8] there is a dearth of personal testimonies or reflections from women who are intellectually disabled. This is a subject that theologians should approach in all its fullness, exploring issues of sexuality, discrimination, and the denial of female identity within a call to vocation. Surely, as Pope Francis says, we must be a Church for "*tutti o nessuno*: everyone or no one."[9]

The Vocation of Women with Intellectual Disability—a Double Discrimination?

Church teaching on women's vocations focuses mainly on the role of women as caregivers, mothers, wives, providers of charity, people who have special dignity, providers of intimacy, with their main vocation as wives and mothers. While Pope Francis has recognized the need to create more roles for women in the Church, much of his thinking sees women as those who bring "harmony, provide balance in families and have the unique role in bringing life into the world."[10] Women who are intellectually disabled are often unable to identify with such descriptions, which can make them feel excluded, lonely, and isolated. It is not because they are not *able* to be mothers or have children but because, more often than not, a culture of "able-ism"[11] sees them as inferior, as women who have no access to marriage or indeed have no capacity to be a mother. As such, they face an attitudinal and intellectual barrier that denies their "womanhood," and this denial is evidenced in the poverty of the stories and catechetical programs that are accessible for their creative learning skills. As Anne Masters observes in her work on disability, they are seen as eternal children in a state of innocence, and this can become a form of stigmatization.[12]

As a disability adviser, I have experienced the pain of listening to stories of women who cannot understand why they have not been able to serve on the altar because of their disability and more importantly because of their gender. I have had the privilege of sharing in the vocations of disabled women who faithfully live out their call by serving as eucharistic ministers, accompanying people as they die, and praying constantly for those who suffer. This has shown me that, as Pope Francis says, "Difference is precisely our wealth."[13]

Where the expression of women who have been disabled is sought out and embraced, the Body of Christ is made complete. It is enriched by their creativity and grows by responding to their lament.

Notes

1. For further reading on the Church and disability, see the special edition of *Culture e Fede* (*Cultures and Faith*), 24, no. 3 (2016), available from cgangemi.kairos@gmail.com.

2. Pope Francis, "Message for the 54th World Day of Prayer for Vocations," November 27, 2016, https://w2.vatican.va/content/francesco/en/messages/vocations/documents/papa-francesco_20161127_54-messaggio-giornata-mondiale-vocazioni.html.

3. Anne Masters, "Don't Worry: He's in a Perpetual State of Grace," in *Culture e Fede*, 186–90.

4. Statement from *Living Fully 2016: Disability, Culture and Faith—A Celebration*, June 23–26, 2016, 1, http://rcdow.org.uk/att/files/caritas/living%20fully%202016%20statement%20and%20charter.pdf.

5. Jos V.M. Welie, ed., "Caring for Persons with Intellectual and Developmental Disabilities: Ethical and Religious Perspectives," *Religion and Society Supplement Series*, The Kripke Center, Suppl. 12 (2015): 129, https://dspace2.creighton.edu/xmlui/bitstream/handle/10504/65685/2015-34.pdf;sequence=3.

6. Statement from *Living Fully 2016*, 6.

7. Statement from *Living Fully 2016*, 8.

8. Kathy Schiffer, "Women with Down Syndrome Respond to God's Call," *Aleteia*, March 21, 2016, https://aleteia.org/2016/03/21/women-with-down-syndrome-respond-to-gods-call/.

9. Pope Francis, "Address to Participants in the Convention for Persons with Disabilities Promoted by the Italian Episcopal Conference," June 11, 2016, https://w2.vatican.va/content/francesco/en/speeches/2016/june/documents/papa-francesco_20160611_convegno-disabili.html.

10. Cf. "Pope Tells Vatican to Appoint Lay Women and Men to Curia," at *Deutsche Welle (DW)*, December 22, 2016, http://bit.ly/2furKeQ.

11. See Jana Bennett, "Women, Disabled," in *Disability in the Christian Tradition: A Reader*, ed. Brian Brock and John Swinton (Grand Rapids, MI: Eerdmans, 2012), 427–66, at 435.

12. Masters, "Don't Worry."

13. Pope Francis, "Address to Participants in the Convention for Persons with Disabilities."

PART THREE

CHANGING LIVES, CHANGING RELATIONSHIPS

Sexuality and Mothering

"I came that they may have life, and have it abundantly."

(John 10:10)

"For whoever does the will of my Father in heaven is my brother and sister and mother."

(Matt 12:50)

Sexuality and Discernment

Learning from the Stories of Young Catholic Women in the United States

Emily Kahm

When we discuss "discernment" in terms of vocation, we seem to be talking about a process of moments that eventually leads to a single, correct outcome. Yet there are many aspects of Catholic life, sexuality being one, in which discernment is constant throughout one's lifetime.

I conducted a study of young women's experiences of how sex education affected their skill at discerning what is best for themselves and those with whom they have relationships. Of fifteen women interviewed, nine still identified as Catholic and ranged from highly traditional to very progressive, but six had left the faith tradition of their childhood for other traditions or were detached from religion entirely. From their stories, I gleaned common themes about how they thought their religious upbringing had affected their sexual understanding in young adulthood.

The Church has carefully codified standards for appropriate expressions of sex and sexuality; the level of detail is, in fact, almost unique among moral topics. Yet moral discernment in sexuality should not be reduced to the decision to have sex prior to or after marriage, or to the specific sex acts that married couples are permitted to enjoy. We must keep in mind that sexuality, according to the *Catechism*,

> affects all aspects of the human person in the unity of his [*sic*] body and soul. It especially concerns affectivity, the capacity to love and procreate, and in a more general way the aptitude for forming bonds of communion with others. (*CCC* 560)

This teaching recognizes that sexuality is about much more than sexual intercourse, or even romantic relationship; it is part of our fundamental aptitude for relationship with others. So it may not be surprising that for these young women, sexual discernment raised complex questions that went beyond what moral rules can address: how to know if someone likes them; what is the role of kissing, hugging, and affectionate touching; how lovers communicate their wants and needs to one another. These concerns were sometimes mixed up with questions of when to have sex, how they felt about "hooking up" in college, and the morality of contraception, but these topics were almost always secondary to the pressing concern of how to be in a good relationship.

Most of the young women I interviewed talked about a fear-based style of sexuality education—one that focused heavily on risks of pregnancy and disease and failed to explain the inherent goodness of sex, at least in a way that was believable. Isabella, a twenty-one-year-old at a Catholic college who showed great commitment to her faith, explained, "[Sex is] portrayed in a negative way, mostly. You listen to talks and you hear the Church teach that sex is a good thing! But I don't really think that it's always portrayed as good." Rose, a nineteen-year-old who had left the Catholic Church for a progressive Evangelical community, described sex education at her Catholic school: "I think it was honestly about the consequences. And it was very looked down upon. Now that I'm thinking about it, the only sex talk we ever had was about diseases."

These accounts suggest approaches that would make sexual discernment difficult for these women in the future: knowing that they weren't supposed to have sex did not help them with their dominant concerns about sex in adolescence or explain how they were supposed to live as sexual people in the moment (e.g., by cultivating good friendships). They primarily learned that sex was something they weren't supposed to be concerned about yet, even while their parents and teachers were clearly concerned about it on their behalf. This fear-based education laid the groundwork for a fraught understanding of sex as they entered into their first romantic relationships.

As these women lived through their teenage years, most of them decided that their parents and teachers were not trustworthy resources for information about sexuality, and that if they wanted to learn about the topic, they would have to do it secretly, by themselves. Valerie, a nominal Catholic with little interest in practicing the faith, described one event at her Catholic school as an example of why she did not trust the adults in her life with questions about sex:

> They wanted us to ask questions, but wouldn't nec-
> essarily answer them. They would have this kind
> of open forum, like if you didn't want to ask it out
> loud you could write it down on a piece of paper
> and hand it in so it was anonymous, but some of
> the questions they wouldn't answer.

It is likely that this situation was a simple misunderstanding. One of Valerie's peers might have written a question that was inappropriate or overly personal and that is why the teachers put it aside. At the time, however, Valerie took this as evidence that her teachers were failing to be as honest and forthright as they claimed they would be. Nora, who was raised in a highly traditional Catholic household, remembers looking up *sex* in the dictionary "because no one was going to tell me, it wasn't something I was going to ask." Others turned to the internet or the limited information they could glean from their peers, some of it inaccurate. A few experimented in sexual relationships as a way of "figuring it out." Because the adults around them talked about sex as a scary, negative thing, these girls were unable to talk about sex openly, and some of them felt ashamed for being interested in a topic that seemed taboo. This tendency to keep quiet about matters of sex and relationships created difficulties for some of them in future relationships, where they felt uncomfortable talking directly to their partners about what they did and did not want.

These women had all worked hard to educate themselves about sexuality on their own as young adults through conversations with friends and partners, by doing their own research, and sometimes through college courses. Yet even for those who wanted to engage with Church tradition and theology, their ability to do so was limited by their own nervousness about the topic and a lack of safe communities in which to start conversations. When I asked them to articulate how they made difficult decisions about sex and relationships, all of them said they relied on a "gut feeling" in the moment to tell them what was right and wrong. This intuitive way of making decisions was not necessarily wrong, but it was curious that such diverse women, from those most steeped in Catholic tradition to those most distant from their religious roots, all spoke about the same means of discernment. The seriousness of their Catholic upbringing or faith did not appear to make much of a difference.

Learning Discernment

The way we teach about sex and sexuality in American Catholic culture is inadequate because there is so much fear of adolescents or young adults making "bad" choices. The theology is frequently oversimplified to a set of specific "do and don't" rules that some will adopt but most will dismiss. When the time comes to make choices, these women lack a clear sense of how their relationships and sexual lives relate to their spirituality, their ethics about friendship, or their moral reasoning.

These same women, however, had clear ideas about how they wish they had learned about sex and sexuality and how they will teach their own daughters. Perhaps unsurprisingly, almost all of them talked about the importance of open and honest conversation starting from an early age, and of how having adults as a nonjudgmental sounding board would have benefited them. Rose, for example, was able to go to the mother of a friend after ending a sexual relationship that left her confused about how she wanted to date in the future:

> I just give it to her point-blank. And she goes, "Okay. I've been there too. Let's talk about what you're feeling."...I didn't want a lecture, I just wanted someone to listen to me and be like, "No, you're not going crazy. You're fine. This is where you're at. And no, you haven't messed things up."

Rose's sense of safety in this conversation came from her confidence that this woman would not shame her for her choices, but rather would help her reflect upon them so that she could learn what she wanted in a relationship.

Jessica, a twenty-two-year-old practicing Catholic, described a similar situation when explaining how she wanted to teach her own future children about sex and sexuality:

> I would try to open up that dialogue, and say, "You know, if you have questions, talk to me. If ever you feel pressure, you can come talk to me." And I think I would put less of an emphasis on kind of that black and white like, "Don't do this, don't do this, don't do this."

Because she had found that the list of moral rules she had learned did not help her understand how to navigate her own relationships, she deliberately takes the emphasis away from rules and focuses instead on the process of discernment, ensuring that her children could have a safe place to seek information and to express their worries.

These women's instincts align with some of the best practices of religious education in the United States more broadly, such as Thomas Groome's methods of faith sharing that encourage adults to see themselves less as the arbiter of information and to concentrate more on "'being with' participants in a subject-to-subject relationship."[1] In other words, one fundamental aspect of good religious education is cultivating a loving, respectful relationship between the learner and the teacher. In this relationship, the more experienced person can be a sounding board that helps the learner explore their own thoughts and feelings and come to realizations on their own. Religious education, from this perspective, involves helping younger people practice discernment, not handing them pat answers.

This framework may be difficult for some parents and religious educators to apply effectively to sexuality education because many sex and relationship decisions come with inherent risk, and adults rightly wish to protect adolescents and youth from the pain of brokenheartedness and the angst of contracting infections or experiencing an unplanned pregnancy. It is much more clear-cut to simply communicate that sex is off-limits as a subject and an activity. Yet studies have indicated that Catholic young adults in the United States behave no differently from their secular peers when it comes to rates of sexual activity in college, and one surprising survey indicated that "hookups" are actually more common on Catholic campuses that prominently emphasize their Catholic identity.[2] The fear-infused style of education that many young women experienced growing up Catholic has clearly not translated into greater alignment with Catholic teachings.

My research suggests that communication is vital for helping young Catholic women to learn skills of discernment with regard to sexual relationships and to move forward from situations that caused them distress or grief. Parents and religious educators may need to take a step back from the temptation to provide simple rules—"No sex until you're married!"—and focus instead on helping young people to think through their choices. This means trusting that those young people will eventually come to recognize and seek to live by the truths of the tradition.

Notes

1. Thomas H. Groome, *Sharing Faith: A Comprehensive Approach to Religious Education and Pastoral Ministry* (Eugene, OR: Wipf & Stock, 1998), 143.

2. Jason King, "How Does Catholic Identity Affect Hookup Culture?" *First Things*, February 9, 2017, https://www.firstthings.com/web-exclusives/2017/02/how-does-catholic-identity-affect-hookup-culture.

Staying In and Reaching Out

Ruth Hunt (Stonewall, UK) and Jeannine Gramick (New Ways Ministry, USA) in Conversation with Tina Beattie

Ruth Hunt, Jeannine Gramick, and Tina Beattie

Tina Beattie met with Ruth Hunt and Jeannine Gramick in the Stonewall offices in London in July 2017.

TB: *You're both Catholic women engaged in frontline campaigning and advocacy work on LGBT issues. How did you become involved in this work?*

RH: I guess that my Catholicism has shaped my fundamental spirit of "treat others as you'd like to be treated"—with kindness, compassion, and love, keeping in mind those who are in pain and suffering and how that gets alleviated.

I came to Stonewall in 2005 as quite a junior member of staff, and I wasn't particularly out about being Catholic. One morning, I got a call from a journalist asking about the stopping of the LGBT-affirming Catholic masses in Soho,[1] and did Stonewall have a view. I said it's a real shame because it's good that LGBT Catholics have a place to go. The journalist said, "Do you know any LGBT Catholics?" and I said, "Yeh, I'm a Catholic," but thought nothing of it. As soon as I became Chief Exec, the headline was "Practicing Catholic takes over as Chief Executive of Stonewall."

Becoming CEO changed the way I talked about my faith. Without sounding too grand, I almost had a kind of "Here I am, Lord" moment. It was my duty to learn how to speak well about faith, and the complexity within that, and how it reconciles with sexuality. I found myself quite isolated, but I very much considered it the right thing to do.

The LGBT community were pretty hostile, but my way of working is inherently collaborative, and I work with gentle hands. I nudge. That's my influencing technique, and it's served me well for the last twelve years. We're one of the most effective campaigning organizations in the country. Of course, privately there were some dark nights of the soul, but I couldn't leave Catholicism—it's impossible. You can't stop being Catholic. So it's just something I have to reconcile.

JG: I came to be involved in LGBT ministry when I was a graduate student way back in 1971 when I was in my twenties. I was at the University of Pennsylvania for my doctoral degree, and I met a gay man. It was that friendship with him and his lesbian and gay friends that drew me into this work, because he kept saying to me, "Well, Sister, what is the Catholic Church doing for my gay brothers and sisters?" In 1971, the Catholic Church wasn't doing anything. Actually, I take that back—it was doing something very harmful. He had stopped going to the Catholic Church because priests had told him he was going to hell, and his friends had had similar experiences.

We began to have home Masses at his apartment or at the homes of his friends on a weekly basis for gay and lesbian Catholics. My learning experience was through the stories. Stories are so important for changing people's attitudes and understanding. After I finished my studies, I was assigned by my community to lesbian and gay ministry. That went on for decades, even despite some opposition from bishops in the United States.

TB: *You've both had struggles with the Catholic hierarchy. How do you deal with that?*

RH: There can be a whole ongoing circular debate about St. Paul and celibacy and marriage as a sacrament and sex—we can do all that—but when it descends into cruelty, it becomes so much the opposite of my Catholic faith that it becomes a conviction to challenge that. I had to get to a place—it's easy to sound trite—but it's "what would God want me to do," and God would not want me to turn a blind eye and be silenced by the power imbalance that exists in the structure.

Stonewall does a lot of work with faith schools. The reality is that Catholic schools have LGBT kids, and the biggest cause of mental distress amongst LGBT young people is being rejected and the expectation of rejection. So even before they've done anything that we can get complex about from a Catholic perspective, the thought of them losing that spiritual family is heartbreaking, utterly heartbreaking. You have to be kept warm and safe in that space. So I will go to any lengths and upset any people to help those who show that perspective.

JG: To me it's about the gospel. Most people look at sexuality when we talk about church teachings on LGBT issues, and I say, what about Church teachings on LGBT people with regard to the social teachings of the Church, which rest upon the dignity of the human person? Every person is a child of God. So I gain my strength from the gospel, from my prayer life, from the voice of God coming to me through people, and I hold on to and want to proclaim the social teachings of the Church.

TB: *How does one promote what the Church teaches about the ethics of sexual love, whether in heterosexual or homosexual relationships?*

RH: I believe that I'm living in a way that is utterly compatible with my faith to treat my partner with the utmost respect and love and fidelity and sometimes it's hard. That was mental gymnastics that I had to do on my own, as someone who had grown up without positive LGBT role models, without representations of LGBT people in the media, without spiritual and pastoral support. We talk about mental health and damage in LGBT communities. It's because everybody's trying to find their own way without any anchoring, and what the Catholic Church provides is an anchor, a moral anchor, a Christian anchor, an anchor where God can express himself through you and with you and in your deeds and in your words. A whole community is bereft of that love, and denied that love, because of an antiquated idea about exactly what St. Paul meant when he talked about sex.

If we could talk honestly about what good relationships look like, and, for example, the fact that gay couples are providing amazing homes for some of the most vulnerable children, and there is nothing more Christian than that. That is so Christ in action. This rigid idea about what family looks like and what love looks like and what tradition has taught is deeply damaging.

JG: Ruth is articulating what I hope everyone does, and that is to follow one's conscience. To me, that is a primary teaching of the Church that we haven't held up, although Pope Francis is holding it up. The leaders of our Church are to articulate for us the wisdom of the community. So to me, when people say Church teaching, I equate that with the wisdom the Catholic, the Christian community has gained over the centuries, and that wisdom is presented as the teaching of the Church. In the final analysis, as Ruth beautifully articulated, you use that teaching to say how does my life incorporate that, how does it square with that, and we use that to make our own conscience decisions. We have to be mature in the faith, and that means making one's own decision, not doing it because someone told me to.

I like what Pope Francis has said. He has said that the Church is there to help people form their conscience, not to replace their conscience. We need spiritual directors, we need priests, sisters, laypeople, those who are in positions of spiritual leadership, to help people to form that conscience, to make that decision, not to replace conscience.

TB: *I wonder how the issues we're discussing relate to gay Catholics attracted to the priesthood or religious life.*

JG: Anecdotally I know that formation directors in some men's communities in the United States will say, "Oh, half of the people in my community are gay." In women's communities I think it's a smaller percentage, only because—well, why? I think if I give you my own interpretation, it's that God is presented to us as male. A male God is attractive to a male person who is gay, or a female person who is heterosexual. I think unconsciously that is the reason why many gay men who have a very spiritual component, who are very good men, are more attracted to a male God, and I think heterosexual women are very attracted to a male God. I think that the conception of God as male has influenced over the centuries the spirituality, or the lifestyle, of gay men and heterosexual women.

TB: *Do you think gay men and women face different challenges in accepting their sexuality?*

JG: In the Church, probably in society, male and female have never been equal. Male has always been superior and the female inferior, and I'm tempted to believe that much of the hesitation or condemnation of same-sex relationships is a result of either a conscious or unconscious thought that if two men are in this relationship, one is making himself inferior. He's putting himself in the position of a woman, and that's degrading to him as a man. Similarly, if you have two women, well, one must be aspiring to a male position. How dare she think of herself in a higher position? I think unconsciously, this has been operating over the centuries, and I think we need to bring it to the surface, to challenge it. I think this impacts, too, on the transgender issue. The forces in the Church, the powers in the Church will say, "This is unnatural," as has been said of lesbian and gay relationships. What does it mean to be unnatural? Our notions about what we know to be natural are based on scientific information, and we have much more scientific information now than we had in the thirteenth century, but our outlook on LGBT issues has not changed since the thirteenth century.

RH: I think generally, female sexuality, whether it's hetero or homo, is always passive, because we live in a patriarchal society. So for a woman in any context to assert her views, whether that's about something to do with pleasure, or about whether she wants children, or whether she wants sex, is quite difficult. There are all sorts of barriers here about a woman's ability to live the life she wants to live: having the financial means to do that, the courage to do that in the stages when everybody else is getting married and your family expects you to get married, the obligation you have to your children first and foremost. Whereas it is easier in a way for men to say, "Well, this is my sexuality, and I am used to asserting what I want," though that's not straightforward either. There are plenty of men who married women and then deeply regretted it. That doesn't feel right, fair, or Christian to me, to know your sexuality but go ahead into an opposite-sex marriage and bring children into the world. Knowing that you're lying to your partner is to me more of a problem within the Catholic faith than being gay and working your way out on that.

So we create these binary options that actually aren't right for everyone. A lot of people knew they were trans but lived a lie, and that's a lot of different lives you're messing up. How much better would it be if that fifteen- or sixteen-year-old was able to tell the truth, because he'd had an affirming message from his priest that it's okay to be you? How many lives would be made less stressful? So it's all about patriarchy, I'm afraid.

TB: *What are your final thoughts before we finish?*

RH: I think the bottom line is that they can't continue to avoid making a decision on moving these issues forward. People need compassion, and they need a space to be close to Jesus Christ. You can't put barriers up to that. It's anathema to the Catholic faith.

JG: I would like to consider worldview. Until the Second Vatican Council, the Catholic Church had this very authoritarian worldview, but there is a different worldview since Vatican II, and Pope Francis is trying to revive this. The truth is that there is truth, but we're in search of the truth. We don't yet have the fullness of truth. We are not a fortress so that we have to close ourselves off and fight the world. The world has something to teach us.

Notes

1. This refers to Cardinal (then Archbishop) Vincent Nichols's decision to stop twice-monthly Masses for LGBT Catholics in London, which he had previously supported, on the basis that they should attend Mass in their local parishes. See *The Tablet*, January 5, 2013.

Whose Life Matters?

Violence against Lesbians and the Politics of Life in the Church

Nontando Hadebe

The partially clothed body of Eudy Simelane, former star of South Africa's acclaimed Banyana Banyana national female football squad, was found in a creek in a park in Kwa Thema, on the outskirts of Johannesburg. Simelane had been gang-raped and brutally beaten before being stabbed 25 times in the face, chest and legs. As well as being one of South Africa's best-known female footballers, Simelane was a voracious equality rights campaigner and one of the first women to live openly as a lesbian in Kwa Thema.[1]

The brutal rape and murder of Simelane is an example of "corrective" rape, a term used to describe the beliefs by perpetrators that rape serves as a tool for correcting lesbian and gay sexualities. Simelane was a young woman with dreams and ambitions like other young women, but she was brutally killed because she was born different. There were no protests from churches, only a silence that seemed to affirm the belief of the perpetrators that being homosexual is not only "un-African" but also "un-Christian." These are the two dominant discourses that allow for the violation and sacrifice of life on the altar of religious and cultural "preservation."

The Catechism is clear in its rejection of homosexual acts:

> Basing itself on Sacred Scripture, which presents homosexual acts as acts of grave depravity, tradition has always declared that "homosexual acts are intrinsically disordered." They are contrary to the natural law. They close the sexual act to the gift of life. They do not proceed from a genuine affective and sexual complementarity. Under no circumstances can they be approved. (*CCC* 2357, quoting *PH* 8)[2]

At the same time, it says that homosexual persons "must be accepted with respect, compassion, and sensitivity," and that "every sign of unjust discrimination in their regard should be avoided" (*CCC* 2358).

However, the language of depravity and disorder is in itself violent, and is not likely to inspire compassion, acceptance, inclusion, and embrace. Such terms produce what the *Catechism* seeks to avoid, namely, rejection, violence, and discrimination.

There are mixed responses to homosexuality from the Catholic Church in Africa, ranging from support for criminalization to a growing level of acceptance. For example, in a pastoral statement, the Episcopal Conference of Malawi states,

> We, the Bishops of the Catholic Church in Malawi
> are aware of the pressure that the Government

has endured so far from foreign nations and agencies who attach their financial support to values and practices that are contrary to our culture. We applaud the efforts and the courage the Government has demonstrated so far to resist the pressure to adopt such foreign values and practices, i.e., homosexuality and abortion. We wish to affirm that such practices are not only against our cultural values but also contrary to our laws and beliefs.[3]

Research done by the Other Foundation in ten southern African countries, however, paints a more positive picture:

One of the most unexpected findings of the country reports is that, across the board, the Catholic Church at a national and local level has been among the most open to dialogue. This was noted, in particular, in Lesotho, where the church is particularly strong, and in Angola and Mozambique: here, Portuguese Catholicism is traditionally "tolerant" and, unlike in the rapidly growing Pentecostal churches, there is no theology of demon-possession, leading to often-violent practices of deliverance and exorcism.[4]

The same research found that the LGTBI people face most rejection in the family:

According to the Social Inclusion Benchmarking Index questionnaire, the greatest area of exclusion, for LGBTI people, is also the most primal: the family. In focus groups run by this project in Swaziland, this was described as the greatest exclusionary factor, and the area of greatest pain. The dilemma faced is whether to risk rejection by one's family, or whether to lead a double life: the Rock of Hope Needs Assessment survey found that 80% of its members remained in the closet because of fear of family rejection.[5]

Many theological issues emerge from the experiences of LGBTI youth, not only in southern Africa but globally. Here, I focus on the following: patriarchy and violence against LGBTI people; the human dignity and equality of all persons who are made in the image of God, irrespective of their sexuality; the giftedness of each person and interconnectedness of all of creation as affirmed in Pope Francis's encyclical *Laudato Si'*; and principles of solidarity and justice in Catholic social teaching as the basis for inculturation.

First, the relationship between violence against LGBTI people and patriarchy arises from the perceived failure of such people to conform to the gender roles of their cultures. Connell argues that each culture has a dominant masculinity—hegemonic masculinity—that represents the ideals of what it means to be a "real man" in a particular culture and era.[6] Gay, bisexual, transgender, and intersex men do not fit into the ideals of hegemonic masculinity and are therefore subject to violence and discrimination. Similarly, lesbians threaten patriarchy because of what Amanda Swarr identifies as the "tripartite threat they pose: to heterosexuality (through their relationships with women), to gender norms (through their expressions of masculinities and disregard for femininities), and to sex (through challenging expectations surrounding somatically female bodies)."[7] Patriarchy is also implicated in other forms of violence, particularly violence against women. The World Health Organization has described violence against women as a global threat to women's health, citing global estimates that "indicate that about 1 in 3 (35%) of women worldwide have experienced either physical and/or sexual intimate partner violence or non-partner sexual violence in their lifetime."[8]

Thus the dismantling of patriarchy is critical to building a world in which the dignity and value of each person is protected and celebrated as critical to the promotion of cultures of peace, free from all forms of violence and where all lives without exception are valued equally.

Second, Pope Francis affirms the equal dignity of all persons made in the image of God and recognizes the intrinsic value, mystery, and interconnectedness of life. In *Laudato Si'*, he writes,

> Everything is related, and we human beings are united as brothers and sisters on a wonderful pilgrimage, woven together by the love God has for each of His creatures and which also unites us in fond affection with brother sun, sister moon, brother river and mother earth. (*LS* 92)

Finally, the integration of values of solidarity and justice in inculturation is necessary to counter the claim that LGBTI is un-African, which is used to justify criminalization and vilification. The fundamental beliefs of African traditional religions affirm the dignity of all persons and the value of life.[9] Studies by African scholars have revealed the presence of sexual diversity in precolonial Africa, suggested by words and phrases that referred to same-sex orientation. For example, Shoko notes that among the Karanga—as in other African languages—are an abundance of Karanga words and phrases that refer to "homosexuality or variation of same-sex patterns."[10] Some examples of these words include the following: "*ngochani*," which refers to "people of same-sex orientation,"[11] "*munhurume-kadzi*" (man-woman), which

149

refers to "a male who lives as female gendered person,"[12] and "*munhukadzi-rume*" (woman-man), referring to "a woman who lives the life of a male gendered person."[13] African languages thus provided insights into the diversity of sexualities in precolonial Africa, challenging the myth that sexual diversity is "un-African." Religious leaders therefore cannot justify their support for the criminalization and exclusion of African LGBTI persons on the grounds of culture. The value of life in both Christianity and African culture should be the basis for countering all forms of violence against any section of the community.

The brutal murder of a young woman because of her sexual orientation is a story of many young women who look to the Church for protection and affirmation of their identity as the beloved daughters of God. Their suffering is not so different from that of many other young women who experience violence at the hands of partners. Patriarchy constitutes a threat to the lives of women. Dismantling it and replacing it with values that affirm the dignity, equality, and interdependence of all persons will make the Church a safe and life-giving place for young women.

Notes

1. Annie Kelly, "Raped and Killed for Being a Lesbian: South Africa Ignores Corrective Attacks," *The Guardian*, March 12, 2009, https://www.theguardian.com/world/2009/mar/12/eudy-simelane-corrective-rape-south-africa.

2. References are to Scriptures such as Gen 19:1–29; Rom 1:24–27; 1 Cor 6:10; and 1 Tim 1:10.

3. Episcopal Conference of Malawi, Pastoral Letter, March 13, 2016, http://www.ecmmw.org/new/2016/03/13/ecm-pastoral-letter-english/.

4. Mark Gevisser, *Canaries in the Coal Mines: An Analysis of Spaces for LGBTI Activism in Southern Africa* (Johannes-

burg: The Other Foundation, 2016), 18, available to download at http://theotherfoundation.org/canaries-in-the-coal-mines/.

5. Gevisser, *Canaries in the Coal Mines*, 26.

6. Robert W. Connell, "Arms and the Man: Using the New Research on Masculinity to Understand Violence and Promote Peace in the Contemporary World," in *Male Roles, Masculinities and Violence: A Culture of Peace Perspective*, ed. Ingeborg Breines, Robert Connell, and Ingrid Eide (Paris: UNESCO, 2000): 21–33, at 24.

7. Amanda M. Swarr, "Paradoxes of Butchness: Lesbian Masculinities and Sexual Violence in Contemporary South Africa," *Signs: Journal of Women in Culture and Society* 37, no. 4 (2012): 962–88, at 963.

8. World Health Organization, *Violence against Women: Intimate Partner and Sexual Violence against Women*, Fact sheet, November 2016, http://www.who.int/mediacentre/factsheets/fs239 /en/.

9. Mbiti, "Aspects of African Heritage and Spirituality," *St. Augustine Papers* 7, no. 1 (2006): 3–27.

10. Tabona Shoko, "Same-sex Relationships among the Karanga of Mberengwa in the Pre-colonial Period," in *Engaging with the Past: Same-Sex Relationships in Pre-colonial Zimbabwe*, ed. Ezra Chitando (Harare: EHAIA, 2015), 29–49, at 32.

11. Shoko, "Same-sex Relationships," 32.

12. Shoko, "Same-sex Relationships," 32.

13. Shoko, "Same-sex Relationships," 33.

Parenting Is Not for Cowards

Losing Greg

Julett Broadnax

Nothing had fully prepared me for the loss of my firstborn son, but being raised by faithful parents and attending Catholic schools for twelve years was a good basis for at least having values and morals as a good background. Homosexuality was new to me and took a period of adjustment for both of us. However, a wise priest counselor advised me that I had a chance to show my son how God loves us just as we are, and we both were able to put this into practice. That priest's wise words helped me also to realize that God loved me too, with all of my shortcomings—a real awakening for me!

When Greg first told me of the possibility he had AIDS, it was 1986 and I had very little knowledge of this disease. In fact, I was probably in denial that this was even a possibility. So when we received the news from his partner that Greg was in the hospital with pneumocystis pneumonia and the possibility of no survival, I was in shock, and we were on a plane to Atlanta within a few hours. Staying at his bedside as he was suffering was a trial by fire—so helpless to do anything but pray. My prayers were rote prayers, the rosary. I asked if I could call a priest and Greg said, "No Mom, you pray for me," barely able to have enough oxygen even to reply.

A few days later, I was at Mass at the cathedral when Greg was resuscitated and intubated after being deprived of oxygen. By the time I returned to the hospital, he was in a coma. I can still remember saying to my husband, "I now understand why sometimes people die after the death of a loved one, for my psychic pain is so severe, I do not know if I can survive."

That afternoon I did call the cathedral and asked for a priest to come and anoint my son, and the same young priest who had said Mass earlier arrived to anoint him and pray the rosary with family members. The priest lent me a CD player so that I could play some of Greg's favorite arias and hymns—which was an easier way for me to pray by his bedside. He said Greg was probably afraid of rejection and that was why he said not to call a priest, as he had listed himself as Catholic upon admission.

After five days, I had to confront his primary doctor about removing him from life support, as Greg had told the doctor to keep him alive by any means. His teen stepsister begged me not to remove the respirator because a spiritual friend had advised her that he would recover. I really did not need this young girl's emotional upheaval during that time. It was enough dealing with my own emotions. When I suggested that the machine was what was keeping him alive, the doctor finally agreed to do an EEG and the results showed no hope of survival. They removed him from life support, and he died peacefully within a few hours.

No amount of support from family or friends was sufficient to help me heal from this trauma. I attended daily Mass and ranted and raved at God for taking my child. I recalled my Dad saying that God only lends us our children before he brings them home again. It took a year of counseling, lots of prayer, and reaching out to help other AIDS patients and their families before I came to accept this loss and achieve healing.

My grief was compounded when then-Cardinal Ratzinger stated that homosexuality was an intrinsic disorder. I found that such a destructive statement. My son was a very precious gift, created by God in his image and likeness. My wise pastor said that the only difference between himself and Greg is that Greg died before the pastor did. Greg would have turned sixty-three the week I wrote this, thirty-one of them spent in heaven, for I was assured by my pastor that God loves him at least as much as I do.

What Does It Mean to Mother?

Susan Harford

For many, my status as "mother" or "grandmother" is questionable. I require the qualifiers "adoptive" and "birth." Am I a second-class mother? Some in my Roman Catholic faith pity me for not procreating. Others in my faith regard me as saintly for taking in someone else's child. And still others regard me ultimately as a failure—for reasons that will become apparent later. All of them are wrong.

My status has forced me to contemplate prayerfully what it means to be "mother" and what "mothering" entails. Now, after decades in the role, I feel no less a mother than any woman who has given birth and raised a child, and no less a failure or success either. Motherhood has been and continues to be a magnificent human and spiritual journey to which I was called—even if the calling is not rooted in biology.

Most people (parents or not) admit there's no such thing as a perfect mother. Yet most of us have expectations of what a mother should be and do, within a margin of error colored by our culture, our family traditions, our religion, parenting literature, and many other outside influences. We measure ourselves against these, and judge others by these expectations. We make decisions throughout the milestone years as best we can with what we know. Mothering comes naturally, if not always clearly, and not without pain. My circumstances demand openness to cultures and traditions I shall never fully understand in order to provide my child and grandchild with the fundamental bonding and full acceptance that allows God to unfurl the unique gifts given to each of them.

I am a white, Catholic adoptive mother of twenty-three years in an open adoption with my daughter's Vietnamese birth family; I am also a birth-grandmother in an open adoption with my daughter's daughter now being raised by a Jewish couple. When one is released from the confines of genetic code and long-held family cultural traditions, the spiritual aspect of mothering—as evidenced by our maternal paragon, Holy Mother Mary—becomes paramount. By this I do not mean that our only care is the salvation of our child's soul and his or her relationship to God. Rather I am referring to what Mary did—her mothering process.

First, motherhood is both an act of faith and a presence. "How can this be, since I am a virgin?" asks Mary of the angel in Luke 1:34. Anyone who reads this as merely a technical question regarding conception misses the enormous role providence plays in every maternal choice. Again, biology is not the key factor. Motherhood is a calling that requires discernment, acceptance, and faith that you will be able to meet the demands and rewards of being a constant, if imperfect, presence for your child. "Let it be with me according to your word" is not just an act of obedience but one of profound trust.

Second, mothers navigate social waters *with* our children, not *for* them. "Woman, what concern is that to you and me? My hour has not yet come." So responds Jesus in John 2:4, the wedding at Cana. Mary carries on instructing servers to follow Jesus's instructions and so Jesus begins to reveal himself. How many of us have set our children up to give of their best, whether in school or clubs or family events?

Is that not our role? My mothering integrates three differ-
ent family cultures (Irish Catholic, Vietnamese Catholic, and
Jewish) along with the Persian Muslim, Anglo-Saxon, Hindu
Indian cultures characteristic of my diverse neighborhood.

The seven gifts of the Holy Spirit (Wisdom, Understanding, Right Judgment, Fortitude, Knowledge, Rever-
ence, Awe) have been the developmental framework for all
social situations in our household. These gifts seamlessly
fit into and also outstrip conventional social norms in every
situation my daughter and I have encountered so far. They
allow everyone in the room to shine. They have guided us to
forge meaningful bonds with my daughter's birth family by
showing us how to unite into one family for the sake of my
daughter—and unexpectedly for ourselves.

Third, mothers help their children to reveal and develop
their God-given gifts. In some cases, the discovery of these
gifts is shocking, mysterious, and glorious simultaneously.
When one is an adoptive parent, it is easy to understand that
our child's gifts transcend our experience. "Nurture" notwithstanding, there are epigenetic character traits and capabilities that emerge. My daughter's love of design and craft
was clear by age three when she said to me, "Mom, I know
why God gave me to you, because I have style." If only you
could see me in my daily "uniform," you would see the truth
of this statement. Suffice it to say she continues to surprise,
dazzle, and sometimes worry me with her ventures. The Gospel of Luke 2:41–52 is seminal for me. I feel the frantic worry
of Mary and Joseph as they search for their son Jesus for
three days at the festival—only to discover him preaching.

Fourth, mothers must bear witness to the ways our children face hurt and brutality. We must stand steadfast with
them despite our own agony, uncertainty, and inability to
control outcomes. We see Mary like this when she couldn't
reach Jesus for the crowds (Luke 8:19–20), later on the road

to Calvary, and ultimately as she stood at the foot of the cross. With motherhood comes heartbreak.

Finally, mothers perpetuate family lineage usually expressed in genealogical terms rooted in biology. What, then, for adoptive families? Lineage most certainly surpasses biological boundaries, and yet, many adoptees yearn to know their birth families. So what is lineage? What does it convey? My daughter had a child out of wedlock (hence my motherly failure, according to some) and gave up her maternal rights in an open adoption with a Jewish couple. What will be my grandmother role now?

Start over with an act of faith and presence. Come, Holy Spirit.

Motherhood as a Mirage

The Role of the Catholic Church and African Culture in Shaping Zimbabwean Girls' Vocations

Revai "Elizabeth" Mudzimu

In Africa generally and in Zimbabwe in particular, girls often find themselves caught in a conflict between traditional and modern attitudes toward motherhood. Catholic girls and women who want to become mothers have to grapple with their African culture and Catholic teachings, while at the same time wanting to respond to the promises and challenges of globalization. There is an idea that motherhood is an essential aspect of African womanhood, and failure to have children or to perform well as a mother can result in stigmatization.

I refer to motherhood as a "mirage" because the way Church teaching is communicated can create an illusion about what it means to be a mother without preparing girls for the reality of mothering. Pope Francis calls for a Church that is *with* people in their struggles and shows them God's mercy. This means that priests, sisters, and teachers of the faith need to understand people's lived experiences and their cultural contexts. Rather than a "one-size-fits-all" approach, teachings need to be adapted to their contexts. If the vocation to marriage and motherhood is to be meaningful, Church teaching needs to be disseminated more effectively to the grassroots and become more integrated into the current social, economic, cultural, and technological environment.

Africanness in Catholicism or Catholicism in Africanness? A Dilemma

The Church teaches that marriage is a mutual bond between a man and a woman, built on love, and ordained for procreation and the education of children. It promotes the vocation to motherhood only in the context of marriage.

Zimbabwe is a patriarchal society in which women are expected to be subordinate to men. This gives men control over every aspect of women's lives. Cultural practices serve to legitimize male control over women in ways that sometimes contradict Church teaching. For example, polygamy violates the idea of marriage as a mutual bond between two people, but in African cultures it is often seen as a sign of wealth. The payment of a bride-price to a girl's family can seem like a transaction in which men buy and own women as personal property. Girls who grow up in rural areas are educated only to become good wives, and some even have their labia enlarged with herbs in order to enhance their husband's sexual pleasure. Proverbs are used to promote the idea that there is no security outside marriage; for example, *"Mudzimai iruva riri mubindu rinochengetwa neruzhowa rwemurume"* (A woman is a flower in the garden; her husband is the fence around). The man is regarded as the breadwinner, which results in the woman giving up her economic rights. Some women are beaten up by their husbands if they fail to perform their so-called wifely duties, and they often keep silent for fear of losing their only source of security, which is their marriage.

The Church teaches that human life is sacred and must be protected from the moment of conception. While it encourages responsible parenthood, it does not allow the use of contraception or abortion under any circumstances. This means that some girls become mothers against their will—as a result of rape, for example—and others become single mothers as a result of failed marriages. Such situations raise a question about Church teaching in regard to single mothers, and with regard to the exclusion of divorced and remarried Catholics from the Eucharist. Single mothers often feel they do not belong in Zimbabwean parishes, since they do not fit into the youth groups or into the women's groups. As a result, some leave the Church in search of more accepting communities where they will be respected.

These various aspects of African culture and Catholic teaching pose a challenge to the idea of inculturation. Is the Church Africanizing Catholicism or Catholicizing Africanism?

Vocations Entangled in the Web of Globalization

The greatest threat to the Church's teaching in Africa today is the influence of globalization on young people. Young Catholic women and girls experience a threefold ideological pressure from their culture, modernity, and Catholic teaching. How does the Church position its teaching in such a situation? *Gaudium et Spes* calls for the Church to "read the signs of the times" (*GS* 4). Teaching according to the signs of the times means taking into consideration the pivotal concerns in people's lives. With regard to motherhood and sexuality, the focus on sexual and reproductive health and rights (SRHR) is one aspect of globalization. The goal of SRHR is for women to attain sexual health, sexual rights, reproductive health, and reproductive rights as essential to their human dignity. If the Church does not address these global issues in its teaching, young people will learn from Google and end up taking all sorts of bad advice regarding sexual and reproductive relationships. If girls and women are taught about their sexual health, sexual rights, reproductive health, and reproductive rights, they will be enabled to make informed decisions and will gain confidence.

From "Namby-Pamby" toward Invigorated Teaching

I am aware that the Catholic Church has a divine commission, and that Church doctrine cannot be changed. I also agree with those who contend that the mandate of the Church is to *christify the world, not to mundanize Christ*. However, for the Church to be relevant in the modern era, it needs to contextualize its teaching and that contextualization should be conciliatory. If young people are to commit themselves to marriage, Church teaching needs to acknowledge the challenging situations they face, as Pope Francis repeatedly argues. Inculturation is effective only when it is built on people's lived experiences and uses an emic perspective—that is, seeking knowledge within local cultures and traditions and not imposing values and ideas from outside. The local church needs to move away from its "namby-pamby" way of teaching to become reinvigorated, so that it really becomes the custodian of knowledge. This also means acknowledging that issues concerning women are best understood by women, and that religious and laywomen need to be involved in teaching girls. By creating space for women to feel at home in their culture and in their church, we enable them to become participants in the making of *"herstory"*—history as experienced and interpreted from the perspectives of women. This can only come about through encouraging the full and equal participation of women in theological reflection and decision-making.

Church teachings can promote and sustain girls' vocations, but challenges arise from the passivity of the local church, from conflicts with African cultural perspectives, and from the influence of globalization. This is why there is a need for inculturation, even as we recognize that the dynamics of power in church and culture are patriarchal. Church teaching and institutions need to respond to calls by Pope John Paul II and Pope Francis to engage women in their cultures and churches as coworkers and not as objects of discussion. (See *Christifideles Laici* and *Evangelii Gaudium.*) To achieve this change of focus there needs to be new vigor in the way Church teaching is interpreted and communicated.

I Mourn My Faith

A Single Mother's Story

Martha Mapasure

Everything I was, knew, and lived was Catholic. I was born and raised in a strong Catholic family and community. I was baptized and confirmed in the Catholic Church. I was educated by Catholics in Catholic schools and universities from primary level through high school and university. Eager to serve in the Church, I studied theology, and after completing my degree, I was fortunate to get a lecturing job at a Catholic university. I was involved in many church activities: giving retreats, serving as lector, singing in choir, and serving as eucharistic minister—the ministry I loved most. I was also a secretary of the parish council and a parish youth leader. I was a member of several Catholic organizations: Catholic Commission for Justice and Peace (CCJP), St. Vincent DePaul, and the Society of the Legion of Mary. I was a role model and an inspiration to parishioners, especially other young people like myself. Attending Mass and going to meet with Christ in the Holy Eucharist was my daily bread. I would never have imagined a day without the Eucharist. I loved and enjoyed my work both at the university and at the parish. I was proud to be a Catholic and could never have imagined being a member of any other church. I mourn my faith.

Life was about to change for me. My Catholic pride was soon to be taken away. I got pregnant and I was not planning to get married, so my child was to be born out of wedlock. What does this mean for Catholics? I had committed a grave sin and violated the Church's law about marriage. Being the young devout Catholic woman I was, I wondered what I was going to do. What was I to tell my family, my parishioners? How was I to face those young people who looked up to me, to whom was I going to turn? Nervous and hesitant, I broke the news to my mother first. I knew she would always support me, no matter what. This time, however, I was wrong. The "sin" I had committed was too grave. She was very disappointed and angry that I had brought shame, disgrace, and embarrassment not only to the family but also to the whole Church.

She tried to persuade me to abort the pregnancy before everyone noticed, and most importantly to free our well-respected Catholic family from shame. I could not believe that my own Catholic mother was asking me to do this. "What about the Catholic law that forbids abortion?" I reminded her. "Oh that, don't worry about that, my baby, no one has to know, it's a better sin than having a child out of wedlock, my dear," was her response. Better sin? I tried to figure out what that meant, if it made sense at all.

I decided to keep my pregnancy. No matter how much I begged my mother for forgiveness for my mistake, she refused to support me and constantly told me that it was not a mistake but a sin, and that I no longer deserved to be a Catholic. I lost my mother's love, trust, and support at a time when I needed her most.

The Catholic Church offers the sacrament of reconciliation whereby one's sins are forgiven by confession. I decided to make a public confession in church at a Sunday Mass. I thought this would bring forgiveness, redeeming and restoring my image, especially as a youth leader. The parish priest vehemently forbade me to do this. He encouraged me to make a private confession instead, and he began to list all the things I was to refrain from. I was immediately to stop the following: receiving holy communion, participating as a eucharistic minister, serving as lector at liturgy, giving retreats, being a youth leader, being the secretary of the parish council. In other words, I was stripped of everything that made me a Catholic. I could only attend Mass and nothing else. In addition, I was to stop wearing the uniform of the Society of Legion of Mary, which is only supposed to be worn by decent and unmarried youths. My heart was broken. I began to feel the loss and to mourn for my faith.

I dreaded going to Mass, especially to Sunday services with a huge congregation. I knew people were gossiping about me every time I entered the church. It was horrific. I stopped attending Sunday Masses and only attended weekday Masses, which are mostly attended by old people who really do not have the energy to gossip. I felt lonely, unloved, and rejected in the Church where I used to find joy, hope, love, and fulfillment.

A church is supposed to be a place where one feels safe, secure, loved, and welcome, but my experience was the opposite of this. Everyone—my family, the priest, my fellow youth mates, and the community—resented me. The whole church turned its back on me. I became a stranger, and I felt like an outcast in my own mother church.

I did not deserve to be treated like this, especially by the Church. I decided to leave. Today, I am a member of the Anglican Church, but even though it embraced me as I was and allowed me to participate in the church and to partake in the Eucharist, I mourned my faith. I still mourn my faith, and I will always mourn my Catholic faith.

Young people face many difficulties and challenges

in the Catholic Church, especially young females. There is nothing as depressing as becoming pregnant and not knowing what to do. Pregnant women need all the support of the priests, parish council and community, and most of all from the family. Yes, there are Church rules and laws that have to be observed, but as human beings, we are prone to error; that does not mean we deserve to be ill-treated and judged.

The Church should be there at all times and in all situations to love and support its members. Many Catholic youths today are afraid to get pregnant, especially without the promise of marriage, but they are using contraceptives, which is against Church law. There is a need to sit down and come up with realistic and useful solutions for young people, and this can happen only if the Church engages and consults with the youths themselves.

As a parent, I am obliged to raise and teach my child about my faith, which is his faith, so that he grows loving, knowing, and valuing his faith. I was fortunate to be raised in a strong Catholic family, and it saddens me that I have now to raise my child in a different faith, the faith that I converted to and was not raised in. It again pains me that my child has to be baptized in a church different from the one I was baptized in. I would have wished otherwise. I would have loved my child to have had the pride and joy of being a Catholic, to share the rich experiences I have had of being Catholic. These, however, will remain wishes; I am an Anglican now and this is the faith my child will grow in. I will only have a history to tell my child, of how I was once a strong and proud Catholic and what made me leave, mourning all the practices of my faith.

Crossing Borderlines

Parish Friendships with Homeless Single Mothers and Their Children

Thérèse M. Craine Bertsch

Hearing the call, "Rebuild my church," Pope Francis challenged us to address the political reality of structural sin. He did so while having showers installed in the Vatican for homeless people to use. Francis knows we encounter God in the sharing of friendships and resources. What does this mean for parishes? Homeless single mothers cannot form ties to a church they cannot get to. Where are their parish friends who share the daily lives of poor and homeless single mothers? My research into American homeless mothers reveals that despite trauma, hurt, and intimidation, they are deeply spiritual and refuse to be victims. Their understanding of family emerges from their life's circumstances, despite societal structures that fail to support impoverished families. These mothers have much to contribute to parish life.

In the United States, past generations were sometimes kept afloat, even in poverty, thanks to affordable urban housing, public transportation, and accessible jobs, but suburbia today is designed for the bourgeoisie who take flight from integrated urban neighborhoods. Our social structures utterly fail poor homeless mothers, and this failure is surely an example of structural sin. Practices such as outsourcing manufacturing jobs and targeting poor city communities for drug arrests, gentrification, and the incarceration of the poor, particularly black men, have contributed to the collapse of urban neighborhoods and have paralleled the dramatic rise of birth rates outside of marriage.

As a young and pretty, white single mother of five children and the former wife of a high school teacher, I had an empathetic social network. Family and parish friends gave me my first four cars. Parish life offered me support and opportunities to use my gifts and helped me with childcare and transportation. Not so for poor single mothers. A job interview is daunting without a permanent address and transportation. Childcare is difficult for those living in sheltered apartments, because visitors are forbidden and older siblings cannot babysit.

In time I became director of a family homeless shelter housing seventy-six families and over three hundred children. I watched the daily parade of pain as young, single homeless mothers arrived after losing permanent housing time and time again. As staff, we were frustrated by judgments made against women who were powerless, vulnerable, and exhausted by work, but we had no influence.

Without sufficient resources, social welfare provided just enough sustenance while holding these families hostage in the "system." Yet it is the lack of affordable housing and the slashing of housing entitlements in the United States that has caused homelessness, frequently resulting in the "shunning" of poor single mothers and their children, and isolating them from parish life. It is important to name poverty and homelessness as the "structural sin"—the root cause of such abandonment and misery.

In a survey I conducted for my doctoral research, I learned what homeless mothers had to say about their day-to-day lives:[1]

Agnes (explaining her decision to enroll for a nursing course rather than spending a full year at home as she is entitled to do after the birth of her baby): I don't quit.…I have two children who need me. I want to go back to school and become a Licensed Practical Nurse (LPN). I can stay home until the baby is a year old, but I'll do this when the baby is three months old. I don't want to wait.

Crystal: I thank God for my child.…All the stuff I've been through…I get to see my child after coming home from school. My child smiles and makes me happy. My child will give me a kiss on the cheek and say, "Mommy, I fixed your heart." My goal now is to get permanent housing and a job as a home health aide. I enjoy my job and I don't like not working.

Michele (despite years of reported abuse): I hope to return to work. I'm a hard worker.…I was diagnosed with MS and I had a hard time being on my feet at my last job.…I feel good about my life.

Queen: My baby is my life. People have always shut me down when I wanted to talk about my own mother and tell people that I loved her. I love my mother unconditionally; regardless of how many kids she had, regardless of what the Bible says. She always did what was best for us, not herself. She never exposed us to any drug activity or

outside life. She never took drugs in our presence.
I always understood that my mother had a sickness; it was the drugs.

Aida Hurtado suggests that women of color "develop
informal political skills" in their struggles in day-to-day life
and are "more like urban guerrillas trained through everyday battle with the state apparatus."[2] One example of this
that I shared with my master's-level social work students is
that I seldom paid my December mortgage bill. It provided
funds for a happy Christmas. I made it up over the next two
months. What business does not function in that way?

Summarizing these different tactics of resistance from
my doctoral thesis, I wrote in a journal article,

> Women surrendered children to family members,
> fought back when accused of child neglect, refused
> to adhere to shelter policy forbidding them to work,
> attempted to find local jobs—even off the books—
> rode bikes and paid exorbitant fees to private taxi
> companies to get to their jobs. Some women felt that
> shelters offered them safety, others left in response
> to shelter policies or workers that attempted to
> regulate their desire to work....The women also
> pushed back against these regulatory practices and
> those who enforced them and over-extended their
> authority. Their stories reveal how "social locations
> are fundamentally structured by power relations"
> which are often not responsive to their needs.[3]

As Pope Francis observes,

> As long as the problems of the poor are not radi-
> cally resolved...by attacking the structural causes

of inequality, no solution will be found for the world's problems or, for that matter, to any problems. Inequality is the root of social ills....Doubly poor are those women who endure situations of exclusion, mistreatment, and violence, since they are frequently less able to defend their rights. Even so, we constantly witness among them impressive examples of daily heroism in defending and protecting their vulnerable families. (*EG* 202, 212)

Pope Francis reminds us that religion is about relationships, not proselytizing or giving goods and services from a distance. Our lives are meant to be shared. He calls for loving outreaches in parishes, so that they become places for building friendship and sharing across lines of gender, class, and race.

Notes

1. See Thérèse Craine Bertsch, "The Standpoint of Homeless Single Mothers on Recurrent Episodes of Homelessness" (DSW diss., Adelphi University, New York, 2012). Available from ProQuest Dissertation and Theses database (UMI No. 3536603).

2. Cited in Chela Sandoval, "U.S. Third World Feminism: The Theory and Method of Differential Oppositional Consciousness," in *The Feminist Standpoint Theory Reader: Intellectual & Political Controversies*, ed. Sandra Harding (New York: Routledge, 2004), 195–209, at 203.

3. Thérèse Craine Bertsch, "Crafting My Own Story: Homeless Mothers' Standpoints Using Thematic Narrative Analyses," *European Scientific Journal* 2, no. 20, special ed. (September 2014): 60–74, at 69, retrieved from http://eujournal.org/index.php/esj/article/view/4131/3967, quoting Nancy Hartsock, "Comment on Hekman's 'Truth and Method: Feminist Standpoint Theory Revisited': Truth or Justice?" in *The Feminist Standpoint Theory Reader*, 243–46, at 243.

A Matter of Conscience

My Encounter with Abortion

Alison Concannon Kennedy

I had an abortion. I was told this by the nurse who admitted me into the local hospital's antenatal care clinic during my third pregnancy.

"One live birth and one abortion," she said, looking to me for confirmation.

"No!" I reacted, "I've only had one baby—the other was ectopic."

"That's what I said," she replied. "One live birth and one abortion."

I had never before thought of my ectopic pregnancy as an abortion. When I queried the term used by the nurse, she explained that its removal was a termination of the pregnancy, an abortion. "Miscarriage is a spontaneous rejection of the embryo," she added, "termination a surgical intervention to remove the fetus."[1] I was shocked and an overwhelming sense of guilt came over me.

My third pregnancy was a surprise. I had been scheduled to be admitted into hospital for removal of the troublesome adhesions left over from the ectopic pregnancy—and I was shocked to discover through the routine pre-op pregnancy test that I was pregnant! The doctor had reassured me that the pregnancy should progress without any unforeseen problems, although I might be a little uncomfortable as growth of the baby would inevitably separate the adhesions. (To clarify, an adhesion is a form of scarring tissue in the internal lining of the abdominal cavity and pelvis resulting from inflammation, sometimes connecting organs together. The inflammation may be due to blood, infection, or surgical intervention such as an ectopic removal. It sounds painful and, yes, my adhesions were causing me considerable pain, hence the need for the operation.)

Instead of the removal of the adhesions, however, I found I was now facing pregnancy, and although I was excited at the prospect of another child, the nurse's seemingly innocent accusatory definition caused my thoughts to turn to the unfortunate baby that had embedded itself in my fallopian tube, a child I'd never had an opportunity to know or properly grieve for.

I wondered where that baby's body was; how was it disposed of? Where do aborted fetuses go—surgical waste, incinerator? Then, another thought: what happens to the embryo when a woman miscarries in the first trimester (three months from conception), long before she has confirmation of pregnancy? (In those days we did not have today's reliable do-it-yourself methods of testing. We had to wait for two missed periods before seeking medical advice.) Could miscarried babies end up in the toilet? Miscarriage or termination: what dignity in death for these little attempts at life?

I continued to ponder: What was life? When does life begin? Whom does life belong to? I had always trustingly supported pro-life issues, signed petitions, attended talks. But I had always been disturbed by how some organizations used graphic bloody images to promote their cause.

As that nurse was speaking to me, I thought back to a leaflet I'd picked up at church some months after my ectopic pregnancy, picturing a so-called aborted fetus. I had gone home from church and cried. Had something I'd created ended up looking like this? I decided I would no longer support any organization that used the image of a dead baby's body alongside their pro-life message, no matter how just they believed their cause to be. It was totally insensitive to the women who had lost their babies through miscarriage and, like me, ectopic pregnancy, even, in my view, unfair to those repentant women who had willingly terminated their pregnancy. There were, after all, other "living" pro-life pictures and films that were becoming available, making a far more convincing witness to the wonder of a growing child in the womb—which also made me cry, although this time at the precious beauty and wonder of creation.

The conversation with that nurse at the antenatal clinic irreversibly changed my outlook on pro-life issues. What she told me made me aware that, irrespective of my Church's teaching, I had seemingly made a choice, the choice to end the life of the child that had ruptured through my fallopian tube in its desperate bid for life. Yes, my baby could not have survived and I would have inevitably died, but that nurse's clinical assessment was the sudden realization for me that I had signed the document giving permission for a surgical intervention. I had agreed to an abortion. I was guilty.

It has taken years to come to terms with the grief associated with the loss of a baby, and always in the overwhelming shadow of guilt that I had possibly chosen the time for my baby to die. But that guilt also nurtured an empathy with all those women who, for whatever reason, have made a choice to end their pregnancy. The issue is not black and white, as some activists would have us believe.

At the time of my ectopic, I was naïve. Although I had asked my doctor whether I could be pregnant, I believed him when he dismissed my recurring symptoms (pain and spasmodic bleeding), attributing them first to an infection and later, after three unsuccessful courses of antibiotics, to neurosis. When I finally collapsed and was rushed to the hospital for the emergency operation, I was at least fourteen weeks pregnant—and I actually believed that the baby in my tube could be moved into the womb! I was at the time slightly delirious and, as I said, medically naïve and trusting.

Could scientific inventions, such as artificial wombs, mean that life-endangered women would in future be able to transfer the nurturing of their baby to a clinical host? In Tokyo, researchers have developed a technique called EUFI—extrauterine fetal incubation. What opportunities for preserving fetal life would such a development mean? What impact could this potential life-saving host have on fetal viability, on the legal gestation limit for abortions? Could life then become viable from the embryonic stage through to birth? Would EUFI be a suitable host for the continued gestation of a removed ectopic pregnancy? I can wonder and I can speculate. Yet, with so many possibilities, I know I am not suitably qualified to judge the ethics of such developments.

What I do know is that there will be many willing to make judgements—those persons who, unlike me, can detach themselves empathetically from the impossible choices some women, along with medics, have to face. I also recognize that we cannot by rule of law remove the choices that conscience needs to develop. The experience of choice nurtures morality, freedom of choice being the gift of our loving Creator. I do know that I shall always want to speak about the sanctity of life and that is my dilemma with the approach of some pro-life organizations—"speak" or "protect"? Speaking offers wisdom from experience, whereas protection can be an authoritarian abdication of responsibility, susceptible to vigilantes who have little or no personal experience other than a conviction that they need to defend the unborn whatever the cost.

What of the miscarried or aborted child? If I am to believe what my faith professes, then those children go straight to God. It is the one truth I believe can give comfort to all who feel responsible for a human life unlived. We shall one day meet those children, uncorrupted by our worldly failings, and say we are sorry that they did not have the opportunity to experience the fullness of life on their journey to eternity. In that understanding I have found peace. It is a peace I wish for all those who have to make that difficult choice, and I know that I cannot and would not want to judge their decision. I am not saying that we do not speak for the sanctity of life, but I do question the methods that are used by some in that mission.

Notes

1. What that nurse told me was technically misleading. Many years later, I obtained the following clarification: "*Any fetal loss before viability (the point at which a baby can survive outside the uterus) is technically an abortion, although legal definitions of the word* abortion *vary by jurisdiction. An induced abortion can be surgical or medical and both of these are what people colloquially mean by the word* abortion *or* pregnancy termination. *A spontaneous abortion is also called a miscarriage. Ectopic pregnancies are a variant of a spontaneous abortion as they cannot go to viability and will often miscarry into the abdominal cavity and may cause maternal death or injury. Pregnancies that will inevitably be lost before viability (due to heavy bleeding or progressive contractions, for example) are called inevitable abortions, so in a sense an ectopic pregnancy is an inevitable abortion (or colloquially, an inevitable miscarriage). A miscarriage that leaves some tissue behind is called an incomplete abortion. A pregnancy that has died before viability, but has not yet miscarried and whose mother has no symptoms, is called a missed*

abortion. Termination is used to describe the purposeful ending of a pregnancy before viability and would not be a term used to describe the removal of an ectopic pregnancy." (Martin Walker, MD, FACOG, [BM, BS, DM, FRCOG], Medical Director, Eastside Maternal Fetal Medicine, Seattle, WA, USA)

"The Writings of Querulous Women"

Dr. Anne Bieżanek's Catholic Birth Control Clinic[1]

Alana Harris

On November 29, 1963, the British tabloid newspaper *The Daily Mail* carried a headline: "Church Defied. RC Woman Doctor Sets Up Family Planning Clinic."[2] The article continued:

> Tall, auburn-haired, and the mother of seven young children, the 36-year-old doctor said: "I am taking a stand on something we Catholics cannot side-step any longer."[3]

Dr. Anne Bieżanek's decision to open one of the first *Catholic* birth control clinics in the world in the front room of her home surgery in Wallasey, Merseyside, would continue to be headline news in the UK and in the United States for the next twelve months.

The bare facts of Bieżanek's life—although completely unknown today—were daily fare for a 1960s newspaper-reading and television-viewing public. She was raised in a Quaker/Anglican household and educated at the progressive

Dartington Hall School (and then Dollar Academy when her family moved to Scotland). She completed a medical degree at the University of Aberdeen and began medical practice in psychiatry in 1951, marrying early to Polish émigré Jan Bieżanek. Most explanations of her public activities in the early 1960s, however, dwelt on the string of ten pregnancies and seven children in thirteen years that led her to question the Catholic Church's reproductive teaching.

Bieżanek's idiosyncratic renegotiation of spiritual and sexual politics was groundbreaking in articulating a "modern" Catholic approach to love and sex and in anticipating the cacophony of such voices elicited by Pope Paul VI's 1968 encyclical, *Humanae Vitae*.[4] Alongside the pioneering initiative of her birth control clinic, which she deemed a "Christian aid programme,"[5] Bieżanek published a justification of her actions and their implications in *All Things New: The Declaration of Faith*. This is a revealing spiritual autobiography and psychological portrait of its author. The opening chapter narrates the fervor and emotional intensity of her conversion to Catholicism, her naïve, romanticized attraction to war-torn Poland (and by extension to its national faith and refugees), and the desire to commit unequivocally and zealously to her new faith. Only against this backdrop is it possible to understand fully the agonized wrestling with conscience and Church teaching that underpinned her decision to take the pill on prescription in 1962 and then open a clinic for Catholic wives the following year. The book is also remarkable in its fearless and, at that time, profoundly countercultural discussion of mental illness—encompassing Dr. Bieżanek's work in psychiatric institutions throughout England in the 1950s and her encounter with patients tortured by religious "scruples,"[6] through to her own confession of her breakdown and self-committal to an Edinburgh mental hospital when she was pregnant with her sixth child.[7]

The second half of the book is a spiritual treatise that undertakes a scholarly but accessible reconceptualization of Catholic teachings on birth control through the lens of the Bible, the writings of St. John of the Cross, and popular Mariology. The framework that sustained Dr. Bieżanek's wholesale critique of traditional natural law ethics and its restatements (such as Pope Pius XI's 1930 encyclical *Casti Connubii*) was her appeal to a very "high" Mariology. She urged Catholics to recognize the fragmentation of Christian truth at the Reformation and to embrace their safekeeping of a unique part of revelation history that "is giving to the woman, the mother of Christ, a status in the scheme of salvation equal to that of her son."[8] As she asserted,

> Christ's work of redemption cannot be separated from the work of His mother, who under the providence of God literally made Christ's advent possible, and translated it from a prophecy to a reality, by her willingness to fulfil the destiny that had been laid upon her.[9]

Meshing popular Mariology to modern technology, she claimed,

> The advent of oral contraception appears to me to be an event of as great a significance for mankind as was the expulsion from the Garden of Eden.... The contraceptive pill has come to woman, as a heavenly reprieve from that primordial doom. It is my contention that this must be willed by God, and I say that the appearance of these drugs can be taken as a sign of God's final pardon...[a] reprieve for the daughters of Eve...won for them by "the Second Eve."[10]

In the English Catholic Church of the early 1960s, Bieżanek's transgressive writings and provocative actions made her notorious, and clerical commentators disparaged or hailed the force of her intervention within increasingly controversial debates about birth control and the "primary ends" of marriage. Prompted to write to the Bishop of Shrewsbury by her public actions and the publication of *All Things New*, Father Joseph Howe of St. Ann's Cheadle (a town in the northwest of England) attributed the catastrophic degeneration of moral standards to such public commentary, which he castigated as the writings of "querulous women [which] offend against taste."[11] Father Alban Byron, SJ, writing in the Catholic Missionary Society's journal, *Catholic Gazette*, violently disagreed with almost all of Bieżanek's contentions but acknowledged that *All Things New* "is the most extraordinary marriage book I have ever read."[12] Much more positively, Canon Harold Drinkwater, a respected catechist and popular author in his own right, praised the book for "eschewing all those tactful euphemisms and soft-pedaling, those delicate nuances and innuendos, those discreet circumlocutions, which so often oil the chariot wheels of truth and which those of us who write under constant censorship get so good at."[13]

Writing a few months later in *Search*, he went further in claiming,

> Let nobody imagine for a moment that the author is some kind of nagging eccentric or notoriety-seeker....Here is a book in the same category as Newman's *Apologia*...an *agonia*, on the mind of the Church of today, as it re-enacted itself in one lonely human soul.[14]

When we reconstruct the chronology of events from a voluminous correspondence, the difficulties for all parties seem to have arisen in early 1962, when Bieżanek confided her extreme difficulties to her assistant parish priest, Father Gaskell, in negotiating her husband's insistent and some- times violent demands for unfettered sexual intimacy.[15] Fearful of yet another pregnancy, but equally afraid of the intense disruption to marital stability caused by sexual absti- nence, she asked for an alternative line of conduct. Father Gaskell is reported, in *All Things New*, to have refused to help Bieżanek separate from her husband and, moreover, to have advised that in taking the contraceptive pill she would be refused confession and communion.[16] Distressed by this impasse, his response to her question "What then am I to do?" was "I do not know."[17]

In the months following May 1962, when Dr. Bieżanek had started practicing contraception, she reportedly refrained from receiving Holy Communion when attend- ing Mass each week at her parish church, St. Alban's. She resumed receiving communion in December that year (galva- nized by her daughter's First Communion), but a crisis arose with the announcement of a parochial visit by the Bishop of Shrewsbury, Bishop Eric Graser, in February 1963. Bieżanek told the priest in charge of her parish, Canon George Hig- gins, that she intended to request a meeting with the bishop, which prompted him to write a letter warning the bishop to "be very wary in whatever you decide to do," and adding, "None of us here want to have anything to do with her."[18]

On February 13, 1963, Bieżanek wrote the first letter in an extensive correspondence with Bishop Glaser that lasted over three years. The letter opened in the formulaic terms usually found within the confessional:

> In the last 12 months I have run into difficulties
> in my married life that have compelled me to take
> extraordinary steps. Steps at variance with my

conscience and the teaching of the church. My reason for acting thus has been the protection of my own health and sanity and thereby the protection of the life of the family.[19]

Bishop Graser proceeded to have a meeting with Dr. Bieżanek during the course of his February parochial visitation, but rather than containing the situation, their conversation seems to have hardened the lines of opposition. Writing shortly thereafter on February 25, 1963, Dr. Bieżanek thanked the bishop for his time, courtesy, and patience, but she continued,

> I do not accept your self-appointed right to act as judge, jury and executioner in this matter, a matter that involves not only the stability of my home but the destiny of my immortal soul and those whom providence has appointed me to influence.[20]

This correspondence provides insight into the shifting and less hierarchical relationship evolving between priest and people in the lead-up to the Second Vatican Council. Despite the anger and self-confident defiance of this letter, a regular—almost weekly—and intimate, indeed familiar correspondence continued between the two. Within this remarkable exchange of letters we see the opposing struggles of two "devout" Catholics attempting to negotiate diametrically contrasting positions within the landscape of increasingly unstable Church teachings.

The correspondence that bishop and laywoman exchanged through the spring of 1963 mostly consisted of Dr Bieżanek updating "dear Eric" on her Family Planning Training in Birkenhead and describing the Catholic women who came to her for help in fitting diaphragms without their husband's knowledge. In a letter written in July, Dr. Bieżanek concluded with "a declaration of war":

> I intend to run, from this house, a private clinic for the purpose of helping Catholics overcome their matrimonial problems. I do this on my own authority and stand between them and anything the clergy choose to say to them on the subject....I am not one little bit afraid of you or the machinery behind you. You will, all of you, break your teeth on me....[21]

The opening of her clinic two months later in September, dedicated to Spanish mystic and healer St. Martin de Porres, and her reception of a stream of Catholic clients in the early months were not seen as an "act of war." It was, rather, the report in November's *Daily Mail* with which this article opened and a short interview on Granada TV's *Scene at 6.30* that prompted Canon Higgins publicly to refuse her communion on December 1, 1963. In the weeks following, other parish priests similarly passed her over at the altar, with the *Daily Mail* reporting, "Crowds gathered around her when she left at the end of the service," mostly to offer "support" and "encouragement."[22]

These events were the breaking point for her husband, Jan. In *All Things New*, she described his contentment with her contraceptive arrangements until "the public rebuff," which he felt as a form of corporate shaming, branding her as a heretic, whore, and sinner.[23] For Jan, as for Canon Higgins, it was the publicity—the airing in public of things that were "secret and sacred"—that elicited acts of outrage and vengeance. What followed was a very public dissection, an almost "kitchen-sink drama," of their marital difficulties. The *Daily Mail* reported in January 1964 that "Husband Drops

Ultimatum on Clinic,"[24] only to be followed in May by "My Marriage Had Broken Up, says Birth Control Doctor."[25]

Bieżanek's last public and highly audacious gesture of defiance came on May 31, 1964, when, having written to the Archbishop of Westminster, Archbishop (later Cardinal) Heenan, to announce her intention to "resolve the issue" through an ethical adjudication at the communion rails, she travelled to Westminster Cathedral to attend Mass and receive holy communion. She was flanked by hordes of reporters, in what the *New York Times* described as "the most publicized and photographed mortal sin ever committed."[26]

Recalling these events herself from the distance of a lifetime, Dr. Bieżanek felt shocked at her own audacity and summarized her early interventions in the birth control debate as the equivalent of the "little boy who'd shouted 'the emperor has no clothes on,' you know, that's really what happened."[27] Dr. Bieżanek's refrain would be taken up in earnest, and monumentally amplified, four years later when many laymen and women, alongside some clergy, petitioned Rome and commandeered the media to voice their own disillusionment with the disjuncture between dogmatic teaching and ordinary, married practice. While her own *cause célèbre* was, as she admitted, a "nine day wonder,"[28] these confrontations in the press and the politicization of the sacraments anticipated further confrontations in churches across the country, wranglings in the confessional, and a deluge of angry correspondence in letters' pages following the leaked Majority Report and Paul VI's encyclical.

When I interviewed Anne Bieżanek in her home in Wallasey, just a month before her death on November 30, 2010, she opened our conversation with a startling reference to Charles de Gaulle. In response to my asking about her conversion to Catholicism in her late teens and the way she "crossed swords" (as she put it) with the English Catholic hierarchy, she responded,

> I read something that was written about General de Gaulle—[that] he had a precocious sense of destiny. I said, "Oh yeah, that's me, I have a precocious sense of destiny." And, I sort of bored ahead, I was going to, I [don't] know, I was going to be canonized or bust. Really serious stuff.[29]

Notes

1. This is an abbreviated version of Alana Harris, "'The Writings of Querulous Women': Contraception, Conscience and Clerical Authority in 1960s Britain," first published in *British Catholic History* 32, no. 4 (2015): 1–30. Editors' Note: We have made every effort to obtain permission from the publisher to use this quotation, but at the time of publication, we are still awaiting a response.

2. *Daily Mail*, November 29, 1963, 7.

3. *Daily Mail*, November 29, 1963, 7.

4. For a survey of these reactions across Europe (including a detailed study of Britain), see Alana Harris, ed., *The Schism of '68: Catholics, Contraception and* Humanae Vitae *in Europe, 1945–1975* (Basingstoke: Palgrave Macmillan, 2018).

5. Anne Bieżanek, *All Things New: The Declaration of Faith* (London: Pan Books, 1964), 59.

6. Bieżanek, *All Things New*, 35.

7. Bieżanek, *All Things New*, 15, 40–41.

8. Bieżanek, *All Things New*, 143.

9. Bieżanek, *All Things New*, 143.

10. Bieżanek, *All Things New*, 145–46.

11. Bieżanek, *All Things New*, 145–46.

12. Alban Byron, "A Sad Story: Dr. Biezanek's Fight against the Church," *Catholic Gazette* 56, no. 1 (1965): 8–9.

13. F. H. Drinkwater, "The Problem of Contraception," *Clergy Review*, February 1965, 166–68 at 167.

14. F.H.D., "Book of the Month," *Search: Michael de la Bedoyere's Independent Christian Newsletter* 3, no. 9 (January 1965): 346–48 at 348.

15. Letter from Anne Bieżanek to Bishop Eric Graser, February 13, 1963.

16. Bieżanek, *All Things New*, 51.

17. Bieżanek, *All Things New*, 51.

18. Higgins to Graser, February 13, 1963.

19. Bieżanek to Graser, February 13, 1963.

20. Bieżanek to Graser, February 25, 1963.

21. Bieżanek to Graser, February 25, 1963, 2–3.

22. "Communion Ban on Birth Control Doctor," *Daily Mail*, January 13, 1964, 3.

23. Bieżanek, *All Things New*, 61–62.

24. "Husband Drops Ultimatum on Clinic," *Daily Mail*, January 23, 1964, 9. See also "Marriage Shock for Birth Control Doctor," *Daily Mail*, January 21, 1964, 9; "Future of Dr. Anne," *Daily Mail*, January 22, 1964, 3.

25. "RC Birth Control Dr. Says: My Marriage is Broken," *Daily Mail*, April 24, 1964, 1.

26. "Briton Who Heads Birth Control Clinic Defies Ban on Rites," *The New York Times*, June 1, 1964, 31.

27. Interview, 3.

28. Interview, 13.

29. Author, Interview with Dr. Anne Bieżanek, October 29, 2010.

Adults for the Faith

Priesthood, Femininity, and the Maternal Church

Cristina Lledo Gomez

Take and eat, take and eat. This is my body given up for you.

Take and drink, take and drink. This is my blood given up for you.

This is the refrain from Michael Joncas's (b. 1951) and James Quinn, SJ's (b.1919), beautiful hymn *Take and Eat*, written in 1989 to a melody by Joncas. The song was sung during communion at my parish Mass recently, as people took up the invitation to take and eat of the Body of Christ and to take and drink of his Blood.

This refrain makes me reflect on being a mother, particularly on the act of birthing: how much the body suffers and how much blood is shed to give life to another. No wonder that the symbol of birth is widely used to represent creation, re-creation, and transformation, including in our own scriptures (see 1 Thess 5:2–3; Rom 8:20–22; John 16:21–22; 1 Pet 1:3; Gal 4:19).

The excruciating pain of birth is followed by the elation of holding one's child in one's arms. Mothering is an experience of this constant marriage of pain and elation. For some women, the pain of childbirth is nothing compared to the sleepless nights and chaotic days of early parenting. It is not surprising that many mothers experience postnatal depression, especially when they are single parents or are isolated from family.[1]

As a mother leaves behind the physical demands of early childhood, she finds herself negotiating the sometimes even more demanding emotional needs of her growing children. Whereas early mothering involves providing a safe environment for exploration, discovery, and growth, in later years the task is to expand the boundaries of that domestic "womb" until the child no longer needs it and can create his or her own boundaries. Containers, boundaries, a "womb," are important because boundless freedom can become imprisoning when chaos reigns.

At the same time, boundaries and structures must allow room for growth in spirit, mind, and body. For example, when buying a child's shoes, one leaves a bit of space for the feet to grow; when teaching, one provides the basics but also sprinkles in a few innovative ideas to stretch the mind, and the good storyteller will provide comfort and familiarity to an audience but also end with a challenge or invitation to spiritual growth.

These maternal experiences and perspectives mean that I have real difficulties when I read accounts of the motherhood of the Church by some of the most respected twentieth-century theologians and priests. For example, Henri de Lubac emphasizes that the type of motherhood he is speaking of with regard to the Church is the opposite of human mothering. He writes,

Whereas in the physical order, the child leaves the womb of his mother, and withdrawing from her, becomes increasingly independent of her protective guardianship as he grows, becomes stronger and advances in years, the Church brings us forth to the new life she bears by receiving us into her womb, and the more our divine education progresses, the more we become intimately bound to her.[2]

Whether from a psychoanalytic perspective or from the perspective of organizational behavioral theory, this is a disturbing analogy. From a psychoanalytic perspective, it suggests somebody whose psychosexual development has halted at a point at which his sense of the feminine is projected onto a mother figure—in this case, the Church. A developed psychosexual self is able to integrate the feminine principle, the anima, with the masculine principle, the animus. However, the failure to achieve such integration can lead to the mother or mother figure becoming his muse, one to whom he wishes to be bonded forever—to reenter her womb and remain there. This diminishes the capacity to form meaningful relationships beyond the muse. For example, a man who chooses the celibate life might project the feminine principle onto the mother and, by extension, onto all other women.

This desire to unite with the feminine principle can conflict with a man's vow of celibacy, if it leads him to seek emotional or sexual bonding with a woman. Seeing all women as mothers enables him to relate to them in a nonsexual way, but this inability to integrate with his own femininity may result in limited contact with females or worse perhaps, relationships with females that unconsciously reject, ignore, or even denigrate them—unless they are viewed as sexually safe mothers.

American psychologist Kaaren Jacobson uses Jungian analysis and Freudian constructs in her research on men and organizational behavior.[3] Her research highlights the need for organizations to promote the following: (1) healthy human development; (2) the feeling function; (3) participatory forms of organization and decision-making; and (4) consciousness of collectivism, within the organization, in order for it to succeed in its aims or mission.[4] In *Organization and the Mother Archetype*, Jacobson used a form of archetypal Jungian analysis on men who identified with their organization as a child to a mother. She found that their identities were tied to the "mother" organization and that they manifested characteristics such as self-emasculation, obsessive security concerns, rule-conforming behavior, and an unwillingness to take risks or to assume responsibility for one's actions.[5] She argues, "Ultimately, these men lose their capacity for independent moral action [and] are unable to develop genuine feeling relationships either inside or outside the organization."[6]

In organizational behavioral language, this is described as "group-think." At its extreme, a person identifies with the group to such an extent that he or she loses his or her individual moral capacity and instead takes on the group's articulated values and ideas.

In *Remaining a Catholic after the Murphy Report*, Kevin Egan argues that "group-think" is one of the major factors that enabled well-meaning and intelligent people to allow sexual abuse to thrive in institutions.[7] To move forward from the aftermath of the sexual abuse scandal, Egan argues that there must be (1) accountability by bishops, (2) identity for priests, and (3) adult faith for laity.[8]

With regard to accountability by bishops, Egan says they must relate to the pope, the college of bishops, and the laity as adult to adult rather than as parent to child in relation to the laity, or child to parent in relation to the pope. Organizational behavior theory indicates that the parent-child relationship leads to "clericalism" in churches,[9] and this is the autocratic model that Pope Francis wishes to dismantle. The very practice of calling priests "Father" reinforces the parent-child relationship, and yet this practice was not present in the early Church. It had later monastic origins and only became universal in the English-speaking world through the Irish Catholic influence in the nineteenth century. It has never been used in Latin.

For priests, finding an identity beyond the mother Church is key if they wish to avoid being part of a "groupthink"—to such an extent that their own moral consciences are silenced. When priests overidentify with the Church, there is the danger of protecting the institution and its leaders above all else, rather than discerning and acting responsibly in each situation or context.

Finally, if adults are formed for adult faith and adult relationships, equipped with tools to engage with one another as well as with Church teaching and practice, there is the possibility of a different future. This future entails working toward transparency, accountability, healthy relationships, and boundaries. These are the signs of an adult Church, and they are the practices called for by many church members seeking renewal.

Jacobson observes that ironically, a "positive movement toward the feminine requires separation from the mother archetype."[10] That is, by finding one's identity beyond one's mother, the mother Church, or the image of woman as essentially a mother, the male comes to see women in a positive light. In conjunction, he comes to accept the feminine principle within himself and is able to integrate it with the male principle. The result of this is an integrated human being who can engage in healthy relationships with all sexes and who has the ability to exercise his individual moral conscience. On the other hand, she writes that "identification with the mother promotes ineffectiveness in the organization's pursuit of its mission."[11] Clinging to the mother archetype is detrimental not only to the individual and the community but to the very mission of spreading the good news of God's reign—as has been demonstrated in our recent scandalous history.

This is the work of "mothering" in and for our churches: to call people to adult faith, adult responsibility, and adult interaction. The work of Jacobson, Egan, Ruddy, and commissions investigating institutional sexual abuse can cast light on the inability of some of our Church's leaders to engage with women and affirm women's roles in the Church. Their studies help us to recognize ways in which both clergy and laity reinforce clericalism and unhealthy relationships and cultures within the Church. Finally, their work challenges us to eschew the inward-looking, security-concerned, infantile Church that Pope Francis continues to criticize, when he writes,

> I prefer a Church which is bruised, hurting and dirty because it has been out on the streets, rather than a Church which is unhealthy from being confined and from clinging to its own security....More than by fear of going astray, my hope is that we will be moved by the fear of remaining shut up within structures which give us a false sense of security, within rules which make us harsh judges, within habits which make us feel safe, while at our door people are starving and Jesus does not tire of saying to us: "Give them something to eat" (Mk 6:37). (*EG* 49)

Pope Francis calls the whole Church to evangelize by going out of itself, in joy, rather than like "someone who has just come back from a funeral!" In a weekly audience, he said,

> All who are baptized, men and women, together we are the church. So often in our lives we do not bear witness of the motherhood of the Church. So often we are cowards! Let us then entrust ourselves to Mary, that She…may teach us to have the same maternal spirit toward our brothers and sisters, with the sincere capacity to welcome, to forgive, to give strength, and to instill trust and hope.[12]

As we seek to be Christ for others, to become his body and blood, we need to ask what it means to die to the old self, the old way of being Church, and rise to new life, a new way of being Church as mature individuals in community with one another for the Church and the world.

Notes

1. See "Postnatal Depression," in *Beyond Blue*, accessed October 21, 2017, https://www.beyondblue.org.au/the-facts/post natal-depression.

2. Henri de Lubac, *The Motherhood of the Church: Followed by Particular Churches in the Universal Church and an Interview Conducted by Gwendoline Jarczyk* (San Francisco: Ignatius Press, 1982), 69. See also Hugo Rahner, *Our Lady and the Church* (Bethesda: Zacchaeus Press, 1961); Robert C. Koerpel, "The Form and Drama of the Church: Hans Urs Von Balthasar on Mary, Peter, and the Eucharist," *Logos: A Journal of Catholic Thought and Culture* 2, no. 1 (2008): 70–99; and Pope Benedict XVI, Hans Urs von Balthasar, and Adrian Walker, *Mary: The Church at the Source* (San Francisco: Ignatius Press, 2005).

3. Cf. Kaaren Hedblom Jacobson, "Organization and the Mother Archetype: A Jungian Analysis of Adult Development and Self-Identity within the Organization," *Administration and Society* 25, no. 1 (May 1993): 60–84.

4. Jacobson, "Organization and the Mother Archetype," 78–81.

5. Jacobson, "Organization and the Mother Archetype," 61–62.

6. Jacobson, "Organization and the Mother Archetype," 62.

7. Kevin Egan, *Remaining a Catholic after the Murphy Report* (Blackrock, Co. Dublin: Columba Press, 2011).

8. Egan, *Remaining a Catholic after the Murphy Report*, 109.

9. See Robert P. Vecchio, Greg Hearn, and Greg Southey, "Types of Organisational Culture," in *Organisational Behaviour*, 2nd ed. (Sydney: Harcourt Brace, 1996), 692–93. See also Christopher Ruddy, "The American Church's Sexual Abuse Crisis," *America* 186, no. 19 (2002), 7–11.

10. Jacobson, "Organization and the Mother Archetype," 62.

11. Jacobson, "Organization and the Mother Archetype," 62.

12. Pope Francis, General Weekly Audience, St. Peter's Square, Wednesday, September 3, 2014.

PART FOUR

THEOLOGICAL AND PASTORAL VOCATIONS

"Mary treasured all these words and pondered them in her heart."

(Luke 2:19)

"There were also women looking on from a distance; among them were Mary Magdalene, and Mary the mother of James the younger and of Joses, and Salome. These used to follow him and provided for him when he was in Galilee; and there were many other women who had come up with him to Jerusalem."

(Mark 15:40–41)

Vocation

An Ongoing Journey

Jeannine M. Pitas

I still remember the day when Father Rob, one of the priests at Infant of Prague Parish in Buffalo, New York, came to talk to my third grade class. We were preparing for our first communion by memorizing prayers and participating in various discussions with our teachers. Sitting quietly in my starched white shirt and plaid jumper, I watched Father Rob write a word on the board: *vocation*.

"There are three vocations," he informed us, "marriage, single life, and religious life." He then went on to explain the features of these three paths and informed us that one day, we would each need to choose one of them.

Hearing this as an eight-year-old, I instantly felt confused. How could there only be three vocations? Most adults I knew were married, but their lives were not at all the same. They worked in different areas and spent their free time in different ways. The unmarried adults I knew also seemed quite different from one another. Indeed, something seemed wrong with this simple triptych of vocations. Did all of the options need to be mutually exclusive? I found myself wishing there could be a way to be married and a religious sister at the same time. Also, what about the work I'd be doing?

At age eight, I wanted to be a singer and an actor and an elementary school teacher; later, I added psychologist, scientist, and writer to this list. Why did I have to choose just one straight path through life?

Later, as an adult, I would realize that while I only get one path, it is not a straight one. Meanwhile, the simple triptych of possible vocations that I learned about as an eight-year-old does not square with the reality of most people's experience. I know a single mother who became a nun. A few years ago, I met a Roman Catholic woman priest who was excommunicated from the Church for following what she believed to be her true vocation, and I also met the priest who was defrocked for supporting her movement. I know a sixty-year-old single woman who had hoped to marry but was not offered that chance, and who has since focused almost entirely on two things: her daily work as a teacher and catechist and her task of caring for her elderly father. I know many married people, young and old, who have gone through a divorce and then sought love again. Very few people walk a straight path.

I always feel more secure when I can plan for the future. The profession I have entered, university teaching, is something I first considered as a college student, inspired by my own professors, and then prepared for over the long course of a PhD in comparative literature at the University of Toronto. While seeking to enter this profession, I was also trying to prepare myself for what I hoped would become a lifelong marriage to my college sweetheart, whom I had met at age twenty and corresponded with for six years before he moved to Toronto to be with me.

Much to my initial sorrow, however, God had a different plan for me. Amazingly, graduate school and the subsequent job search worked out, but the relationship did not. In the autumn of 2015, I found myself moving to Dubuque, Iowa, beginning work as a professor, dealing with the reverse culture shock of living in my own country after ten years abroad, and living alone for the first time in my life. At thirty-two—the age that for so many others involves marriages, new babies, and mortgages—I was starting a new life as a single person.

This transition was not easy. As a first-year professor, I felt completely overwhelmed as I struggled to prepare all my literature and Spanish classes from scratch, grade papers on time, and keep up with the constant administrative minutiae demanding my attention. Two months into the school year, when my beloved told me that he could not envision a future with me, I found it hard just to make it through the day. Meanwhile, finding friends in my new community proved to be a challenge. So many other people in my age-group had their time filled with work and their children's activities, as well as the friends they already had. They did not need my company in the way that I needed theirs.

Eventually, this situation started to change. About eight months after moving to Dubuque, I was encouraged to visit Hope House, an urban Catholic Worker house of hospitality that provides a food pantry, regular community meals, and long-term shelter for about twelve people who need it. Although I had previously heard of the Catholic Worker Movement and found it intriguing, I did not begin volunteering there because I saw it as a vocation. Instead, I arrived at Hope House as many others do: out of a deep need to receive the corporal and spiritual works of mercy. Though I did not lack money, food, or physical shelter, I needed something just as crucial: companionship, spiritual guidance, community, and love.

From the first day I stepped into Hope House, the warm greetings I received let me know I belonged. Though I hesitate to call myself a Catholic Worker (the term I have been using thus far is "Catholic Worker groupie"), I feel so grateful to this community that has warmly accepted me as one of their own. Indeed, the experience of praying, laughing, and learning with these dedicated people has been a catalyst for transformation.

In 1817, the poet John Keats asserted that artists should strive to live and create their work in a spirit of "negative capability," which he defines as "being in uncertainties, mysteries, doubts, without any irritable striving after fact and reason." Applying this idea to vocation, it seems like a more realistic (if less desirable) approach to following God's call. Dorothy Day, cofounder of the Catholic Worker Movement, herself lived in this way, beginning her adult life as a bohemian writer, leaving a common-law marriage to become a single mother, and ultimately entering a kind of unvowed religious life in the Catholic Worker Movement. In a similar way, most of the people I have met in the Dubuque Catholic Worker community did not set out to become Catholic Workers. Instead, the movement found them. Meanwhile, when I look at my students, I see a similar ongoing process of discernment, particularly in those older ones who are returning to the classroom after years of work.

It is still hard to accept that my own vocation has not fit neatly into the scheme I was presented with as a child. I am not a religious sister, but through the Catholic Worker Movement, I have come to engage in similar activities to some of the women religious I know: regular prayer, direct charity, and advocacy for justice. I am not a parent, but I would argue that as a teacher, I am still actively engaged in the work of raising up the next generation. Over time, I have come to embrace the ambiguities, uncertainties, and occasional contradictions in my life, and this has helped me better to embrace the contradictions of others, to approach the people I encounter with curiosity rather than fear.

A few years ago, I had the privilege of walking the Camino de Santiago, an eight-hundred-kilometer medieval pilgrimage route through northern Spain. Some pilgrims stated that this journey is a metaphor for life. While I see the truth in that, I would argue that more often, our journey is not like the Camino. Instead, like those ancient Israelites who followed Moses through the wilderness for forty years, we humans traverse a wild landscape with unclear paths and no adequate map (and certainly no GPS). But as scary as this may seem, it is also a thrilling adventure. And, if we can remember occasionally to stop, take a deep breath, and take in our surroundings, we will be amazed by the beauty we encounter.

The First Ten Years

Becoming a Woman Theologian

Jessica Coblentz

I treasure those spring afternoons I spent lying in the grass of my parents' front yard. When the sun had finally broken through the stubborn clouds of the Seattle sky, I postponed my math homework to lounge with a book. I was a peculiar sixteen-year-old: I read St. Augustine, whose *Confessions* I had happened upon while browsing the local bookstore. I had thought I recognized the author, which in retrospect is quite unlikely. My inexplicable impression of familiarity was fortuitous, however, because I recognized myself in the story of the North African bishop as I began to read. The young man's singular drive toward a higher purpose—a Higher Being—captivated me. I shared his insatiable desire for something more in my life, and his testimony prompted me to wonder whether I, too, could make my life about God. I had no idea this would lead me into professional ministry and Catholic theology, but, like Augustine, it did. This is a glimpse of some defining scenes from the first ten years of this vocation.

※ • ※

I am twenty-four years old, and a middle-aged priest has been reassigned to the parish where I have worked as a part-time young adult minister for the past year. After pleasant small talk, we turn to how we might collaborate on this ministry in the year ahead. The kind man suggests how we might proceed as a team: "I'm happy to come in and give talks—you know, theology presentations—and you can cover the logistics. I'm not interested in event planning."

As I listen, I realize there is so much he does not see as I sit before him. Despite knowing my resumé, he does not see my full-time graduate studies at an Ivy League divinity school, where my theological studies are supported by the institution's most prestigious merit-based scholarship. He does not see my undergraduate degree—*summa cum laude* and Phi Beta Kappa—in religious studies from a reputable Catholic university, where I studied under some of the guild's leading Catholic theologians. He does not see my internship at the largest archdiocese in the country, where I advanced innovative formation programs for ministers serving young adults in parishes. I have a lot of theological education and specialized ministry experience, yet he sees a church party planner.

※ • ※

A few years later, I am invited to offer a workshop at a regional formation day for parish religious educators. I have graduated into a PhD program at one of the country's leading Catholic theology departments, and after a long week of coursework, I spend Saturday morning driving hours to the site of this formation day. I have made a crisp Power-Point presentation and printed handouts with up-to-date resources. All day, I offer enthusiastic and practical presentations to a room of professional and volunteer ministers.

The room clears at the end of my final workshop, and I go to pick up the stack of remaining handouts. Written in bold ink on the top sheet is an anonymous note addressed to me. I read it. Startled, I read it again—and again: "You are too attractive to be taken seriously. It's distracting. I appreciate your enthusiasm, though."

※ • ※

It is the third week of doctoral studies, and my longest day of class ends with an evening course on the Trinity. The brilliance and quick wit of the instructor draws a room full of admirers; nearly every seat in the classroom is occupied. Male students far outnumber the women. Class introductions confirm that I am in fact the only woman enrolled in the class of around thirty graduate students.

The professor sits in a chair at the front and outlines the evening's lecture. He speaks intently, softly even, and the class leans in for the unfolding excursus. Everyone stops taking notes when the door at the front of the classroom opens and a woman walks in. The professor pauses, mid-sentence, to offer her an inquisitive look. Saying nothing, the woman pivots and closes the door behind her. The professor turns back to the class and says, "Well, I think we scared her away." His eyes twinkle and my classmates roar with laughter.

A polite smirk masks my discomfort, and I wonder if I heard something different than my peers. The professor suggested that we—"we, *men*"—scared *her* off; that's what I thought the joke implied.

The lecture picks up, and I replay the incident again and again. It distracts me from the trinitarian processions. It preoccupies me in the days that follow, too. I find myself circling around a basic insight of contemporary hermeneutics, which posits that an interpretation reflects something about the interpreter. My interpretation of the incident reveals something about me. Regardless of the professor's intentions and my classmates' interpretation of his jest, it reveals how the gross disparities between men and women in the theology department, and in Catholic theology more broadly, have led me to intuit that I, a woman, am not a part of the "we."

☙ • ☙

It is a Tuesday night at a quaint Irish pub near Boston, and I have arrived to give a talk on women in Catholicism. The topic not only aligns with my theological expertise but also affords an opportunity to draw on my own experiences and on the wisdom of my many Catholic female friends and mentors.

Following a generous introduction from the lay minister who organized the event, I frame the talk as a reflection on women in the Church since Vatican II. I celebrate how Church leaders and teachings have affirmed the important contributions of women in the life of the Church since then. I detail the expansion of liturgical ministries, the development of a theology of the laity, the emergence of women theologians. I also note the continued misgivings of Catholics whose experiences do not resonate with the Church's prevailing depictions of gender. I choose my words carefully, making no mention of the divisive "f-word"—*feminist*—and saying nothing of women's ordination. I proceed respectfully and concretely, avoiding generalizations. "While Pope John Paul II's writings on the body have been praised for all these reasons, some people have expressed concerns about his emphasis on…"

The parish priest interrupts: "You haven't mentioned his devotion to the Virgin Mother. Anyone who disagrees with Pope John Paul's view of women clearly does not understand his devotion to Mary. He loved women."

I respond graciously, but assertively, "You are right that the Pope's devotion to Mary is well known. In fact, it is not disconnected from many of the concerns that have been

raised about his view of women." I present these critiques
as a matter of ongoing theological debate and pastoral concern. "Some Catholic women identify with these and other
Catholic perspectives on gender, but many Catholic women
do not, which can be a source of personal and spiritual strife.
How can we support Catholic women..."

The middle-aged cleric interrupts my presentation yet
again, exclaiming, "These feminists and women's ordination
advocates are so unfair to the Church! They do not know
what they are talking about, and..." I wear a blank expression. I have academic expertise on women in the Church.
I *am* a Catholic woman. Were this my classroom I would
never tolerate this insolence, but I remind myself that I cannot win against a man in a collar who is surrounded by his
congregation.

When he stops speaking, I call on a young woman
who has raised her hand. I open the presentation to further
discussion, and I continue to call on others in the crowd,
responding to their insights and raising questions in turn.
When the priest interrupts another woman, I gently request
that he please let her finish. This happens once more, and I
get through it.

When I finally depart, it is well after sunset and the
winter streets are empty and dark. I settle into the driver's
seat of my car and burst into tears of frustration. I refuse
to grow accustomed to this disrespect, even as it no longer
surprises me.

※ • ※

I've nearly completed my PhD, and I continue to be
active in a vibrant church downtown. After a couple years of
volunteering as a lector and eucharistic minister on Sundays,
I am asked to serve on the community's liturgy committee,
a multigenerational group of lay ministers led by one of the

Franciscan friars on staff. We plan holy days and manage the hundreds of volunteers who serve at the community's forty eucharistic liturgies each week.

When we meet to organize the annual formation day for liturgical ministers, we discuss who might do the day's central theological presentation. I suggest the name of the friar who presented the first year that I participated, then the lone friar on the committee inquires, "Why doesn't Jessica do it?" He gestures toward me. "You're a theologian. You're certainly qualified! I don't want to put you on the spot, but would you be interested in doing it?"

I'm startled but quickly agree. "Yes—yes, I'd love to do it." The conversation moves onto another agenda item, but my mind returns to what just happened. That my own church community would call upon me—a theologian—to provide a presentation on theology had genuinely surprised me. I am sad that so many Catholics have dismissed my contributions over the years that I am now astonished by the vocational affirmation of my community.

The clericalism I projected on them also saddens me. That I presumed the disregard of other Catholics is unfair to them as individuals. I know this friar to be a thoughtful and supportive individual who cares about the gifts of all people in the community, yet a decade of ministry and theological education has provided plenty of reasons to expect fellow Catholics, especially priests like him, to ignore my vocational call and hard-earned competencies.

※ • ※

The presentation goes well, and I am invited to return as the formation day presenter the following year. I must decline, however, because I'm moving away. I have graduated with my PhD and received a coveted full-time, tenure-track position as a theology professor. I'm elated and humbled by the opportunity. Despite theology's unceasing intellectual difficulty and the academy's demands of personal sacrifice, I am fully alive doing this work, and each day I treasure the privilege of getting to do it. I pack up my belongings and once again move across the country in response to this call.

On my first day in the office, someone asks if I am a new secretary. "No," I reply, "I'm the new theologian."

From the Particular to the Universal

Musings of a Woman Theologian

Maeve Louise Heaney

The Irish poet Denis O'Driscoll, a quiet, humble man who died unexpectedly at the age of fifty-eight, wrote with elegant irony in a poem titled *Memoire*: "It has been absolutely fascinating being me. A unique privilege. Now my whole life lies ahead of you. No thanks at all are called for, I assure you. The pleasure is all mine."

I aspire to this kind of epitaph: a life that has embraced living to the full, in the concrete and real circumstances we are given, "for just such a time as this" (Esth 4:14). Contributing to this book is one attempt to do just that, offering a theological reflection on the vocation to be a theologian, or rather a particular biographical lens into what it feels like to be an early to mid-career woman who identifies as a Catholic systematic theologian formed and forged in a plurality of cultural and ecclesial contexts.

I am not a feminist theologian—by conscious decision at various stages of my writing and for a variety of reasons. This in itself reveals as much as it conceals. I do not presume to speak for anyone other than myself or those I have journeyed with. That being said, I think it is fair to say that one of the strengths of feminist thought and of women's contribution to theology is respect for and attention to the particular as a means of accessing the universal, rather than seeing the two in conflict. It is also, I believe, one of the main strengths of the Catholic Women Speak Network: "We do not speak with one voice, nor do we deny our differences and disagreements. We regard these as creative aspects of the process of learning and growing towards one another in faith. We speak as women not as 'Woman.'"

So my aim is to give access to what it feels like to be called to be a theologian in our current Catholic scenario, with its challenges and opportunities, in the hope that my reflections give some insight to others, male and female, who may find themselves called to the same vocation and who will share the same world in the future. And this *is* my guiding thread: theology as a vocation—a calling, and an ecclesial one.

I came to theological research and teaching in what feels like a seamless journey born of a call to know Jesus, to evangelize, and to form others to do the same, and to find the theological foundations that would enable this to happen. At the risk of overcomplication, I am framing my reflection within my own approach to theological thinking, because it this perspective that explains why it is important that we think not only about theological *things*, but also about *who we are* that think them, and where we are coming from.

My field of theology is theological aesthetics—theology's approach to everything related to art and beauty and, in particular, music. The framework I use is that of twentieth-century Canadian Jesuit Bernard Lonergan, who wrote little on art and even less on music, but whose overall approach to theology I find convincing. With the shift of culture and cultures we are all part of, it seems as if the ground is moving under Christianity's feet, and we need to find solid ground to build on and negotiate our way into the future. That solid ground, Lonergan suggests, is in place when those of us who *do theology* not only express theories or ideas, but develop them from within a conscious *awareness* of various aspects of our lives—specifically:

1. our religious experience,
2. our freedom (the fact that we are ultimately responsible for who we are/become),
3. how we come to know reality (epistemology), and
4. our affective life: attentiveness to the aesthetic, embodied, and symbolic dimensions of life that condition our presence in the worlds we inhabit.

These areas of awareness, or *conversions*, as he calls them (*religious*, *moral*, *intellectual*, and *psychic*, respectively), protect and guide our quest for truth in dialogue and contrast, always within a community of theologians. They frame the mainly autobiographical account that follows: how being a *woman* theologian has affected (enabled or hindered) my various ongoing "conversions" and how these conversions help me make sense of that vocation.

Starting Point
(under the Broad Heading of *Psychic Awareness*)

I am a heterosexual woman who, despite herself, felt called to consecrated life. I start here because, although we know and teach that sexuality is an intrinsic aspect of our anthropological makeup, just how deeply that marks every aspect of our theological service is, I believe, still largely unrecognized. I could summarize my journey in Catholic theology as a learning of that lesson.

I came to theology by way of ministry in evangelization, in a community that was founded by Father Jaime Bonet in 1963 with the intention of promoting women for preaching.[1] Our founder believed that all the baptized have the right and duty, as prophets, priests, and kings, to preach the gospel and form apostolic communities, within the Church and faithful to its leadership. This belief included a vision of women being involved at every level of ecclesial leadership. It meant that for many years preaching, forming, and leading communities of faith and training others for the same activities were unproblematic for me.

Change came from outside *and* from within that family. My interpretation of this change is that the men of the community, who were dealing with a generation of very strong founding women, began to ask questions about their own identity as men and priests, perhaps feeling unsure or vulnerable. This process found an echo in the gradual shift in ecclesial awareness running through the Church that I sensed emerging in the 1990s.

The exception in canon law allowing laypeople to preach in exceptional circumstances was closed, so we obeyed—in retrospect, perhaps too rigidly. My community's sense of ecclesial belonging, which has served us well and saved us more than once, has also led us to be very conscious of any hierarchical perception of our ministry. The women of my community, including myself, often feel our voices are heeded less than those of the men. Perhaps this is all for the common good of the community and the Church, but it is disappointing, leaving some of us feeling somehow betwixt and between.

Still within the realm of psychic awareness is the fact of being consecrated, that is, a religious who, as distinct from forming a family, has committed to the vows of poverty, chastity, and obedience in a community. I am aware that these vows make me appear "safe," although I would be safer still if I wore a habit. For over thirty years of religious life, the time I have spent choosing what to wear has not decreased—to reflect faithfully who I am, who God is for me, and what I stand for. Aesthetics are not superficial. My bag is always bigger than that of my male colleagues. Perhaps this is part of my artistic sensibility, but it is also intrinsic to my way of being a Catholic female theologian: if too attractive, they get scared; too dowdy, and I allow them to forget that I am a *woman* theologian.

Having lived and worked in Ireland, Spain, England, Italy, the United States, Germany, and Australia (admittedly all relatively westernized countries), I know how much culture matters. Rome was perhaps the most eye-opening of these places. As I progressed in my studies, ever more the sole female presence in theological circles and seminars, I felt at one and the same time that colleagues appreciated my presence and the voice I brought, *and* they were surprised the moment they realized I "had a brain." Any feminist awareness I have was sharpened in Rome.

Religious Conversion

My religious experience is contemplative and eucharistic. It was born of a question about whether Jesus was really in the tabernacle—answered during long hours in front of the Blessed Sacrament. My community taught me to pray, introducing me into a profound, trinitarian spirituality that is, when I am faithful, the air that I breathe, the source of my music and thought. It is the *only* reason I am a religious and continue to belong to Church and community. My need for the Eucharist is visceral.

As time went on, holding together that sense of Jesus's presence and its realization in our eucharistic celebrations has meant learning to close my eyes to things that threaten my peace. I mourn the lack of female preaching in our churches and comb the cities I live in for a real voice in the midst of the clamor. I have internally railed against the washing of *men's* feet on the feast day that inaugurates Jesus's intimate presence. I have tried to close my mind to the lack of consistency between liturgical theology's grounding in the Body of Christ and literalized metaphors of the Church as "Mother." When invited, I attend the ordinations of my friends who become priests or bishops. In fact, I think friendship may be one of our only ways forward (see John 15:15). I am not sure what this "conscious *in*attentiveness" to what does not make sense to me in these celebrations of our faith might do to my spirituality or witness, whether perfection in patience or the gradual purging of any preaching worth its salt. Religious life exists, in part, to bring a prophetic witness of eschatological freedom to the Church itself. Furthermore, my specific charism is that of prayer and ministry of the Word (see Acts 6:4). Prophetic preaching implies paying attention to the Word of God and the world, so as to name what is in place and what is not. I fear becoming accustomed to the role women play in the Church, and therefore not being faithful to the essence of religious life.

Moral Conversion

My formation was an odd, perhaps graced mixture of prophetic vision and submissive religious obedience. The incurved woman of Luke 13 is one guiding image: from a straight-backed seeker at seventeen years old, I passed through being a much more spiritual but bent-over young woman, to my current daily attempt to stand tall and free, to become all that the triune Presence I sense within calls me to be.

That journey has been tremendously difficult. The ecclesial belonging of my community is strong. I used to call us "radical," planted in a faith experience that gave us freedom. I have generally worked well with people from across the liberal/conservative spectrum. This may be partly due to my sense of political survival, but it is also the fruit of my genuine attempt to choose the particular over the universal, or to access the latter through the former, to accept each person's gifts and insights, to respect what we all bring to the table. James Joyce's definition of the Church, "Here comes everybody," holds some truth.

I have chosen not to engage the issue of the ordination of women, even before the 1990s, mainly because I sensed the polarization it provoked or within which it was received and felt that we, the universal Church in all its complex, vast cultural and theological richness and diversity, were and perhaps are still not ready. I include myself in that we. Symbol is stronger than and prior to words. I also believe, however, that it is urgent to untie the knot between ministerial priesthood and power, in its three *munera*—priest, prophet, and king. It would not be difficult theologically to move forward in true collaborative ministry, without causing division, through some sensible reflection on the theology of ministry.

When asked to collaborate in the formation of young men for priesthood, I have always said yes, because the request presented itself as a sign of trust from people I respect. I genuinely embrace the opportunity, even while I am aware that I work within a structure that does not always or fully convince me. Is our approach and methodology in formation work really paving the way fruitfully for what the Church needs to become? While unsure if this is the right way forward, my collaboration allows me to bring a woman's voice into the heart of the formative process of those who will, in the not too distant future, lead our assemblies. And I choose to care for these men, hoping mine will be a positive presence that will stay with them and shape their future understanding of women in the Church. But it has often not been easy.

I am grateful for the women who have gone ahead, on whose shoulders I stand—for the ones who push the frontiers—perhaps because I don't have to or perhaps because we need to work on all fronts. But I think freedom and faithfulness to the ongoing call is at the heart of our journey, a conviction that leads me to the last point.

Intellectual Conversion

In my case, this conversion has to do with art and music and their place in my vocation to theology. Women are still not fully present at the intellectual table as creators of the mental constructs through which we think. But becoming part of that world *cannot* mean sacrificing *how* we come to know what we know. While not wishing to canonize essentialisms, I think it's fair to say that women compartmentalize less than men in the various ways we make sense of life, and we bring to theological discourse perspectives that stretch us beyond ourselves. Art and music challenge theology to open to other patterns of experience beyond theory's hegemony. Music enriches and transforms the worlds of meaning we inhabit, and how we experience, interpret, and understand those worlds: it has a place in theological thought. This is not a woman's insight. It is simply my theological conviction.

Despite the challenges, I feel graced to work in this vineyard that is theological thinking. But I continue because I cannot *not* do so, as long as this call sustains me and there is the hope that my presence is changing something.

While I was studying for my doctorate, I followed the Ignatian Spiritual Exercises. One day I was meditating through a form of prayer called imaginative contemplation, in which one enters into a scene in the life of Jesus. That scene was the Last Supper—foundational text for the institution of the Eucharist. I remember sensing deep pain about the whole scene and situation: how did we come to the conviction that there were only men there, at this, the very center of my experience of Jesus and my continued presence in the Church? I vividly remember intuiting, in a prayer experience that stays with me still, that the pain was his, with the words "I never meant it to be like this." Those words ground and sustain my hope that this community of friends that is the Church will find or develop another way of doing things.

Notes

1. *Verbum Dei* is what they call a "new form of religious life" that includes women, men, and married couples on (nearly) equal standing—not as a third order but as an intrinsic third branch of a "fraternity" (for whom inclusive language is still a challenge!).

Seminaries and Priestly Formation

A Woman Theologian Reflects

Cettina Militello
(translated from Italian by Luca Badini)

Forgive me for tackling issues relating to training projects and to vocational discernment, raised by the forthcoming 2018 Synod on Young People, Faith, and Vocational Discernment, from the very personal perspective of someone who has been teaching theology courses in ecclesiastical institutions for about forty years. Those courses are attended mainly by candidates for the priesthood, who must undergo theological studies. For many years, I have witnessed the methodical demolition of everything I have proposed to my students through my teaching, especially on the topic of ecclesiology.

I have punctiliously strived to lead them to the ecclesiology of Vatican II, an ecclesiology informed by communion and by the interrelationship among all members of the people of God: women and men, clergy, religious, laywomen and laymen. My efforts have been consistently "sabotaged"—if you will allow me to use that term—in a way that leads my students to see themselves, and their future ministry, not as a collaborative service, but rather as a powerful mark of diversity and privilege.

I have seen many of them, though not all, attend theology courses only as a burdensome requirement, which is not comparable to the rules, the common prayer, and formation meetings of their proper vocational training. Only these last experiences, not theological studies, have importance in preparing for the priestly ministry.

In fact, the ecclesiological model of powerful and hierarchical verticality and absoluteness from which the Council freed us is once again being proposed as the true face of the Church, as the authentic way of making understandable its mystery. I really do not know how to break the vicious cycle perpetuated by such an awful education. Frankly, I believe that it can only be done by abolishing the seminary system altogether.

This once commendable system was a result of Tridentine reform. It had a positive effect by giving back to the clergy a basic theological education that they had been deprived of for such a long time. Educating them in a communal setting also gave them secular knowledge, which was denied to the majority of people. During the Middle Ages and early modernity, education was a privilege of the dominant social classes. And since becoming a priest involved acquiring a social status (as for religious men and women), the offer, in the absence of mass education, of basic information was entirely meritorious, and it no doubt had positive sociopolitical consequences. Moreover, the numbers were quite different. Despite the extremely high infant mortality rate, the lack of access to birth control resulted in a high number of men aspiring to clerical status.

This is no longer the situation today for our young Catholic people: there are fewer of them and they no longer enter the seminary during school age. Minor seminaries, which used to enroll boys from ten to fourteen or fifteen years of age (that is, still within compulsory school age) are now very few in number and without social importance. Today, in the vast majority of cases, men enter seminary when they became adults, after having already obtained a diploma of secondary education or a university degree, or at an age when others attend university.

In other words, nowadays candidates for ordination are generally fewer and older than in the past, and, at least it is to be hoped, they come with an education and even more with an ecclesial background—the latter being the likely source of their ministerial vocation. Now, all such candidates are put in the same basket, homologated, forced into a communal life, under the authority of the officials governing every seminary—rector, vice-rector, spiritual director, and so on—following a five-hundred-year-old system that we stubbornly continue to deem necessary. Diocesan seminaries may be closing down, but at the same time, interdiocesan or regional seminaries are open. The seminary system itself is left untouched.

In seminaries one often finds, on the one hand, a perverse effort to instill in candidates for the priesthood a visceral dislike of every form of intellectual deepening of the faith, and on the other, training for a way of life that will be unattainable to them. In effect, as priests, they will live lonely lives. At times, as newly ordained priests, they will have to endure the harassment of an elderly parish priest who will not believe his luck in being able to mold in his own way the young curate placed under his authority. Situations like that cannot be described as "communal life."

None of the routines and practices that give structure to seminary life (such as the daily schedule, communal prayer, communal meals) will be there for them during the harsh loneliness of their future ministry. They will be alone in decision-making, alone in their living quarters, alone in eating, alone in personal prayer, and so on. On the other hand, they will be accompanied by the presumption that they chose the best kind of life for a Christian, a life superior to and different from the life common to the people of God who are entrusted to them.

Accordingly, they will act in a despotic and authoritarian fashion. What is more, they will regard their ministry as a career, because this is what has been suggested to them. They will thus strive to be assigned to the most important and wealthiest parish; they will aspire to climb up the hierarchical ladder: auxiliary vicar, parish priest, pastoral vicar, auxiliary bishop, ordinary bishop; or canon, monsignor, cardinal.

Pope Francis has frequently pointed to careerism as a wound of the Church. However, it is impossible to heal such a wound if what is prevalent is a despotic understanding of ministry. Such understanding is, paradoxically, more alive among young people today, who find in it a remedy to the sense of fragility and weakness that so often defines them. The "sacred" power that they regard as the essential element of ordained ministry makes them feel both strong and safe.

It must also be noted that a seminary is a male-only institution. To this day, women there fulfill only auxiliary tasks. Even granted the existence of a mixed commission of men and women tasked with the vocational discernment and accompaniment of seminarians, the requirement of celibacy makes the latter suspicious toward women, whose presence is perceived as that of a possible antagonist to their vocational choice.

The seminary can therefore be characterized as a "homophile" space, often ideologically homosexual. It goes without saying that it can and indeed does happen that those who enter it are homosexual, maybe unconsciously, and later openly. Without wanting to isolate and exclude anybody a priori from the ordained ministry, there is no doubt that such a separation results in an objective relational difficulty *with* and a distance *from* women, which easily becomes misogyny. Unfortunately, it can also become a form of violence that might find an outlet in pedophilia, the fruit of a delirium of omnipotence reinforced by an aura of sacredness that appears to place the priest above any law.

The Church of the future, the multifaceted Church so dear to Pope Francis, must urgently ask herself questions about vocational discernment and accompaniment. Both processes must be anchored in the people of God, because ordained ministers will have to be at the service of those people.

I believe it is necessary to close seminaries. Candidates to ordained ministry should first obtain at the very least a BA in theology, not simply because it is obligatory for admission to ordination, but because they need the intellectual tools to give an account of the hope that they have. I also think it is necessary to create places of cohabitation, strong in what forms us as humans, between, on the one hand, candidates to ordained ministry and families; and, on the other, candidates to ordained ministry and bishops. That way, admission into ministry will happen in a context of absolutely normal relationships. It is, in any case, evident that what will make a difference (and not just within the Church) will be the theological understanding of "being for others" that is the true nature of service, of *diakonia*, which is not arrogance and arbitrariness but rather the permanent service of helping all the people of God to exercise their common priesthood.

Who Will Heal the Wounds of the Church?

Women's Lay Ministry and Priestly Power

Jennifer Owens-Jofré

I remember the way my mother and my aunts used to break the limbs off the aloe vera plant when my cousins and I skinned our knees as children. Their mother, my Mamita, had shared with them about its healing properties as her mother had shared with her on the outskirts of Santa Cruz, Bolivia, many years before she had brought her husband and her four children to live in Southern California. Too afraid of its prickly edges to handle them myself, I stayed away from the plant, even though I knew of its power to heal. I remember the clean smell of the plant's insides, how the light sting upon contact with my grazed knee would give way to the cooling that signaled healing.

I discovered at a young age that I also had a passion for healing. As a teenager, I recognized the quotidian work of the parish to which my family had belonged my whole life as a balm for my community, and I wanted to be part of that work. I was a cantor at Sunday evening Masses, co-led retreats with teams of other teenagers and adults, co-facilitated small faith sharing groups alongside adult leaders for teenagers preparing for the sacrament of confirmation, gave reflections on the readings of the day during communion services at my high school, participated in anti–death penalty protests downtown, and shared food with homeless and unemployed folks with the local Catholic Worker community. I was a church kid, and I loved it.

It was no surprise to my parents that I began graduate studies in divinity on the other side of the country just before my twenty-fifth birthday. It was my first experience of education outside the Catholic system, and I took classes alongside Zen Buddhists, Southern Baptists, Latter Day Saints, Sikhs, Presbyterians, Quakers, secular humanists, and many others. Most of my Christian classmates were preparing for ordination in their respective denominations, and some of them were puzzled by my presence as a Catholic woman preparing for lay ecclesial ministry. "It's different in the Catholic Church," I tried to explain. "Lay Catholics can do everything priests can do, except offer the sacraments. We lack the power to forgive sins, and we can't consecrate the Eucharist, but we can baptize people in case of an emergency." I would go on about the power of what happened at the Second Vatican Council and with the emergence of liberation theology.

When I moved back across the country to begin doctoral studies, I joined a local parish. It was relatively small for an urban church, but the liturgy was vibrant, the preaching was engaging, and the community welcomed me. Within two years of joining the parish, I was hired as an intern to work with confirmation preparation and young adult ministry. I sought permission from our then-pastor to grow our outreach to young people by starting a Sunday evening Mass. We sang contemporary Christian music, offered the spirit of welcome for which the parish had become known, and focused the preaching on issues relevant to the lives of many who came through the doors. This Mass began on a monthly basis, then it became a weekly fixture on the parish calendar under the parochial administrator—a sort of interim leader the diocese assigned to the parish, who had all the responsibilities of a pastor without the official title.

While my ministry responsibilities at the parish shifted over time, I continued to find meaning in my ministry there because I had the privilege of accompanying parishioners, young and old, through some of the most trying, most life-giving times in their lives. I was able to walk with them as they prepared to be baptized, to go to Reconciliation for the first time, to receive the Eucharist for the first time, to be confirmed. Further, the parochial administrator allowed me a place on the preaching schedule. Time and time again, parishioners shared with me what a difference it made in their experience of communal prayer to hear the Word of God broken open from a woman's perspective—and a feminist one at that.

At the start of Advent during my last year at the parish, a new priest was assigned to us as second parochial administrator. Early on, it was clear that changes were afoot. He was chair of the parish council, where my role was to liaise with staff. At my first meeting, I started to express a perspective different from his. He spoke over me and told me to stop speaking, saying my point of view was no longer welcome. When I asked to speak with him afterward, he told me that I was welcome to observe the meetings, but my participation would no longer be necessary. I let him know that I would not attend future meetings.

Early that summer, two colleagues on the pastoral staff and I—all of us women who had earned advanced degrees and who had experience in theology and ministry—received letters saying that we were being laid off. Our part-time positions were being combined into one full-time position, for which we were invited to apply. I could not help but feel I was let go, at least in part, because I am a young woman who speaks her mind. Our parochial administrator had a hierarchical approach to leadership in ministry, whereas my women colleagues and I had been vocal about our desire for the collaborative style of ministry we felt would serve the parish best. None of us applied for the full-time position. He did not inform the members of the parish of his decision. Two years later, the congregation has shrunk to the point that the diocese is joining it to a nearby parish administratively, in the midst of rumors that a total joining of the two parishes (and the closing of the smaller) is not far behind.

Part of what was so heartbreaking about my experience is that much of the ministry I was permitted to do was completely dependent upon the priest in charge. Regardless of how much training I had acquired, irrespective of how hard I had prayed about the insights I aimed to share, my ministry ultimately was in the hands of whatever priest was assigned to the parish at any given time. I struggled not to internalize the sense of powerlessness I experienced during my ministry there. Even when I preached on Sundays, I was keenly aware that the opportunity to do so could be eliminated at any moment, which, in the end, it was. I look back on that experience of ministry with a bittersweetness and a full heart that no one can take away.

As I reflect, the memory of the aloe vera plant emerges as an apt metaphor for the Church since Vatican II. We need skilled aunts and mothers to break her limbs carefully, to cut past the prickly edges of the kyriarchy that plagues her, to bring holy and healing salve to our wounds.

A Church That Welcomes Young People?

What a Difference a Priest Makes

Katie Humphrey

In my thirty-plus years as a Catholic, I have had varied and mixed experiences with parish priests. Writing this piece has given me a chance to reflect on just how vital, in myriad ways, a parish priest is to the spiritual growth of individuals and communities. I was extremely fortunate, in my home parish, to grow up with several supportive, open-minded, collaborative, and compassionate priests. From a young age, I was involved in helping with Sunday school and first communion preparation, and after my confirmation, I went on to support and grow the youth church in our parish. This included catechist training, youth church meetings, trips, outings, and opportunities for children and teenagers to take part in Mass, fundraising, and church events. What I learned in this time, and the experiences I had, developed my personal spirituality as well as my love for and deeper understanding of theology.

The involvement of and encouragement from our parish priest at the time was invaluable, not just emotionally but also financially. I was employed for one day a week during my year out before university to direct the confirmation groups and continue to encourage and develop young people's involvement in liturgy, music, annual events, retreats, and fundraising.

Trust was a huge part of building the youth church, and there were a number of challenges for an eighteen-year-old woman in a Catholic community. This was particularly the case at the parish council meetings, when I encountered people who didn't want change or who didn't understand the importance of younger people in the church. Nevertheless, we had the support of our wonderful parish priest and our pastoral worker who would encourage our ideas. Such affirmation showed that the church could become a welcoming, encouraging, and approachable place for younger people. They could grow spiritually, ask questions, and be a part of a nonjudgmental community that valued their contributions. I am honored that these people who shaped so much of my development and understanding of Catholicism are still in my life.

When I went away to university, I knew that I had left the youth church in the hands of supportive people who would help it to grow and ensure that our church was a safe, welcoming place. When I returned for family visits, it always filled me with joy to attend meetings, events, and confirmation ceremonies and feel the vitality and warmth.

Sadly, this did not last. One wonderful priest retired, one died, and one moved away. The new recruit was an old-fashioned, closed-minded man who felt no desire to encourage young people, and especially not young women. Mass went from being an opportunity to worship and to celebrate the wonderful community we had, to a difficult and sometimes painful hour of judgment and backward theology. The lay community stepped in, despite his resistance, to ensure that there was still music, bidding prayers, readers, and community events. The strength that our community had had for so long is what kept the church doors open. The impact this new priest had was a clear example of how hierarchical structures and a failure to build good relationships with the laity contributes to declining Mass attendance.

I have visited a number of churches over the years, and I have noticed a real energy, positive and negative, between congregations and their spiritual leaders. A vitally important part of a reflection on vocation in our Church must be about collaborative leadership in parish communities, which needs priests to be supportive of lay initiatives and to cultivate a shared sense of mission. As the number of priests continues to dwindle, parish life will depend more and more on strong, trusting relationships between priests and laity. Rather than discouraging women, young people, and innovative thinking, we need a culture of openness, affirmation, and collaboration. This is also important for encouraging a new generation of priests into the Church.

For these reasons, I welcome a Synod on Youth, Faith, and Vocational Discernment. I hope it will open doors and create greater opportunities for those who have thus far been marginalized in the Church.

I Sang the *Exsultet*

Representation Matters

Ruth Fehlker

I am a pastoral lay worker, working for the Diocese of Münster in Coesfeld, Germany. I hold a master's degree in theology and I have trained in pastoral theology and pastoral psychology.

Two years ago, I was asked to sing the *Exsultet* during the Easter Vigil. I had been working in the parish for only a few months and did not know, at that point, that I was the first woman to sing the great Easter Vigil hymn in that church. After the service ended, I stood by one of the church doors, wishing people a happy Easter as they left—I was astonished by their reaction. So many women (and a few men also) were visibly moved, some with tears in their eyes. This had little to do with the quality of my singing, I realized, and everything to do with the fact that they had witnessed a woman proclaiming the joy of the resurrection.

This was an especially powerful moment for me, but in my profession I often contribute to the liturgy in various ways. Preaching during the Sunday Eucharist is part of my ministry. To me this means that I am able to think aloud, to share my ideas, thoughts, feelings, and questions concerning Scripture and faith with the congregation. I can share that

I have hope but few answers (if any at all), that I often feel puzzled, overwhelmed, and fearful, but I can express the joy I find in life and in God. Again, the response is overwhelmingly positive. My questions sometimes resonate with the listeners because their lives and questions are similar to mine. This sense of familiarity enables us to start a conversation, and we learn from one another.

I lead funerals, and in doing so, I encounter grieving families from all walks of life and faith. I am able to serve them, as the one "holding space" for their grief, to help them give their farewells a shape, to help them put into words their hope for resurrection, however they understand this hope.

I work with youth group leaders, altar servers, and those preparing for confirmation—girls and boys, young men and women—who grow up seeing men and women working together in the Church, sharing their faith, sharing their questions and their hopes.

For the past three years, I have been lucky enough to work in a team of pastoral workers—men and women, laypeople and priests—who are quite different from one another. We come from different backgrounds, have different temperaments, different strengths, and different ways of expressing our faith, but we trust one another to work toward a common goal. This sense of purpose has enabled us to realize that each of us appeals to some people, none of us to all, and that it is important that we are there: witnesses of Jesus Christ, each in our own way.

I know that my situation is privileged—especially within the Catholic Church. Few women get to be so visible and fewer still have their voices heard. I work as part of a team that wants my voice to be heard.

This is an amazing gift. I cherish it, but I also really hope that my experience might give hope to all those whose voices are not heard, who are in danger of losing that hope, and that our Church can truly be a place where all are heard.

Obviously, my profession and my position in the church has its difficulties, but my situation is more fulfilling than would otherwise be possible. I am reminded of the woman at the church door who told me that Easter morning when I sang the *Exsultet*, "Seeing this—it gives me hope for our Church."

Affirming Laity

Women in Parish Life

Marion Morgan

I was brought up in the Church of England on the outskirts of London just after the Second World War. Working within the church was a tradition in our family. My Welsh grandmother was still serving as secretary of the Sisterhood group in her local Presbyterian chapel in her eighties. So when, at the age of twenty-seven, I was received into the Roman Catholic Church, it was natural for me to expect to be involved in its running.

I was received in 1969 when I was living in Bristol, at a time when my parish was trying to implement the changes brought in by Vatican II. The parish priest was delighted to have my help. We started a group for ecumenism, a group for social issues, and there was also a group for liturgy. Laypeople, including myself, started to read at the Masses. I joined the newly formed mixed choir.

What I had not anticipated was the reaction of the people. Some were happy to join in. Others were openly hostile. Combined with an attitude of respect for the priest was an underlying current of resentment against all he was trying to do. Many of the good and willing women had been brought up not to "push themselves forward." They could not understand how it was possible for women and priests to work together. Rumors abounded, particularly as many priests were leaving at that time to get married. (In my case the rumors were completely unfounded!)

I left my job to study for a degree in theology at the local university. I was amused when a priest commented, "Theology is very difficult for a woman." I found such paternalistic attitudes within the Church amusing most of the time, but I had not suffered under them as I was growing up. I had left my many hang-ups behind when I left the Church of England, and I always found the Catholic priests I met to be kind people.

After completing my degree and a postgraduate diploma in Pastoral Theology, I wanted to serve my parish, so they created the post of Pastoral Assistant. The bishop granted us a small honorarium and some money was raised from supportive parishioners, but there was still opposition.

I think that some lay volunteers in the parish felt downgraded because I was being paid. There is something liberating about generously giving your time and energy as a volunteer, but a paid person working with you can make this seem second best. After a year, all surplus funds had to be put toward church-building work, which brought an end to my paid employment.

I stayed in the parish but worked elsewhere for three years until I eventually became Executive Secretary of the local Council of Christian Churches. As a theologically trained, regionally based laywoman, I was a rare commodity! I was on national ecumenical committees. I gave talks and contributed to local radio. I was certainly not hampered by being a woman and was treated everywhere with respect and fairness. But I kept my head down and did not tell the parish much about what I was doing.

Eventually I needed a break from "church-speak," so I

resigned from most of my ecumenical activities and became a freelance feature writer for the local free paper. I met women and men from all backgrounds running programs for the disadvantaged, community centers, day centers, and projects for women. I remember one in particular. An Indian lady had set up a sewing project for local Indian women. She was based in an old factory and had several sewing machines and was teaching the women a skill, as well as encouraging self-expression, conversation, and exploration of their culture. I believe she was Catholic, though she was not prominent in her local church. Why should she be? She was already providing a wonderful service for local disadvantaged Indian women.

So what are my experiences as a Catholic woman? I felt no discrimination anywhere except in the parish, and that was not from the clergy, but from a few longstanding parish workers.

It does appear to me, thank God, that those prejudices are now dying out. We have girl altar servers, women lectors and special ministers of the Eucharist, and women increasingly serving in all sorts of capacities. In my parish, the influx of new members from the Philippines, from Kerala in India, from Africa, and from other parts of Europe has changed the whole scene for the better. I currently lead the RCIA program and still sing in the choir and help plan the music.

But there is still some way to go. I would love to see women more confident in their own gifts and talents. If they have a good idea, I would like to see them have the confidence to find helpers and implement it on their own. Of course, one should check it with the parish priest if it involves the church or church premises, but do not expect him to *do* anything. He has enough to do already.

Personally, I have never felt the Church or its hierarchy to be restrictive. But—and I realize it is a big "but"—I am not married and have no children. None of my extended family are Catholic, although some are churchgoers in their own denomination. I have sympathy and respect for those who struggle in different situations. And I have never felt called to be a priest. As far as I can see, there is far more scope in being a layperson!

Finally, a few words gleaned from my seventy years of experience of different churches: don't be shy. Don't be afraid of making mistakes: we all do from time to time. Be bold and adventurous. Be welcoming. Listen to others and learn. But always, always, be courteous.

A Vocation to Hospitality

Reflections of a University Chaplain

Ginny Jordan-Arthur

At the age of twenty-one, I spent a brilliant year working as a chaplaincy assistant. It was meant to be a temporary job to tide me over until I decided what my career should be. At the end of the year, we went to Taizé with a group of students. There on a hill with thousands of young people, I knew I was exactly where I was meant to be. I sat in the beautiful services listening to the simple and moving songs about trust, hope, and compassion, and those quiet days gave my soul an inner calm that later, through doubt, distance, and challenges, has held me.

My line manager was an Anglican priest. She walked with me in those early days of exploring my vocation. She invited me into conversations about pastoral ministry and helped me to continue in my chaplaincy work. She also encouraged me to offer my gifts to my Catholic parish, and I happily led a youth club and confirmation classes.

I enjoyed that work and had a real respect and fondness for my parish priest. However, there was a contrast between my experience of working in an ecumenical chaplaincy with all its processes of discernment, and the level of conversation and engagement in the parish. Not only did I become aware of women's ministry in different church traditions, I also realized that my church did not actively engage with young women in their vocational quest. These early experiences shaped my vision of chaplaincy. I wanted to make space for the women who walk through my office door to explore where God might be leading them.

Those early years of discernment also awakened me to the importance of hospitality. Whenever I was challenged to name what I found life-giving, I came back to the fact that I love drinking tea with people and hearing their stories. I am committed to the theology of hospitality, which doesn't mean just putting on lovely meals for those actively seeking. The practice of hospitality leads me out of my comfort zone.

Someone once joked that I had a ministry of smiling as I nearly always grin at anyone who walks by. Part of my vocation as chaplain is to make all people I pass feel noticed and appreciated. Chaplaincy celebrates the uniqueness of every person through the gift of hospitality. The invitation for all to come to the table as themselves and to be at home is central to my daily life, and it allows me to walk with many people as they explore their own journey. My pastoral ministry often takes me to "thin places," where I sit across from another and see the face of Christ.

As a wife and mother of two young children, and having been in full-time employment for over fifteen years, I no longer count myself among the youth that the Church reaches out to. However, my vocation is forever growing and changing me, and as a university chaplain, I can both open and close doors for the young people I encounter. Many students I speak to are not interested in organized religion, and many experienced exclusion rather than the welcoming embrace of Christ. Others are fully committed to the Church, but they are uncomfortable applying the same level of questioning and thirst for knowledge to their faith as they do to all other areas of their lives and academic study. My role is to support those who are just holding onto their faith, while I also offer a place for those who are so comfortable in the Church that they are blind to some of its challenges. And thankfully the chaplaincy is also the place for the many in-between, and for those making a transition to a more mature, reflective faith as they travel through university.

Those who knock on my door come for a multitude of reasons, but my starting question is nearly always the same: What is life-giving for you? Though I see both male and female students, it is more often the women that I support in an ongoing relationship with them. Many have told me that, while they are happy to talk to their parish priest about matters of religion and to seek the sacraments, they feel embarrassed or uncomfortable talking to him about relationships, sexuality and identity, mental health concerns, and their images of God.

The time we spend together often includes space for quiet contemplation and listening to the Scriptures. We talk about the unconditional love of God, as opposed to the distant, condemning man on a cloud that many still hold in their imaginations. I've watched them grow in confidence in their faith and their relationship with God.

However, the challenge they face is uncertainty about where they belong in the Church. Most of the women I talk to assume their role will be to show up on Sundays and, as and when they have children, to help run parish activities. On occasion, if someone is more committed, she may be thinking of running small groups, youth clubs, or leading worship, but few have spoken of how they might use their voices to challenge what they feel uncomfortable about. Some female students say they are frustrated because they do not feel as valued as their young male counterparts. Some experience the pain of not being allowed to share in the Eucharist with their friends or family in different church traditions. Others are concerned that the Church seems to focus more on personal morality than on social justice, and many find it troubling that celibate men are making decisions about women's bodies. Most express frustration about the lack of women in leadership positions in the Church, including but not limited to ordination.

Many women feel empowered and encouraged to be leaders in the community while they are at university, but once they return to parish life, what roles are they encouraged to take? Do we encourage them to do only flower arranging, cleaning the pews, and looking after the children—roles that are important but that fall disproportionately to women? My experience of supporting highly intelligent and aspirational women is that they hope for a more inclusive Church that will celebrate the diversity within its walls while at the same time reaching out to its ecumenical brothers and sisters. They search for Christian unity and embrace a multifaith community that can build true friendships and deepen a desire to understand the faith of others and to learn from them. As a Catholic chaplain, I also see and support many outside the Church. In all these encounters I see God's face and hope for the day when the Church listens to the voices of all God's children.

Chaplaincy in a Women's Prison

Sarah Pearce

I have been working as a volunteer chaplain at a women's prison for about twenty-one years alongside both volunteer and paid colleagues. Initially, I was nominated by my Quaker Area Meeting, but when I converted to Catholicism about eight years ago, I stayed on and became an addition to the Catholic part of the team. My position was subsequently ratified by my bishop, who had received me into the Church.

Over the years, our originally ecumenical Christian chaplaincy team became a multifaith team. Most of us carry out both the generic statutory duties and the faith-specific work required by the Prison Service. We see all the prisoners when they first come in and just before they leave, we make daily visits to anyone who is confined to her cell for disciplinary reasons, we are responsible for breaking bad news to prisoners, and we have specific duties if somebody dies in custody. When necessary, we facilitate visits from visiting chaplains who come in less regularly because they have fewer members of their faith in the prison. In addition, we offer pastoral care to all prisoners, and also to other members of staff, with whom we work cooperatively. We are involved with trying to help with the huge issue of self-harm. We respond to all applications to see a chaplain, and we will often bring a woman to the chapel to light a candle, for example, following bereavement or on an anniversary. We often pray with women who request it, in a language appropriate to where they are coming from. Sometimes we can help facilitate a woman's resettlement back into the community by linking her to mentoring agencies when she is released. In our faith-specific role, we offer teaching, discussions, and services. This is not an exhaustive list, so we are kept busy, but we try never to seem rushed when engaging with the women and always to be welcoming to everyone who wants to talk to us as well as make everyone feel important and cared for. Sometimes we are invited into a conversation taking place in one of the prison wings, which might start, "Miss, can you explain the difference between Catholic and Christian?" or "I used to believe in God, but then my baby died."

Obviously, any kind of proselytizing is inappropriate. We always make it clear that we are united in our chaplaincy team and respectful toward those who feel they have no time for God. Although the most frequently registered religious affiliation is "nil," this does not necessarily indicate a lack of interest in religion. We encourage women to experience various kinds of worship or meditation if they wish it, with the approval of that particular faith chaplain. For example, at our weekly Catholic Mass, we welcome both those who are registered Roman Catholic and "extras." These might include devout practicing Catholics, or they might be women who have some past experience of Catholicism, or who just want to come and see what it is all about, or who have a friend who comes, or who want to talk in their own language with compatriots, or who want to have a chance to sing some hymns, or who are hoping to pass drugs, or who are hoping to become a Catholic, or any combination of these! We have a strong faith that God can make something good out of everything.

Since my conversion, I have continued in much the same way as before, coming in once or twice a week and doing statutory duties. Now, in addition, I help the priest (or deacon) with the Catholic Mass (or Liturgy of the Word with communion) together with any volunteers they bring from the local parish. This involves helping to welcome the women into the chapel, assisting with decisions about hymns, finding women who would like to do the readings, collecting and reading out the bidding prayers (one of the most moving and often heart-rending parts of the service), and offering to see women the next time I am in on a weekday if they have a particular need for a longer talk. I have also been privileged to help with arrangements for the sacrament of reconciliation when we have been able to offer it, and in preparing several women for baptism or full reception into the Church. Sometimes after the service we may take communion to a woman who has asked for it because for some reason she has been unable to attend.

I have never felt any difficulty or sense of inferiority about the fact that I am a seventy-five-year-old woman doing this work. In fact, playing the role of a grandmother or big sister has often seemed an advantage. Had I experienced anything approaching the extent of some of the desperate situations so many of our women have suffered, particularly childhood abuse and bereavement and trauma, I don't think I would have been able to do the work I do. However, I believe I have known enough loss and sorrow in my own life for God to transform into something useful, and I am incredibly thankful for the privilege of working with these lovely, brave, funny, often incredibly honest women.

Hospitality and Hope

Reflections of a High School Chaplain

Catherine Cavanagh

It's all about the welcome. High school chaplaincy finds its direction in hospitality, in the "being with"—of adults with youth, of one person with another.

This ministry arises from the beatitudes, Christ's call to discover blessings among the least and the lost. High school chaplains find Christ for themselves and for their communities in the chaotic and burdened but also loving and generous lives of the teenagers who populate their schools.

In Ontario, Canada, Catholic high schools are open to all. Whatever their religion or beliefs, whether academic study comes easily or whether learning is a struggle, whatever physical or mental abilities a teenager may have, whatever their family situation, whatever level of wealth, whatever sexuality or gender, there is room for every young person in our Catholic schools.

The wild beauty of life only becomes real within the diversity of our world. Yet the challenges against diversity come both from without and from within. In society, as in the Church, there are powerful voices who would exclude young people for one reason or another—they are pregnant, they are gay, they are trans, they are mentally ill, they are angry, they are poor, they are disabled. They are, in a word, insufficient.

Chaplaincy works against these voices. Christ is found here in the myriad faces and souls: in the anxious and the bold, in the athlete and the academic, in the Catholic and the atheist. Either we are all loved by God, or none of us is loved by God. If God is love, and God *is* love, then chaplaincy is about loving our way to God with all our young people. We do not crucify; we embrace.

I have lost count of how often in my fifteen years as chaplain a student has sat before me and said, "How do I tell my parents…that I'm gay…that I'm pregnant…that I'm failing…that I'm suspended." In that moment, the only response is presence. I do not know that it will be okay if they tell their parents. I do not know how difficult their journey will be. I do not care if they are in any way to blame for their situation. I can only assure them that I will be with them, and that God is always with them.

In high school chaplaincy, we look only for the possibility and potential in youth. The activities and the pastoral care we offer revolve around a welcome based on Christlike love, one that can use humor when appropriate, or compassionate words, or silence.

Chaplaincy provides a model of living together for teenagers to learn from. If we welcome, we hope they, too, will welcome. If we do not judge, we hope they, too, will not judge. If we are present, we hope they, too, will be present. If we love, we hope they, too, will love. And if we rely on Christ, we hope they, too, will someday rest in him.

The pastoral presence we provide in chaplaincy looks both to the here and now and to the future. Chaplaincy calls us to live as if the kingdom were already here, in the belief that if we live it ourselves, perhaps it will come sooner—at least for some of our youth. In our human frailty we do not manage to do it perfectly all the time, but this is our direction and our calling.

The blessings are many and the rewards abundant. Some are immediate, as when a teenager confides in a parent, fearful of rejection, and is gathered up instead in a warm and sustaining embrace. Some blessings are more long term, as when a message arrives from a student long graduated, just to say thank you. And some are eternal, as when that sense of God's presence envelopes and sustains because love is deep and strong and its own reward.

In the end, we pray to have the strength and wisdom to offer whatever pale model we can of what Christ has given us. In chaplaincy we strive for and desire to offer no less than the deepest gifts of the eternal: God's hospitality, God's embrace, and God's love.

PART FIVE

VOCATIONS TO RELIGIOUS LIFE

"And everyone who has left houses or brothers or sisters or father or mother or children or fields, for my name's sake, will receive a hundredfold, and will inherit eternal life."

(Matt 19:29)

From Knowledge and Power to Wisdom and Authority

Religious Vocation in the Life of the Church

Madeleine Fredell, OP

"Before I formed you in the womb I knew you, and before you were born I consecrated you; I appointed you a prophet to the nations" (Jer 1:5). The words of Jeremiah struck me like lightning. I was sitting with three sisters in the small oratory of the Dominican Sisters in a flat in one of the suburbs of Grenoble. It was the Feast of Mary Magdalene. I was looking into the life of a number of religious communities during my summer holidays. This was in 1976 and I felt the call to proclaim the gospel, to preach the word of the living God just as those three sisters did in this block of flats among immigrants and socially deprived people.

We shared biblical texts and prayed together. They took me to their different places of work and various church groups. They introduced me to a dialogue with Marxists (yes, they existed then!) and with Muslims. I was flabbergasted and knew that this was God's mysterious vocation for me.

It took four years before I was admitted into the community of Dominican Sisters in Sweden. I had to finish my university studies and to work and prove that I could support myself. Every romantic dream I might have had about religious life was destroyed during the initial formation period, the novitiate. We were not supposed to evangelize through a religious habit, but to mix with ordinary people. The purpose of the initial formation was to live as baptized among all men and women. A religious sister is not meant to be part of the hierarchy—any hierarchy, not just the ecclesial one. She is consecrated through her baptism, and that is something she shares with all baptized. She is in fact nothing special—a hard lesson to learn over a lifetime, and I shall come back to this later. We were taught that, through our lifestyle and attitude, we should arouse questions in others. Like every baptized person, we are called to be Christ, to represent Christ in everything we are and do toward everybody we meet. Nobody else can do this in another person's place; everyone is called to be Christ in a personal and unique way.

This emptying of the self takes place together with a number of other women who will call forth one's best sides as well as one's worst. They call each other out in mission, God's mission, and that could be anything. The worst mistake is to put the meaning in and of our lives in what we *do*, however good or successful it may be, and not in what we *are*.

I belong to what is called an apostolic congregation, which means that we do not live enclosed lives. Usually our living space is called a convent, literally meaning the place where we come together, where we live. The group of people living there forms a community, and together we share all aspects of life. My religious life is also colored by Dominican history and spirituality.

What holds a community together are the vows, traditionally the vows of obedience, chastity, and poverty. There are differences, however, between religious orders and congregations. Sometimes one of the three classical vows is emphasized in a special way, such as poverty for the Franciscans. Some take vows for life, others renew them on a regular basis. What matters is how we interpret them together as a community *and* on a personal level. They must be life-giving over decades and therefore their deeper meaning may change not only over time, but also for the individual sister or brother.

Obedience is certainly not what that word suggests—it is not about taking orders! If we don't pay attention to our own will, our own capacities, and our own strength or lack of it, we shall fail. We must know ourselves very well to be able to obey. The word comes from the Latin *oboedire*, which means "hear" and "listen to." We listen to God's voice in studying, interpreting, and sharing the biblical message in an intelligent way, but we also listen to God in our sisters and in ourselves. The big challenges in religious life usually come from inside ourselves rather than from superiors and whatever constitutions or rules we are following. Obedience is also the most important of the vows because it is the one that gives a deeper meaning to religious life.

The vow of celibacy is, of course, about living a celibate life but equally about accepting our sexuality and sexual orientation. Each sister must come to grips with herself, with her body, and how it functions. The vow is traditionally called chastity, a virtue to be practiced by all the baptized. It is about the humility to accept ourselves as the person we really are. That sounds great, but it is the most difficult challenge people have to struggle with. We must not compare ourselves with anybody else but *love* ourselves just as we are, with our limitations and capacities. Being chaste and humble is not about comparing oneself with others but about being happy with ourselves just as we are.

To live the vow of poverty is a bit of a scandal today. Religious sisters are generally not poor, although there are communities who literally live in poverty. Sociologically speaking, religious people will be taken care of by the institutional Church in one way or the other if they cannot provide for themselves. Therefore, they can rely on basic security for housing, food, and health care. Poverty in religious life is more about material simplicity. It is also a strong witness to society that I as an individual do not have free disposal over material goods, but that they are the common good of the whole community. The real poverty, though, is that one is quite alone as a sister or brother. We do not have intimate partners or children, we live at a distance from our families, and we have to struggle with the meaning of life in a lonely way. This leads me to what is crucial for a religious vocation in the Church today.

Unfortunately, many religious sisters have lost meaning in their lives. Why is this so? It usually happens later on, when religious life has become a routine—when we no longer marvel at anything. In such cases, a sister might know what she believes—the contents of Christianity, the dogmas and doctrine—but she no longer has faith. The deep meaning of life is gone. The tools for creating meaning in life are not always provided by the Church or by our different religious congregations, and still less in society as a whole. These tools show what religious life is about and the only real mission we are called to. Living a meaningful life is our one and only witness, and it is a witness of deep joy.

The first tool is that faith is about relationship to life itself, to our brothers and sisters and to a living and expanding God. We cannot base our adult faith on catechetical statements, dogmas, and doctrine. Life will change the contents of our faith in ways that may at times be at odds with the official doctrine of the Church. This is something we have to handle without being distressed and without thinking that we have "lost" our vocation. God is always calling us forward. It is painful to change and leave outdated beliefs behind, but we are never abandoned by the living God.

The second tool is that religious profession—especially the final one, which normally is for life—is the opposite of certainty. I remember the day before my final profession when my formator told me that making this step was like throwing oneself from the highest diving board into the void, not knowing if there was any water to receive one. Religious vocation is about uncertainty and expansion into the unknown and therefore about real faith. Not in our wildest imaginations can we plan our future religious lives. Of course, we do all kinds of planning to make life work on a practical level and in relation to others; however, if we strive for meaning in life, we have to relinquish control over the planning.

The third tool is something we forget more often than not. As religious we have to create occasions to marvel over life. Those called to parenthood are given this marveling in a natural way. Each child is a gift, a wonder, a person to learn to know more and more. The ability to wonder and marvel is fundamental for faith and meaning in life. How can this be fostered in religious life? I describe this as beauty and grace—grace in the sense that we learn to be present in our bodies and in the here and now. Grace can only be experienced if we are wholly there and aware of ourselves and fully open to otherness. It is a gift of God and we have to be open to receive it. Apostolic religious people are usually not very good at this. We are so preoccupied with work and—let's admit it, with success and even careerism—that we forget to enjoy grace, the moment free of charge. Some monasteries are known for their beauty and breathtaking surroundings. Some convents of apostolic religious sisters are equally known for their drab tastelessness, often in the name of poverty. This can be extremely harmful for faith.

The fourth tool to foster is curiosity in its deepest sense. Like parents playing with their children, we should play with everything that connects us to life itself. Many sisters are highly trained professionals, especially within medical care and education. They know a great deal within their own fields. During the spare time that has to be provided by every community, sisters should be encouraged to connect with new science, technology, the environment, history, politics, film, theater, dance—whatever puts us on a new track of life and awakens our curiosity. Then faith also becomes a joyful reality to explore from new and different perspectives.

But some might be asking, isn't religious life about prayer, sacraments, and a regular way of life? Obviously, every community needs some kind of structure and regularity for common prayer and the celebration of the Eucharist. A dangerous error, however, is to regard this as something we *do*, rather than what we *are*. The ecclesial sacraments are important, but it is also important to blend with God in God's living and creating Word. This encounter with God can be through marveling at God's presence in nature and meeting God there. It can be an encounter with God in dialogue, *through the word*, with our sisters, colleagues, friends, and everybody who is different from ourselves. Dialogue must be fostered from the first day of religious life.

Religious life is about *being* and not *doing*, even for apostolic sisters. At the same time, we should put our gifts and capacities at the service of humanity. Today, this has become extremely difficult and challenging in two ways. First, when we are working professionally in nonecclesial structures, we also have to live with a certain careerism and stress if we do not want to be separate and different from others. As a professional I have to do the best I can, which means I shall have to follow a certain career and experience stress, but I must not be enslaved by my work. I am a religious sister as some of my colleagues are parents, and we both have to cultivate these realities as well. It is religious life and parenthood that give most meaning to our lives, not first and foremost our professional careers.

The second challenge for many religious sisters is that many of us are working within ecclesial structures, close to the hierarchy. This is a mixed blessing! On the one hand, women want to share in decision-making in the Church and thereby risk a certain conformity to a not-so-healthy and sometimes rigid tradition and culture. On the other hand, if we place ourselves totally outside official ecclesial structures, we shall not be able to change the system itself.

Since the Second Vatican Council, there has been an emphasis on the prophetic calling of religious life. By the way we live, by our simplicity and openness we should point to a realized eschatology. Freedom, equality, democracy, and an almost naïve hospitality should characterize our communities. All people should trust us.

Why have I chosen religious life? The easy, and maybe only, answer is because it captivates me! What, then, is the ultimate purpose of religious life? My personal answer to this is to descend from the throne of power and ascend to the throne of wisdom. I hope that this short essay points toward what that means, even if I am far from having achieved it myself. The meaning of religious life is to go from knowledge and power to wisdom and authority. Once we have attained authority, we no longer need power. Authority means enabling others to grow in their vocations. It comes from the Latin *augere*, "to make something grow." Once we have attained wisdom, theories become one with real life.

I have held the hands of many aging and dying sisters. At the end, there is only one thing left, and that is true for every baptized person. It is to bring Christ's own words to life: "Very truly, I tell you, when you were younger, you used to fasten your own belt and to go wherever you wished. But when you grow old, you will stretch out your hands, and someone else will fasten a belt round you and take you where you do not wish to go" (John 21:18).

A Journey toward Wholeness

Sharing the Fullness of Life with Poor and Marginalized Women

Sister Mary Deepika, SND

My life, mission, and relationships as a religious are well described in the vision statement of the Sisters of Notre Dame: *"Trusting in God who makes all things new, we commit ourselves to live incarnational spirituality, grow in life-giving relationships, be one in diversity."*

My life has been shaped by a passage in the Bible from the Book of Jeremiah:

> My people do not be afraid; people of Israel, do not
> be terrified. I will rescue you from that faraway
> land, from the land where you are prisoners; you
> will come back home and live in peace; you will be
> secure. (Jer 30:10 GNT)

Fifteen years ago, I heard in these words God, my Creator, calling me to come home to myself, to be healed and live in peace. In my relationships and values I had wandered far from God. I experienced a sense of alienation from the Holy Spirit who offers true peace and love. Like the Samaritan woman, my jar was empty and I was seeking life-giving water. I heard the promise of God to rescue the people from distant lands in the context of my own life. I also heard it on behalf of a large number of women and girls who were prisoners in their own homes and villages, bereft of dignity and justice. I discerned that my vocation was to become an instrument in the hands of God so that I could share fullness of life with the marginalized and deprived people whose lives touched mine.

My transformation began when I worked with women from low castes in the villages in Bihar. They were illiterate agricultural laborers—physically, emotionally, and socially broken, abused and discriminated against by society. Most of the younger ones endured violence at the hands of their husbands or in-laws. The older ones experienced neglect and deprivation at the hands of their children. I was in charge of the Centre for Social Services, which had a program for the empowerment of women. Gradually over five years, the women were organized into self-help groups and were empowered socially, psychologically, and emotionally through personal contacts, family visits, training in awareness-raising and micro-finances. It was the custom that women were not known by their own names but only as somebody's wife or somebody's mother. Now, women began to write and claim their names. Women who had no money, despite having labored for nearly eighteen hours a day, started having bank savings. Women who never ventured out of their villages without male accompaniment began to go out alone. Women who had never had a voice in decision-making at home or in public began to attend local government meetings. They experienced new life and vigor. Within myself, too, I felt a sense of renewal and homecoming. I experienced freedom as the chains of prejudice, anger, and resentment slowly gave way to compassion, understanding, and cooperation.

The more I gave of my time, energy, and talents, the freer and more joyful my life became.

Another phase of my life was shared with adolescent girls at a vocational training center in Assam. The center provided training in employable skills for illiterate girls and built up their capacities for better living. Poor tribal families in interior villages could not send their children, especially the girls, to school. The girls spent their childhood doing household chores and helping with farming activities. When they reached puberty, early marriage prevented any further development.

I had to undertake tiring journeys through interior villages to convince parents and girls themselves to enroll at the center, where they could have residential training in catechism, functional literacy, tailoring, and weaving. At the end of a year of training, the girls who had come in with unkempt hair and shabby clothes became professional tailors and weavers. Their self-esteem increased and their leadership skills developed. They learned basic mathematics, health tips, and home management.

They used to compare their growth with that of the lotus. They had been living in ignorance and poverty, not realizing the immense potential hidden within them. The sunlight of basic education and capacity enhancement training helped them to bloom and recognize their worth. As each group of girls was liberated from the clutches of poverty, illiteracy, and low self-esteem, my life, too, was blessed with fruitfulness and love—the promise of the Lord. I grew close to the living God whose creative Spirit was alive in me, as every girl went away from our center feeling secure and confident of a dignified life.

My mission is carried out among the community of sisters with whom I live and work, and among whom I have experienced the hand of God rescuing me from many forms of imprisonment. Often when working in a team I have had to wriggle out of the prison of selfishness and ego-centeredness. I escaped the prison of fear and inhibition when I had to make daily decisions as a leader of the community.

Sharing the Eucharist every morning with the sisters and the wider community is a call for me to recognize the deeper reality that we are one, and to live the implications of that throughout each day, especially the giving and receiving of forgiveness. The process of homecoming to peace and security continues in me and in those with whom I live, as we continue to share our life with those on the margins of our society, especially the women.

New Beginnings and the Reconciling Love of God

Why We Need the Third Rite of the Sacrament of Reconciliation

Judith Barwick, LCM

Close to midnight one Christmas Eve some years ago in a hospital in Australia, Leila, a wife and the mother of two adult children, died after a long battle with cancer. On the same Christmas Eve close to midnight, in the same hospital, a healthy baby girl was born by emergency caesarean section. I was present for this birth and later encountered the family of the mother who had so recently entered eternal life.

The mystery of birth and death was never more poignant for me than on that Christmas night. In each case, there was a bringing to birth. A mother died and was born into eternal life, and a child was born into our world.

In birth and death, and in the dyings and risings of each day, we are faced with new beginnings.

In the beginning when God created the heavens and the earth, the earth was a formless void and darkness covered the face of the deep, while a wind from God swept over the face of the waters.

Then God said, "Let there be light"; and there was light. (Gen 1:1–3)

The Congregation of the Little Company of Mary to which I belong was founded by Venerable Mary Potter to pray with and for the suffering and dying people of our world. This includes a companioning of one another in the many dyings and risings of everyday life. In these shared experiences, we express our hope and trust that new beginnings will ultimately speak of resurrection and new life.

Each of us has our own stories of birth and death, of new beginnings and hopefully of resurrection as well. The death of Gwen, the mother of a Benedictine nun, is one of the stories I cherish.

Gwen was a long-term resident in an aged-care facility and a favorite with the staff because of her quick wit and tenacious spirit. Gwen died quietly in the early hours of a Sunday morning. I was with her when she died. When I telephoned Gwen's daughter Rachel to tell her about her mother's death, Rachel did not sound surprised. She had woken up just after midnight and sensed a need to go to the chapel, to light a candle in thanksgiving for the gift of her mother. Some weeks after her mother's death, Rachel wrote me a note that read,

> On the night of my mother's death the spirit of St. Benedict and the spirit of Mary Potter were at one…at one with Mary in Christ…as the Benedictines and the Little Company of Mary accompanied my mother on the final steps to her eternal union with her God.

Today, not everybody facing the death of a loved one feels as much a part of the community of the Church as

Rachel did, and many Catholics are estranged from the sacraments. How do we help such people to share our longing that we all will become "*at one with Mary in Christ*" by offering them a process of reconciliation that will offer them comfort during times of loss? As a people of God in the community of the universal Catholic Church, how are we really immersed in and responsive to the needs of others? The dyings are constantly before us, and people are crying out for compassion, reconciliation, and healing. Do our pastoral, prayerful, and sacramental practices reach out, touch, and heal in that freedom of the Spirit with which Jesus ministered? Do our pastoral, prayerful, and sacramental practices express the motherly love of God? God's maternal love enables us to move through fragility to strength, through searching to finding, through suffering to healing, and ultimately through death to new life. It invites an opening up to all generations, for every woman and man, every girl and boy, to seek and find fullness of life in God and in one another.

When present with others in the sacredness of new beginnings in birth and in death, I find myself more and more convinced of the importance of the third rite of the sacrament of reconciliation, when people come together as a community to confess and receive absolution. I experience a constant call of the Spirit telling me that, as a "Jesus people," as a Church that seeks to meet people where they are, we should recognize how effective this rite might be for those who experience the sacrament of reconciliation as a stumbling block in seeking to return to a parish community. These are people like Leila's family, experiencing overwhelming darkness as they grieved the loss of a wife, daughter, mother, and grandmother. As with many families, there were members who were struggling to see relevance in some sacramental aspects of church practice, yet at such times many Catholics estranged from the Church seek a parish community that would offer them support and strength.

The baby born on Christmas Eve was born into a family with a long tradition of Catholic parish life, but even so the younger generation was struggling to be part of a Catholic worshiping community. To them, the individual format of the sacrament of reconciliation seemed like a roadblock, a barrier. A community celebration of support through a third rite of the sacrament would be a healing gift for such people.

So many Catholics are walking away from the sacrament of reconciliation, with a gradually diminishing appreciation of the sacrament together with the loss of the grace-filled gifts it offers. This past year, many hundreds of people attended the Holy Week and Easter ceremonies in the parish I attended. In stark contrast, very few participated in the second rite of reconciliation in the preceding week. I strongly believe that Jesus would desire that people be regularly able to approach the sacrament with an ease made possible within the community setting of the third rite.

When I recall the regular availability of the third rite of the sacrament of reconciliation in the 1980s, it was the faith community's sharing of sorrow and forgiveness in silent presence and unity that I found so very healing. My commitment to express sorrow for sin and a renewed fidelity to the gospel was supported by the presence of those around me. The sacramental third rite is a most powerful experience and expression of community in Christ. Individual confession is always available for those who seek a more personal form of reconciliation, but I believe the Spirit of God is calling for the regular practice of the third rite.

May the spirit of all God's people and all creation seek to be "*at one with Mary in Christ*," in birth and in death, in our dyings and our risings. May we as a Catholic Church be enablers of reconciliation, of healing, and of hope. May we be able to find the opportunity for the third rite of reconciliation as a norm in our parishes and our local faith communities.

(For privacy reasons, the names of the people in these stories and the locations have been changed.)

I Came for the Sisters—and Stayed for the Sisterhood

Margaret Susan Thompson

My becoming Catholic is absolute proof of the existence of God—because it never would have been my idea! Indeed, why else would a feminist academic, raised in as secular a way as can be imagined, have taken the path I have? Even after more than thirty years, the whole business is a mystery to me. But what is more Catholic than mystery?

Both my parents were nonobservant Jews who raised me with a clear moral foundation and commitment to social justice that had no evident roots whatsoever in the divine. Two incidents reflect what that involved. The first happened when I was six, as my new stepfather was driving my mother and me from New York to what was to become our home in northern Florida. It was a hot August afternoon somewhere in Georgia or South Carolina, when he suddenly stopped the car alongside a huge cotton field. Asking me to get out, he told me to start picking. I looked at him in astonishment; my mother started to scream. After what seemed like hours (but was doubtless no more than ten minutes), my father called me over, gave me a big hug, and handed me a cold soda from our ice chest. "Some children, not much older than you, spend all their days picking crops in the fields," he said. "You need to know the kind of world you are moving to. You have to understand."

A year or so later, my mother and I were in a downtown department store, the only place in town where one could buy decent shoes and, more importantly, Brownie uniforms. I saw two water fountains side by side, one marked "white" and the other "colored." Trained well by my father, I deliberately went to the "colored" one and took a drink. The manager came over to me and, thinking that perhaps I couldn't read, drawled, "L'il girl, can't you see that you're drinking out of the colored fountain?" I responded, sweetly, "But, sir" (Southern children always said "sir" or "ma'am"), "the water looked clear to me!" Mother and I were told to leave the store and to never return.

So I developed a strong sense of social justice, participating in numerous civil rights demonstrations over the years—and never, despite peer pressure and even direct orders from teachers, standing for the Confederate anthem of "Dixie." But the pull of religion was less explicable, and obviously not a function of parental pressure. Yet it was always there, however inchoate. In retrospect, I always felt a conviction that God was very real and somehow knowable. What that might mean did not become clear until much later.

In fact, much like fundamentalists around whom I was raised, my own moment of (re)birth is both specific and very clear to me. So is my conviction that it came about not in spite of the fact that I am a feminist and an academic, but indisputably because I am those things.

The feminist academic in me began to teach American women's history, which in turn led a friend (not Catholic!) to suggest I include a lecture on nuns the next time I offered the course. Like a good historian, I went to the library, where I found exactly one book on the subject: Elinor Tong Dehey's *Women's Religious Orders in the United States* (1930): big, blue, and filled with florid and edifyingly pious prose about every one of the hundreds of communities located in the United States. I had never heard of most of them but, according to this tome, each seemed to have been founded by a zealous priest and four pious virgins—or a pious priest and four zealous virgins. Nonetheless, I was enthralled, and by the end of that weekend, my scholarly interests were redirected completely from legislative lobbyists to sisters. And so, although I was less aware of it at the time, was the personal and spiritual path that would focus the rest of my life.

It was through that research focus that I came to know the women who would change my actual and not just my academic life, including the sisters who helped guide my way to and through the worlds of both religious life and the Catholic Church. Some were archivists, many of them the first in their communities to attempt to organize their records for scholars like me. Some were the women, living and dead, who populated the congregations that I came to know through the records they left of their lives and that I came to know as well as the people around me. Not surprisingly, as a historian, the Communion of Saints was one of the easiest Catholic concepts for me to grasp and to embrace. Others were members of organizations of post–Vatican II sisters who sent me boxes of information about religious life in the modern world, and who helped me negotiate lingo and lifestyles that were at once foreign and oddly fascinating to me.

One of these sisters, the brilliant, dynamic, fierce, and prophetic Margaret Ellen Traxler, SSND, would become my godmother when I was baptized a little more than a year after this improbable journey began. Until her death in 2002, Margaret's wisdom, love, and sisterhood kept me grounded in ways I could not have anticipated being necessary when this journey began. "Never get distracted by all the Church's clerical garbage; never forget what is really important," she said on the evening before my baptism—and untold numbers of times thereafter. She showed me, by example more than through words, how someone could be both feminist and faithful, couRAGEous in the face of injustice and joyful despite all the obstacles that patriarchy allowed to clutter the way forward. She made me realize that it was among women like her that I felt most at home. Perhaps surprisingly, I never considered becoming a nun myself, though I did become an associate member of a congregation—the Immaculate Heart of Mary (IHM) Sisters of Monroe, Michigan—with whom I had worked as a consultant and historian.

But nuns have not been the only women in the Church with whom I've celebrated and bonded. As time went on, my circles of sisterhood expanded, and came to embrace not only those who were vowed religious, but also so many others in various "states of life" who continued (often only after mighty struggle) to call themselves Catholic—whatever that might mean to them.

These circles are concentric and intersecting, spanning women younger and older, married and single, straight and lesbian, and from countries and continents I know well or may never actually visit. They accept me as I accept them: flawed and flailing, and laboring and loving. Sometimes I am the lost one and they the guides, and sometimes the roles are reversed. We learn from one another and support one other, and sometimes annoy one other, but always care for one another—as *sisters* truly do. As an orphaned only child, no longer married and without offspring of my own, I know these women as friends and, indeed, as family. Because isn't that what sisters are all about?

PART SIX

VOCATIONS TO ORDINATION

"Mary Magdalene went and announced to the disciples, 'I have seen the Lord'; and she told them that he had said these things to her."

(John 20:18)

"Now it was Mary Magdalene, Joanna, Mary the mother of James, and the other women with them who told this to the apostles. But these words seemed to them an idle tale, and they did not believe them."

(Luke 24:10–11)

"I Am Called to Be Both Sister and Priest"

Melissa Carnall

The Community Calls Forth Love

While growing up, I never felt limited by my gender in the Church. I had to "finish" growing up before I experienced that. I was an altar server. I was a teen leader in our youth group. I led our Catholic Campus Ministry during college. I was the go-to for spiritual guidance and prayer in my full-time volunteer program after college. In graduate school at a Catholic seminary for my Master of Divinity degree, I cultivated community, led our student government, and was eventually chosen by my classmates to be the speaker at commencement. My varied communities continually called forth my gifts and encouraged me to use them. This changed, however, after graduation from divinity school.

While I sought employment at various ministries and parishes, my male seminarian classmates were ordained and subsequently placed in churches. As I began work at my new ministry in a parish, I felt pain that my previous experience had not prepared me for. My gender suddenly made a difference. It was only theoretical before. Now it became personal. I could no longer do the work I felt called to, the work for which I was equipped—with the right degree and the required gifts. Preparing couples for their child's baptism and then being unnecessary at the moment of signing their child from death to new life was unbearable. Walking with adults for months in RCIA and then "handing them over" to the priest for their sacraments was like being an aunt when you desire to be a mother and cannot be. Yearning to preach and continually being affirmed for my gift in that area (when I would share in approved settings like Evening Prayer— sometimes with only ten people present) felt and feels like a squandering of a gift that God has given me. It is the Church that holds back my offering, yet the Church calls it forth in me. I hear Love calling me through the people of God, the Body of Christ, and yet, my "yes" is thwarted by that same Body. My own body is not right for the job, I am told.

Falling in Love

"Nothing is more practical than finding God, that is, than falling in love in a quite absolute, final way…."

—attributed to Pedro Arrupe, SJ

I grew up in a nominally Catholic family. We went to church most Sundays, but faith was not an integral part of our life-style and family culture. Yet somehow, I became the one that "liked church," at least according to my older brothers. The Church intrigued me and spoke to a part of me that wasn't addressed elsewhere. Thankfully, I not only liked church as a human institution, I also fell in love with God, especially as my years in high school progressed. God became my main priority, and I tried to make my life decisions based on this ever-deepening relationship with God. I did not yet know the unexpected places this Love would lead me, nor the depth of the joy—and the pain—that would stem from trying to answer the call of Love in my life.

Called by Love

"I am your bridegroom. Marry me." What?? "I am your bridegroom. Marry me." In a sentence structure and word choice not my own, not yet eighteen years old, I heard this call from Christ while at daily Mass on a service trip with my youth group. Theologically, I no longer resonate with nuptial imagery as the only way to understand my call to be a Catholic sister and to live the vows of poverty, chastity, and obedience. And yet, this moment of clarity is one I held onto through years of vocational discernment. When we would discuss religious vocation in my Catholic campus ministry during university, my heart stirred and I could imagine nothing more than giving myself single-heartedly to God and neighbor. I knew exactly ZERO sisters growing up, and I grew up in an age when people thought being a sister was a thing of the past, so this calling seemed to have come out of left field. This moment of clarity was a stronghold amid the turmoil of discernment throughout college. It helped me to weather the challenges from some in my community of loved ones who didn't understand why I would still consider this calling as a valid way of life for a young, vibrant woman. It is, though, and it can be. God still calls people to live life in community, committed to simplicity and wholehearted listening to God, sustained by a deep prayer life. I say yes to this calling from my God, who is Love.

Love Lives into the Unknown

"No, I am not becoming a sister because I can't become a priest," I must clearly and continually respond to answer the question I am often asked. Although related ecclesial vocations, they are separate and different. I heard the sister calling more clearly first. The priest one was a slower realization. I am called to be both sister and priest, like my male friends in religious communities who are called to be brother and priest. The only difference is that I cannot answer my call in a straightforward way as they can because I am a woman. It hurts. And I dare to say it hurts the people of God. I know that my trust is in the One who loves me infinitely and intimately as I seek to live out what these callings mean. To be sister most commonly necessitates being Catholic. To be an ordained priest would necessitate disconnecting from this tradition I know and love dearly, a tradition that is part of my identity, and a huge part of cultivating my relationship with God.

I do not yet know what my life will look like as I seek to answer creatively these conflicting calls—conflicting only because I am a woman. I do know this: God is not daunted by the complexity of these calls. God is the one doing the calling. Love will see me through, even when the Church hurts me by celebrating one of my calls and dismissing the other.

"Who I Am Called to Be"

My Vocation to the Diaconate

Cynthia (Sam) M. Bowns

For many years, I have felt a strong calling to the permanent diaconate. As a young person of eleven, I was drawn to walk with Jesus in the Methodist faith tradition, but I fell in love with Catholicism as a mid-teen. My conversion to Catholicism took several decades as my family was firmly opposed to it. My Italian great-grandfather had died just before I was born, and a callous priest refused to say memorial Masses when his struggling immigrant family could no longer afford to pay the stipends. As a result, the family left the Catholic Church. When I finally converted in my mid-thirties, the family was fractured along religious fault lines for many years. The entire family has now returned to the Church, which is nothing short of a miracle, and is another story.

My Methodist husband was suspicious of Catholicism, but after my conversion he started attending Mass with me, mostly out of curiosity. He fell deeply in love with the Eucharist and slowly came to feel drawn toward becoming Catholic.

Several years after his conversion, a parishioner approached us after Mass and asked whether she could pray that we become a "diaconal couple." It had never occurred to either of us that we would be called to this ministry, but the Spirit had planted the seed, and this was affirmed by our priest and others around us as time went on. During my husband's formation, a deep realization formed within me that this vocation to the diaconate had been with me all my life. I was absolutely sure beyond all doubt that I was called to be a deacon as well.

This recognition of what I saw as my vocation awakened a great sense of joy, but that was quickly replaced by a deep-seated pain that has remained with me. Initially, having come from a faith tradition that does ordain women, it did not occur to me that women could not be ordained to this service. While I am overjoyed for my husband that he can share his personal giftedness with others in the formal ministerial role of deacon, I also experience a strong sense of hurt, anger, and jealousy that has often overshadowed the joy that I have for his vocation, which I believe is my vocation as well.

I have wanted to journey with people in the same way that my husband does, and I take every opportunity that the Spirit gives me to minister as deacon to others. This mutual ministry—with its sense of complementariness in what we can offer—has given us some of the greatest moments in our marriage. I believe that this mutuality is reflected in the fact that many in our parish think of me as a deacon and call me such. I have finally stopped correcting them. If they see and feel this in me, I believe that this is the Spirit's way of affirming my vocation, even if it is not formalized through the laying on of hands by the bishop.

Some years ago, a dear priest who was our pastor and mutual mentor encouraged me to acquire my own credentials. He saw the deacon in me and thought I needed to cultivate my own authority since I could not be ordained as my husband had been. Thanks to his mentoring and support, I spent the next few years studying for a master of divinity degree and qualifying as a spiritual director. He was right: these qualifications have opened opportunities for me that otherwise would not have been available to a laywoman without training, but it still is not the same as ordination, and our wise priest knew this. He gave me the greatest affirmation of who I am called to be by having me anoint him on his deathbed, asking the priest to hand me the chrism. I was humbled and affirmed by this parting gift. I have grown in the conviction that women as well as men are called to this sacred form of ministry, as were our foremothers and fathers in faith.

I have taken the joy and the pain that my experience and vocation have given me and put them in the service of educating men and women on the role that women played in this ancient ministry that was revived by the Second Vatican Council. I advocate for and encourage other women who know in their souls that they are called to the ministry of deacon. My joint ministry with my husband has assured me that there is a great desire in the Church to have men and women, side by side, labor in the vineyards of the Lord. The need is great. When will we see that there is wisdom in using the gifts of the many, rather than the few?

Stories of Hurt and Hope

Women Called to Priesthood

Celia Viggo Wexler

As a young teen, I felt a vague and fleeting call to religious life. I admired many of the women religious who were my teachers at Our Lady of Mercy High School in Brighton, a suburb of Rochester, New York, where I grew up.

But a vocation to the priesthood? That never occurred to me. Priest meant one thing to me—a man wearing vestments, standing before the altar. Yes, I was aware of the movement to ordain women to the priesthood. I certainly did not oppose that, but it did not touch me personally. Compared to the Church's raging misogyny on so many other issues, particularly the reproductive rights of women, the ordination issue seemed less important.

My narrow vision of the issue really did not change until 2012, when I began writing my book *Catholic Women Confront Their Church: Stories of Hurt and Hope.*[1] I wrote the book because I was at a crossroads. I was a cradle Catholic and a professional in the world, married and a mother, but I was demoralized by an institutional Church that neither understood nor respected me. I did not know whether I could continue to be both a practicing Catholic and a feminist. To answer that question, I sought out exceptional Catholic feminists. I found nine extraordinary Catholic women who shared their wisdom and their lives with me. Their stories rocked my insulated Catholic world.

In my quest, I was not looking for feminists who felt a calling to the priesthood, but I soon encountered them. They changed my vision of what "priesthood" ought to mean, and why the Church's resistance to women priests was so damaging not only to them personally but to the institution itself.

To be told repeatedly by the Church, even by progressive Pope Francis, that women can never be ordained to the priesthood, is more than a blow to our egos. This rebuke reminds us that Catholicism continues to perceive us as inferior goods, not really worthy of God's love and acceptance. As millennial blogger and Catholic feminist Tinamarie Stolz recently observed, "As a woman, I could be like Jesus, but not like Jesus enough...to bless the most stable and precious thing I knew—the Eucharist. Theologically, this did not make sense, and spiritually it crushed me, as I felt a strong call to ministry."[2] I have now come to believe that ordination must be every Catholic feminist's issue because it is the central obstacle to the Church actually viewing us as fully human and worthy of full citizenship in the kingdom of God.

I had sought out Marianne Duddy-Burke, the executive director of DignityUSA, because of her full-throated advocacy for LGBT Catholics. Duddy-Burke realized she was a lesbian during her sophomore year at college, but her commitment to Catholicism and desire to be a priest had been part of her character since childhood.

"I felt deeply called to be a priest," she told me. "I used to pray Mass in our backyard and play confession with all the neighborhood kids," she added. She took communion to the sick, bandaged up her pets as surrogates for patients, and dispensed Necco wafers as hosts. When a pet died, she officiated at the funeral service.

This calling took hold when she was about seven, but it did not go away. As she grew older, she believed that the rules on ordination would change. Duddy-Burke was born in 1960 and grew up with a Catholicism directly touched by Vatican II. It was a time of hope for the Church, she recalled. "All kinds of things were changing." Women religious were no longer consigned to teaching and nursing. "They were involved in politics and antipoverty work and housing rights. Of course, women could be priests."

She had seen evidence of those changes in her own life. When she was in third grade, denied the opportunity to be an altar server, she was chosen to be a lector, the youngest in her parish to be selected. When she went to an all-girls' Catholic high school, her constant presence at daily Mass led the nuns to deputize her to help the aged and blind priest who officiated. "It was amazing to be right up there in the inner sanctum with the priest and know all the words and all the gestures," Duddy-Burke said. It felt like "another step" on the way to fulfilling her dream.

She did her graduate work in theology at a Jesuit Catholic seminary. "I knew at this point I couldn't go in saying I wanted to be a priest," Duddy-Burke said. "I just talked about being called to ministry." She thought she could at least partially realize her dream through work as a hospital or college chaplain, but as a gay woman in a relationship, she was denied that outlet.

The loss of the priesthood was all the more acute because her colleagues at school were seminarians. She remembers watching those seminarians, now ordained, presiding at Mass and herself sobbing week after week. "Seeing a priest up there on the altar doing what I knew I was totally capable of, but knowing that I would never have that status was excruciating."

Theologian Teresa Delgado also felt called to the priesthood. "My older sister was very clear about wanting to be

a doctor," Delgado recalled. "She knew that from the min-
ute she was taking apart our Beanie Babies and doing surgery on them." Delgado, too, had this sense of vocation. She
pretended to officiate at Mass, dragooning her sisters to be
members of her congregation. Even before she could read,
she said, she had memorized the words of the Mass. She had
watched her father bring communion to her homebound
grandmother. When her father learned that she "said" Mass
in the basement, he gently dissuaded her from pretending,
telling her that only men could be priests. Her immediate
reaction? She had a tantrum and ran away from home.

The call Delgado felt did not disappear. As a teen, she
would challenge her parish priest about the ban on the ordination of women. "We would go back and forth on this question, and I never felt his responses were satisfactory," she
recalled. During her graduate studies in theology at Union
Theological Seminary in New York City, Delgado seriously
thought about leaving Catholicism to pursue the ministry. "I
did consider the Episcopal ordination track," Delgado said.
"I really did pray about it." In the end, she opted to remain a
Catholic, believing that "any hope for change" in the institutional Church must be driven by critiques from within.

Both Duddy-Burke and Delgado would have made exem-
plary priests. They now believe that the Church must change
more fundamentally, embracing a far more inclusive vision
of priesthood. They and many other Catholic feminists contend that the Church must forsake a narrow vision of priest
based on a patriarchal understanding of top-down power, a
model that puts a man in charge. I, too, have come to believe
that the Mass is not a one-man play, that Christ's presence
in the Eucharist is not an interaction solely between a male
priest and divinity. The people of God who worship at Mass
are concelebrants. We are not mute witnesses to a miracle;
we participate in the miracle.

The institutional Church is flawed, like all human constructs, but it is capable of change. If change is to come, women—among Catholicism's most faithful adherents—will lead the way.

Notes

1. Celia Viggo Wexler, *Catholic Women Confront Their Church: Stories of Hurt and Hope* (Lanham, MD: Rowman & Littlefield, 2016).

2. Tinamarie Stolz, "Handmade by God," Global Sisters Report, August 2, 2017, http://globalsistersreport.org/blog/gsr -today/equality/handmade-god-48341.

Women's Ordination to the Priesthood

From Rejection to Vocation

Colette Joyce

The older I get and the more funerals I attend, the more I wonder what my own funeral will be like. As a cradle Catholic and employee of the Church for many years, I know a lot of priests and deacons, even a few bishops, and I count many good friends among them. My hope is that, when I eventually pass on to my heavenly home, my funeral will be a Catholic Mass and those male friends who survive me will come along to my final rites. However, as a woman who has advocated and prayed for many years for the ordination of women, I can't think of a worse tribute to my life and work than for my coffin to be surrounded by a sanctuary full of men. Could it possibly be different by the time my turn comes around? Will male and female priests and deacons celebrate my funeral together? I really wish it could be so!

The question of why Catholic men are priests, yet Catholic women are not, struck me at an impressionable age. I was sixteen when a non-Christian friend of the family asked me if I thought women should be priests. My answer was a very shocked, "No!" However, both the question and my reaction nagged at me, and I began to give it more serious consideration. I was surprised by how appalled I was by the idea of a woman at the altar. Where did that thought come from? I was a lector myself already by that time, and I loved giving this service in the Church, proclaiming God's Word from the Old and New Testaments. I wanted to spend a lifetime devoted to God. I used to listen carefully to what the priest said and make up sermons in my head, thinking about what I would say if I were in his position. I loved the Mass and concentrated intensely during the consecration of the Eucharist. Every moment of it mattered to me, and I was just beginning to discover that I also loved helping other people, that I even had some leadership qualities that helped groups around me to grow. All these things were starting to suggest to me that I might have a vocation to priestly service except one—I was not a man. This idea of a vocation alarmed me. There followed six years of internal conflict. Why was priesthood an awful thing for a woman to contemplate for herself, and why did I not want to see other women in that role? Why could I not consider priesthood for myself?

At an intellectual level, I began to find some answers. There were two thousand years of history to consider. There was a theological tradition that had always emphasized the significance of the male priest and the male Jesus. I discovered feminism and realized there was a more sinister history of actual suppression of women, and that discrimination against them had restricted their access to the universities and professions. A theology of women as inferior to men, moreover, had been upheld over centuries. I went to university when I was eighteen to do a degree in theology and English, so it took a while to register the significance of traditional views of women. It was only at the end of my studies that I realized I had not read one book or article by a woman in my theology course. All the feminism I had acquired had come from the literary side of my studies. Now I really began to ask serious questions, questions other women and men were also asking, as feminist theology appeared and discussion groups around me began to debate the issue.

At the same time, the background nagging that had begun when I was sixteen became a very loud banging on the door by God. In 1992, I went to India for four months to explore my vocation. After an eight-day retreat at a Jesuit center in Goa, I faced, at last, the inescapable conclusion that I was being called to ordination myself. That call has never gone away.

People have said to me over and over again when I tell them my story that there are plenty of other things women can do in the Church. I know—I have done most of them! I am a lector, a eucharistic minister, a catechist, a church musician. I have run a church refugee center, served on a justice and peace commission, volunteered with the homeless, and promoted good employment practice in faith groups as a trade union representative. I am employed by my diocese as a pastoral assistant in a parish. If women are never ordained in the Catholic Church, it will not affect my willingness and commitment to serve in whatever capacity is open to me. I cannot help wondering, though, if my sense of calling is there for a reason. What if God is asking us, as a whole Church, to listen anew and realize how our history has affected our ability to see the person of Christ in the faces of women? What if the young women and young men of tomorrow have the vocations to serve together in the churches of tomorrow in ordained as well as lay roles? What if we could see this happen by the time of my funeral?

The commission set up by Pope Francis to explore the history and purpose of women in the diaconate has given me great hope that a new conversation is beginning and is possible. Can we continue it?

The Taboo of
Women's Ordination

Kate McElwee

One way to advocate for women's empowerment is to claim that it is not about women priests. The big tent of *women's leadership* is a rallying point for secular feminists, Church reform organizations, and even forward-thinking members of the clergy. All acknowledge that there is great room for improvement in this area. But authority in the Roman Catholic Church is linked to ordination, and it is this that excludes women from leadership and decision-making roles. The stained glass ceiling remains low, since all women in these imagined leadership roles will still report to their ordained male superiors. Hierarchies and systems of subordination are replicated around the world and endorsed by the unmatched political, moral, and spiritual influence of the Catholic Church. Setting aside the question of ordination might seem like a tactical move, but it preserves the roots of oppression and prevents women's gifts from being shared.

The institutional Church still regards it as taboo that women and girls are called by God to be priests, that God is speaking to and through women's bodies and women are listening. Vocal women with a vocation are dismissed as power hungry, delusional, crazy. One of the early projects of members of the Women's Ordination Conference was to publicize

the results of a psychological analysis of women who experienced a vocation to the priesthood. (They passed.)[1]

The inability to believe what women say is one of the
trademarks of any unchecked patriarchy. We know this in
cases of sexual assault, rape, and violence against women:
the structures are in place to silence the voices of women.
Social and cultural pressure, shame, and fear work alongside a legal system that simply does not grant women equal
rights. In our Church, silence is enforced on a papal level
and upheld by bishops' conferences and priests around the
world, eliminating any opportunity for discussion or dialogue.

This is a painful story. The Church has lost generations
of talent and passion by closing its doors to women's priestly
vocations. The Church's credibility as an institution that can
effectively work for justice or peace, or accompany Catholics in their family or sexual lives, is lost because women are
absent from informing policies and serving in positions of
leadership. This exclusion keeps our Church from wholeness
and violates the integrity of all of its members by limiting
opportunities to embrace God's gifts and live authentically
in the gospel.

Part of the solution is to trust women. Trust women
to make decisions about their lives, trust women to have a
relationship with God, and trust women when they share
their stories. Catholic women who experience a vocation to
priesthood cope with an intimate struggle. Some women live
their ministry in pastoral and creative ways, finding peace
and validation in community-supported "calling forth" ceremonies or parallel ordinations. Some transform liturgy and
ritual into a feminist experience, modeling a discipleship
of equals. A lot of women leave, dedicating their gifts to a
different faith community that celebrates and values them.
These women are not victims. Resilient, persistent, and

faithful women cope and take great risks to answer their call because our discipleship is at stake.

Another part of the solution is to know women. Pope Francis encourages a culture of encounter and accompaniment. How can our Church pastorally accompany women who experience a vocation to the priesthood? How can this relationship become a journey for our Church? In listening to women, one can more closely know God's limitless and transformative love. The story of a woman called is a hope for a better world and a prayer for a better Church. Members of the hierarchy need to challenge themselves to build relationships with women and those communities on the margins of society who pursue and live out what they are told is impossible.

When our global Church prays for vocations, pray for the resilient women whose truths change the world and crumble patriarchal structures. Pray that our Church leaders open their hearts to trust and come to know women as partners in faith. Pray for those who are nourished by women prophetically living their vocations in the world. Pray for the voices that break the silence.

Notes

1. See Fran Ferder, *Called to Break Bread? A Psychological Investigation of 100 Women Who Feel Called to Priesthood in the Catholic Church* (Mt. Rainer, MD: Quixote Center, University of Michigan, 1978).

Musings in an Art Gallery

Responsibility, Freedom, and Choice

Sheila Peiffer

Recently, a visit to a small regional art museum near my home prompted an unforeseen meditation on choice, feminism, and gender equality in the Catholic Church.

Eastman Johnson's *Hollyhocks* (1876)[1] shows a number of women gathering blossoms from towering hollyhock stalks, within the confines of high brick walls on all sides. The label explains,

> The theme of the enclosed garden (*hortus conclusus*) is associated with the Virgin Mary in Medieval and Renaissance poetry…and the colorful flowers symbolize abundance and fertility. The activity of picking flowers is a metaphor for the choices the young women will soon face in their domestic lives.[2]

What may have passed for a charming genre painting has become—for me—fraught with implications beyond its slight stature in the world of art.

Many of us raised in the pre–Vatican II Church will be familiar with the *hortus conclusus*, if not by this name, then certainly in the concept of the perpetual virginity of Mary and her "walled-off" womb. The walled garden was initially developed as part of Annunciation settings by medieval and Renaissance painters, although it later evolved into more of a "holy conversation" setting with Mary seated in the garden with various saints, angels, and patrons surrounding her in the controlled and safe space, which may also have included other symbolic features such as fountains, towers, and even the occasional unicorn. The original reference comes from the Song of Songs 4:12, "A garden locked is my sister, my bride, a garden locked, a fountain sealed."

As I gazed at the colorful array of hollyhocks and the young women, I was reminded of another kind of "walled garden" that still exists in the contemporary world, even if we no longer meditate on virgins surrounded by saints and uni-corns. We are often told that women are being (choose your adjective) silly, unreasonable, heretical, to expect equality of opportunity in the Catholic Church. Why should women insist on ordination when they have so many other "blooms" to pick? Indeed, there is often opposition to women's ordina-tion from women themselves who claim that they have all the opportunities they want in the diverse ministries that *are* open to women. But does this kind of internalized misogyny stem from having only known the walled garden? If you are told that you have "choice," but your choice is limited to a particular area in which only hollyhocks grow, do you even realize that you are missing the wild trillium or the tender violet that flourishes beyond the walls built for containment?

At a panel discussion in early 2017, "Catholic Feminists at the UN: Working toward Women's Equality," it was instruc-tive to hear a group of young women protest that they felt completely satisfied by the opportunities presently afforded within the "walls" of the institutional Catholic Church. In this global organization of 1.2 billion people, access to leadership, autonomy, and often even education and healthcare are reserved for and controlled by a cadre of men—yet some women still feel grateful to be able to choose a hollyhock.

As the Church prepared for the 2018 Synod on "Youth, Faith and Vocational Discernment," questionnaires and letters poured into Rome in response to the preparatory document.[3] How many will take note of the document's statement that "promoting truly free and responsible choices, *fully removed from practices of the past*, remains the goal of every serious pastoral vocation programme" (II 2, emphasis added)? Will the Church hierarchy see that women do not have a full range of "truly free and responsible choices"?

The document goes on to assert that "discernment is the main tool which permits safeguarding the inviolable place of conscience, without pretending to replace it" (II 2).

When will all the many young women whose consciences lead them to yearn for full equality in the Church be able to claim their place in the ecclesial community? When will half the Catholics in the world have a choice beyond the color of their hollyhock?

Notes

1. See http://www.nbmaa.org/original-site-assets/timeline_highlights/essays/johnson.html (accessed July 10, 2018).

2. New Britain Museum of American Art staff.

3. See Synod of Bishops, XV Ordinary General Assembly, "Young People, the Faith and Vocational Discernment: Preparatory Document," January 13, 2017, http://www.vatican.va/roman_curia/synod/documents/rc_synod_doc_20170113_documento-preparatorio-xv_en.html.

Part Seven

ECOLOGICAL VOCATIONS

"Who then is this, that he commands even the winds and the water, and they obey him?"

(Luke 8:25)

Laudato Si', Veganism, and the Interconnectedness of All Things

Melanie Newbould

> *"Living our vocation to be protectors of God's handiwork is essential to a life of virtue; it is not an optional or a secondary aspect of our Christian experience."*
>
> (*LS* 217)

In *Laudato Si'*, Pope Francis tells us that it is important for all of us to try to work toward a new lifestyle in which we all care for our common home, the Earth (*LS* 203). He writes that Christians who fail to take environmental concerns seriously require "an 'ecological conversion' whereby the effects of their encounter with Jesus Christ become evident in their relationship with the world around them" (*LS* 217).

It is sometimes argued that individuals are powerless to do anything to help to counteract environmental degradation, climate catastrophe, and the lives of those in geographical regions remote from us, but acknowledgment of the interconnectedness of the whole of creation makes it clear that individual lifestyle choices may have profoundly positive effects. This conviction fits in with Pope Francis's idea of an "integral ecology" (*LS* 138–59), which has been described as "an awareness and way of acting based on the truth of our ecological interconnections with the rest of creation."[1] He writes, "An integral ecology is also made up of simple daily gestures which break with the logic of violence, exploitation and selfishness" (*LS* 230).

For me, these simple daily actions start with considering what I eat. Just mentioning some of the effects of this lifestyle choice and how my choice affects the whole planet serves to illustrate the interconnectedness of all things, emphasized throughout *Laudato Si'*. My eating habits, in particular, have consequences.

Veganism[2] is a philosophy of life in which the individual seeks to avoid the use of animal products. In dietary terms this means avoiding food that contains meat, fish, dairy, eggs, or honey. Vegans also try to avoid using animal products or products that involve some form of animal exploitation in cosmetics, clothing, furniture, and any other aspect of life—as far as one can. Very few of us are perfect vegans. Basically, we try to live in accordance with the philosophy as far as we can while knowing that we sometimes fail.

I became vegan some years ago, before the publication of *Laudato Si'*. For me, the encyclical reinforces and clarifies the reasoning behind my choice. Veganism is a way of trying to live in this world, accepting the interconnectedness of things and attempting to minimize adverse effects. It is an important aspect of my Christian and Catholic faith.

Why, generally, does anyone choose to be vegan? The most obvious reason is the wish to avoid exploitation of animals and to exhibit, as far as possible, compassion for the whole of the planet—all humans and all other animals. Implicit in the philosophy underpinning veganism is that humans are animals and, therefore, we share much with other animals, including many aspects of our genetics, physiology, and anatomy. In *Laudato Si'*, Pope Francis speaks out against "tyrannical anthropocentrism" (*LS* 68). For people like me, this means that we should avoid eating animals. However, many do not share this opinion, and approximately 60 billion land animals and over a trillion marine creatures are killed annually for human food.[3] Though vegetarians hold many of the same beliefs as vegans, they consume dairy products and eggs. Unfortunately, both of these industries involve large-scale slaughter. Many male calves (apart from those used to produce veal) and male chicks are killed in the first few days of life.

While it might, in theory, be possible to farm in a way that minimizes animal suffering, this is not the world in which we live. Both the *Catechism of the Catholic Church* (*CCC* 2418) and *Laudato Si'* (*LS* 130) emphasize that we should be kind toward animals.[4] For me, and for other vegans, it is impossible to be kind to animals if we collude in farming as it is currently practiced.

There are other reasons why we might wish to refrain from using animal products, and these are entirely in line with the points of view put forward in *Laudato Si'*. For example, throughout the encyclical, the importance of the availability of fresh drinking water for all is emphasized (*LS* 27, 30, 164). Farming consumes about 70 percent of the world's accessible fresh water, much of which is used to irrigate land on which crops are grown. A high proportion of such crops are used as animal fodder rather than for direct human consumption.

Land usage is also much greater for meat production than that required to produce an equivalent plant-based diet. The land needed for a varied vegan diet is about a third of that required for the equivalent meat-based diet.[5] The use of land for the production of meat has led to the destruction of many important natural habitats. For example, large areas of the

Central and South American rain forest have been lost to make way for cattle farming, in order to supply cheap beef to North America, China, and Russia. In *Laudato Si'*, Pope Francis laments the destruction of large tracts of the planet such as the Amazon and Congo basins, which he describes as "the richly biodiverse lungs of our planet" (*LS* 38).

How do our dietary choices affect climate change? Different foods carry different implications with regard to greenhouse gas emissions in their production or cultivation and other aspects of the journey to the consumer. If one looks at protein-rich foods, greenhouse gas emissions for beef, cheese, and pork are very high, in comparison to those for legumes, poultry, and eggs.[6] Fruit and vegetables carry the lowest emissions (unless they are transported by air, emphasizing the rationale for trying to eat locally produced seasonal food wherever possible).[7] Some people reading this may decide that they can negotiate many of the environmental pitfalls by choosing nonvegan or even nonvegetarian food and this is entirely possible, particularly when small-scale local organic farms are involved. However, in the context of modern commercial farming, I (and many others) prefer not to condone current methods of animal husbandry and slaughter.

Climate change is predicted to have a major effect on human geography. It increases the probability of extreme weather events[8] and is likely to affect the poor in the global South disproportionately (*LS* 25). Changing climate is predicted to lead to destruction and loss of natural reserves and forests, loss of fisheries and agricultural land, sea level rises and flooding, fires, and an increased risk of disease.[9] Because of these factors, food, water, and housing will be increasingly scarce. The Intergovernmental Panel on Climate Change (IPCC) has stated that there will be a greater likelihood of civil war and other conflicts.[10] Economic migration and displacement of population (and the exploitation and danger that this may involve) may increase. These mobile populations are not always recognized as refugees (*LS* 25). The IPCC points out that those disadvantaged by society are those most also disadvantaged by the effects of climate change. Women, children, and indigenous people are most affected.[11] Therefore, our lifestyle choices are particularly likely to impact the lives of women and their children living in poverty in the global South.

In chapter 5 of *Laudato Si'*, Pope Francis emphasizes how the triune God is present in every aspect of the universe in the form of the Creator, the created, and the bond of love that unites all. The Eucharist is the expression of the unity of all things: "The Eucharist joins heaven and earth; it embraces and penetrates all creation." It is "a source of light and motivation for our concerns for the environment, directing us to be stewards of all creation" (*LS* 236). Just brief consideration of the effects of an individual's food choices illustrates the truth of this. How can we not respond to the call to care for all creation?

Notes

1. Daniel R. DiLeo, "Creation Care through Consumption and Life Choices," in *The Theological and Ecological Vision of Laudato Si': Everything Is Connected*, ed. Vincent J. Miller (London: Bloomsbury, 2015), chap. 12.

2. The word *vegan* was coined in 1944 by Donald Watson, who founded the Vegan Society, accessed July 10, 2018, https://www.vegansociety.com/about-us/history.

3. See "Compassion for Animals—Being Vegan Is the Logical Next Step," accessed July 10, 2018, https://www.vegansociety.com/sites/default/files/CompassionForAnimalsedited.pdf.

4. The *Catechism* does suggest that it is legitimate to use animals for food or clothing (§2417) and also for medical or scientific experimentation.

5. See https://www.vegansociety.com/resources/environment/food-security.

6. Annika Carlsson-Kanyama and Alejandro D Gonzalez, "Potential Contributions of Food Consumption Patterns to Climate Change," *American Journal of Clinical Nutrition* 89, no. 26 (2009): 1704S–1749S.

7. Carlsson-Kanyama and Gonzalez, "Potential Contributions of Food Consumption Patterns to Climate Change."

8. Cynthia Rosenzweig, Ana Iglesius, X. B. Yang, Paul R. Epstein, and Eric Chivian, "Climate Change and Extreme Weather Events—Implications for Food Production, Plant Diseases and Pests," NASA publications, 2001, http://digitalcommons.unl.edu/cgi/viewcontent.cgi?article=1023&context=nasapub.

9. Intergovernmental Panel on Climate Change (IPCC), "2014: Summary for Policymakers," in *Climate Change 2014: Impacts, Adaptation and Vulnerability*, ed. C.B. Field et al. (Cambridge: Cambridge University Press, 2014), 17, https://www.ipcc.ch/pdf/assessment-report/ar5/wg2/ar5_wgII_spm_en.pdf.

10. IPCC, "2014: Summary for Policymakers," 20.

11. IPCC, "2014: Livelihoods and Poverty," in *Climate Change 2014: Impacts, Adaptation and Vulnerability*, ed. C.B. Field et al. (Cambridge: Cambridge University Press, 2014), 797, 799, 800, 802, http://www.ipcc.ch/pdf/assessment-report/ar5/wg2/WGIIAR5-Chap13_FINAL.pdf.

Faith and Nature

Would Jesus Weep for an Eider Duck?

Mary Colwell

In my experience, the Holy Spirit can be compared to a mountain path in mist. The way ahead appears and then disappears, seemingly at random. Sometimes the track is obvious for miles into the distance; at others it is only possible to take one step forward, and hurriedly, before the view is obliterated. If you have ever been caught out on a mountain in low cloud you will know how disconcerting a whiteout can be, and how elating it is when all becomes clear again and the view spreads out before you in breathtaking beauty.

My environmental journey is a mountain trek, but unlike a real mountain, which has a summit to reach and a route back down again, this path seems to wind its way through ever higher ranges that are evermore mysterious—but every step of the way is worth it.

A few years ago, I left work one lunchtime and went to Clifton Cathedral in Bristol to spend some quiet time alone. Suddenly, it was as though the richly colored stained glass windows had melted away and the view outside became crystal clear. I felt that I could see the whole world. Every leaf was shining and every blade of grass was a brilliant green. The flowers were blooming and gently swaying in a wind

305

that was not just blowing but dancing. The music of the birds was clear and bright. I was overcome with a sense of love for this astonishing planet we live on, but at the same time a deep feeling of dread spread throughout my body. The same words kept reverberating in my head: "Is it too late? Is it too late to do something?" I was acutely aware of the destruction taking place throughout the earth, and that doing nothing to help was not an option, but I had no idea what that something was. The instruction was clear, though. For those few moments, the mist had cleared and a path revealed itself that was impossible to ignore—but where was it leading? I did not know but so wanted to find out. All too soon the mist closed in again and the view was lost. The brightness of the vision faded to normality. But I knew the path was there.

I had long been aware that the Catholic Church has spiritual, social, and political influence around the world, that it touches the hearts and motivations of people in almost all countries on earth, and teaches that God is the Creator of the universe. I thought, naïvely, that engaging it in the plight of the world would be straightforward. What is there not to understand about the importance of the richness and variety of life that lives alongside us, "the teeming heart of natural families," to quote Thomas Merton? Why is it hard to appreciate that the integrity of landscapes upon which we all depend—the soils, water catchments, oceans, rivers, and forests—is paramount to our health and well-being? But it wasn't, and still isn't, easy to persuade the Catholic Church to take the conservation of nature seriously. I wonder why. Perhaps one story helps to explain it.

When making a Natural World television documentary, I went to the North Slope of Alaska, about as far north as it is possible to go in North America. I was filming a magnificent bird called a spectacled eider. These ducks live above the Arctic Circle and have very little to do with humans.

We don't eat their meat or eggs, or use their feathers. They live wild lives in remote places where we find it hard to survive. I filmed one of four nests on an island in the middle of an estuary and watched the ducklings waddle down to the edge of the water, led by their mother. They were little more than downy feathers with feet, tiny balls of fluff in a bitingly cold tundra landscape. They bobbed away on the waves of the Arctic Ocean, and I still have no idea how such fragile creatures can withstand the polar extremes. It was a life-changing moment.

A year later, I called the man who had been my field guide and asked him how the birds were doing. He delivered a blow. All four nests on the island had been destroyed and the females shot as they incubated their eggs. Hunters had been through this isolated stretch of river and found good sport. I put the phone down and I wept and I raged—railing against the stupidity, the hard-heartedness, the coldness of humanity.

What would Jesus have done, I wonder, if he had found those nests with the bodies of the ducks, limp and lifeless on cooling eggs? Would he have wept too? Or perhaps this world is just for us and we have the mandate to use it as we see fit. After all, no one will die if spectacled eiders disappear. No one will lose their jobs or become ill. This is not a bird that adds to the bottom line of anyone's financial spreadsheet. It is just a wild duck—that is all—albeit an endangered one.

I asked the Jesus question to a number of Catholic clerics. No one thought Jesus would weep over a duck. Over the selfishness of the humans who killed them, yes, but not the loss of ducks themselves. One said, "Christ would not weep over that which is not human." And therein, I think, lies the problem. Over the centuries Catholicism has become a human-centered faith that has largely lost its connection to the grit and the dirt of the world. It is no longer visceral and inspired by the power of a living, breathing, singing planet. It operates at the more intimate, inward level of the human heart—closed to the natural world. It finds its modus operandi in books and liturgy, not in the dangerously pagan, untameable world of animals and plants, mountains and oceans. Modern Catholicism doesn't inhabit nature, it moves through streets and buildings.

This is a great pity because it used to look at the magnificence of the earth and hear it speak of God. It used to find a glimpse of the Almighty in the joy and pain, the fear and wonder of this planet of living forms. But something happened, and the organic nature of faith became contained.

That is why bringing Catholicism to sit at the environmental table does not work. It is more possible these days to discuss how to mitigate climate change, which will (and already is in some places) affect poorer nations disproportionately, adding to the injustice of the rich versus the poor. But it is not possible to engage the Catholic imagination in conservation of species or landscapes—and this, despite Pope Francis's extraordinary and far-reaching encyclical *Laudato Si'*.

There is one paragraph in particular that took my breath away when I first read it:

> It is not enough, however, to think of different species merely as potential "resources" to be exploited, while overlooking the fact that they have value in themselves. Each year sees the disappearance of thousands of plant and animal species which we will never know, which our children will never see, because they have been lost for ever. The great majority become extinct for reasons related to human activity. Because of us, thousands of species will no longer give glory to

God by their very existence, nor convey their message to us. We have no such right. (*LS* 33)

This powerful piece of writing goes from the heart to the
heart. It is unprecedented in its reaching out to other forms
of life on earth and recognizing their inherent value. It is a
passage on a par with the writings of St. Francis, who called
other species his sisters and brothers in a radical revisioning
of our relationship to life on earth. Yet it goes further. It asks
us to care, not because other life is useful to us, but because
"all creatures are connected, each must be cherished with
love and respect, for all of us as living creatures are dependent on one another." And then it has instructions for action:

> Each area is responsible for the care of this fam-
> ily. This will require undertaking a careful inven-
> tory of the species which it hosts, with a view to
> developing programmes and strategies of protec-
> tion with particular care for safeguarding species
> heading toward extinction. (*LS* 42)

This is a clear mandate for the Church to take conservation
seriously and to be involved directly, as part of faith. Yet, this
section of *Laudato Si'* is largely ignored and is rarely ever
referenced.

Over the last ten years, I have been involved in many
events, talks, and conferences on Christianity and nature.
They have all been uplifting and heartening, but ultimately, I
am not sure that they have achieved what Pope Francis has
in mind. They have raised awareness, particularly about climate change, and that is good, of course. Perhaps that is all
that can be done at present. For me, it was time to move on.

I am now working to save the endangered Eurasian
curlew, a bird like the spectacled eider that has no direct

influence on humanity other than bringing joy into the lives of those who listen to its exquisite song bubbling and tumbling over wetlands and moors. This work does not involve the Church. Experience has told me there is no point, not at present anyway. Perhaps Pope Francis is slowly making the Catholic soil more fertile for environmental messages, so that in time to come they will take root, but for now it is low on the religious agenda. I very much hope things will change.

So I will keep doing what I feel is right and keep looking for the path ahead. I always take with me the words at the end of the Mass—"Go in peace to love and serve the Lord." That instruction is my guide along this mountain track that still appears and disappears with infuriating randomness but is undoubtedly there. And I suspect I share with other women in this book the sense that there is no option but to keep on going on, peacefully and determinedly walking our own paths, and bringing our own stories and insights, trusting that they will contribute to a more holistic and inclusive future.

Epilogue

This collection of women's theological reflections and personal stories offers a fleeting glimpse into the abundant diversity of what it means to be a Catholic woman in the modern world. It shows that phrases such as "feminine genius" and "woman's mystery" are obfuscations that mask the reality of what it means to be female and Catholic in the twenty-first century, as women who draw on a rich tradition of Scripture, theology, history, and experience, but who also face unprecedented challenges because of the ever widening gulf between the Catholic Church and modern culture.

Catholic women are often doubly marginalized—by secular feminists and by Church authorities. Yet none of the women in this book have turned their backs on the wisdom of the Catholic tradition, and nowhere is there any uncritical capitulation to the shifting trends of secular culture. Even those who have been too wounded or alienated to continue to practice their Catholic faith remain deeply committed to the wisdom that they find within it. Not all the contributors are campaigning for radical change in Church practice and teachings—though some are. Our intention is not to privilege any single cause or point of view, but to bring many voices into dialogue in the hope that others inside and outside the Church will have their understanding enriched and their vision expanded by what they read.

For most of the women here, the challenges they face are incentives to action and inspire a deepening of faith through resistance, hope, and perseverance. After all, the heart of the Catholic faith is not the male hierarchy but Jesus of Nazareth, a man who loved and suffered and wept and bled as women do, and whose life is communicated and sustained within every individual through the sacramental faith of the Church. It is worth reiterating what McAleese said in her keynote speech to the Voices of Faith conference published in this book:

> Down the two-thousand-year highway of Christian history came the ethereal divine beauty of the nativity, the cruel sacrifice of the crucifixion, the hallelujah of the resurrection, and the rallying cry of the great commandment to love one another. But down that same highway came man-made toxins such as misogyny and homophobia, to say nothing of anti-Semitism, with their legacy of damaged and wasted lives and deeply embedded institutional dysfunction.

For many women writing here, these words explain our reasons for staying in and struggling on.

Catherine of Siena, writing in the fourteenth century, was no stranger to the cultures of bullying, misogyny, and domination that can fester within the Catholic hierarchy. She used colorful language to condemn the priestly abuses of her time, and she was a critical voice of conscience to the pope. She was also a woman who discovered that the love of God is a transformative power that dignifies the human creature with a deep sense of grace and beauty. She writes,

> You, eternal Trinity, are the craftsman; and I your handiwork have come to know that you are in love with the beauty of what you have made, since you

made of me a new creation in the blood of your Son.[1]

For some of the women here, that sense of being the beautiful beloved of God is a sustaining reality; for others it is a promise that must be renewed daily in the face of overwhelming obstacles. Yet even in the darkness and desolation, there is a sense of the God who dances an invisible dance in the margins of time, and who sometimes touches our fingertips in passing and laughs with us in the delight of existence. This book is an invitation to the cardinals and bishops who will gather in Rome for the Synod on Young People, Faith and Vocational Discernment in October 2018: will you join the dance and share with us in the laughter of God?

Notes

1. Catherine of Siena, *The Dialogue*, trans. and intro. Suzanne Noffke (New York: Paulist Press, 1980), 364–65.

The Feast of Saint Luke

Martha Pollard

On St. Luke's Day 2010, I attended a midday Mass at Old Saint Paul's Scottish Episcopal Church in Edinburgh, an Anglo-Catholic Church. The service took place in the Lady Chapel and, of course, included intercessions. I had at that time been experiencing long-term depression, and during the prayers, I was kneeling and shouting silently inside my head, "When will things change?!" Suddenly I felt hit as if by physical force, and a great weight was lifted from me.

On the Saturday of that same week, I went on a day-trip to the Holy Island of Lindisfarne to give thanks to God. I wrote this poem that day about my emotional experiences during my visit there.

The Dance

Today we danced
an invisible dance
and I loved how our fingertips
just brushed in passing
and how our feet twirled
and our arms
reached to the sky.

I knew you had to go
of course
so I was glad when
you let me touch you
my hand against your face
in the intensity of your gaze.

There I saw the laugh within you
the kind of laugh which glories
in wonder and delight
and longs for all the world
to come and join in too.

And as you turned to go I heard you
Wait here for me, you said
for I shall need you in my spirit
and on return I may be weary
and shall need your love
in which to dance.

Contributors

Anne Arabome (Nigeria/USA) is a member of the Sisters of Social Service in Los Angeles, California. She holds a doctor of ministry degree in spirituality from the Catholic Theological Union in Chicago and a PhD in systematic theology from the University of Roehampton in London. She is presently the Associate Director of the Faber Center for Ignatian Spirituality at Marquette University in Milwaukee, Wisconsin. She has published several articles and book chapters on gender and women.

Judith Barwick, LCM (Australia) is a retired nurse, having trained and ministered in general, midwifery, psychiatric, and gerontology nursing in clinical and management roles for over fifty years. Judith has also ministered in pastoral care. She is a member of the religious congregation of The Little Company of Mary Sisters. She currently resides in Melbourne, Australia.

Tina Beattie (UK) is Professor of Catholic Studies at the University of Roehampton in London and Director of Catherine of Siena College—an online college offering courses in gender, theology, and social justice—based at Roehampton. She is the founder and coordinator of Catholic Women Speak. Her main research interests are in the areas of sacramental theology and gender, Marian theology and art, Catholic social teaching, human dignity, and human rights, with a particular focus on women's sexual and reproductive health and rights. She is the author of numerous books, book chapters, and journal articles. Tina is married with four adult children and two grandchildren.

Thérèse M. Craine Bertsch (USA) is a mother of five children and eight grandchildren. An Extraordinary Minister of the Eucharist, lector, and participant in the RCIA, she has a bachelor's degree from Empire State College, a master's in social work from Columbia University, and a doctorate from Adelphi University. Thérèse is a therapist who pioneered AIDS and substance abuse programs and she has also organized retreats and weekly Taizé prayers.

Cynthia (Sam) M. Bowns (USA) has a master of divinity and a certificate in spiritual formation from Catholic Theological Union. A married mother of three, she is additionally certified as a spiritual companion. Sam first recognized her desire to serve as deacon when she accompanied her husband through his discernment and training as deacon. She has advocated nationally for women's restoration to the permanent diaconate in many forums in the United States and abroad.

Julett Broadnax (USA) is an eighty-five-year-old widowed mother of three sons, one of whom died from AIDS and the other as an adult with diabetic complications. She was educated primarily in Catholic academies and universities. After raising her sons, she did volunteer work at parish, diocesan, and community levels. She later discerned a calling to education/training as an Ignatian spiritual director/retreat leader, and she has practiced for the past twenty years.

Melissa Carnall (USA) received her master of divinity degree from Catholic Theological Union in Chicago, Illinois. Upon graduation, Melissa ministered as a pastoral associate in a parish in Chicago before moving to New Orleans, Louisiana, to minister as a hospital chaplain. She currently lives in an intentional Christian community.

Catherine Cavanagh, D.Min (Canada), works as a Catholic high school teacher and chaplain in Ontario, Canada. She has lived in several different countries and Canadian provinces and is profoundly interested in questions of hospitality, belonging, and difference. She engages in social justice advocacy, including calling for greater gender equity in the Catholic Church.

Jessica Coblentz (USA) is Assistant Professor of theology and religious studies at Saint Mary's College of California. She also holds a 2017–19 postdoctoral fellowship from the Louisville Institute.

Her research recently appeared in *Journal of Feminist Studies in Religion* and *Journal of Catholic Higher Education*. She is also a regular contributor to *Give Us This Day* (Liturgical Press). She earned her PhD in systematic theology from Boston College in 2017.

Leslye Colvin (USA) is Communications Coordinator for Catholic Committee of the South's *Gathering for Mission* (GatheringForMission.org). With a range of experience in promoting mission and expanding outreach, she is passionate about encouraging diversity of thought as it relates to those marginalized. She earned an MA in communications from University of Massachusetts, Amherst, a BS from Xavier University of Louisiana, and a certificate in Catholic social teaching. She belongs to Saint Columba Parish in Dothan, Alabama.

Mary Colwell (UK) is a writer, producer, and public speaker on humanity's relationship with the natural world. She produced radio and TV programs for the BBC Natural History Unit, and in 2003, she gave her first talk on faith and the environment at Clifton Cathedral in Bristol. She is the author of *John Muir: The Scotsman Who Saved America's Wild Places* (Oxford: Lion Books, 2014), and *Curlew Moon* (London: William Collins, 2018). In September 2017, she walked the John Muir Trail, 230 miles through the Sierra Nevada in California.

Mary Deepika, SND (India) is a member of the Sisters of Notre Dame in Patna, India. She is Chief Coordinator at North East Diocesan Social Service Society (NEDSSS), Kharghuli, Assam, India. NEDSSS is the social work wing of the Catholic Church in North East India involved in social development activities in seven states in the region. She is also Regional Secretary of CBCI Council for women in North East India, working with the women commissions of fifteen dioceses.

Carolina del Río Mena (Chile) holds a master's degree in fundamental theology from the Pontificia Universidad Católica de Chile and a bachelor's degree in social sciences and information. She is a journalist and teacher in the Santa María Spirituality Centre and a member of the "Circle of the Study of Sexuality and Gospel" at the Manuel Larraín Theological Centre; she also participates in the Teologanda Program for Study, Research and Publication in Argentina. She is the author of the book *Quién soy yo para juzgar? Testimonios de homosexuales católicos* (*Who Am I to Judge? Testimonies of Gay Catholics*) published in 2015, and coeditor of the book *La irrupción de los laicos: Iglesia en crisis* (*The Emergence of the Laity: Church in Crisis*) published in 2011. She is a member of the laity and mother of four.

Ruth Fehlker (Germany) is from Coesfeld, Germany. She studied Catholic theology at the University of Münster (WWU). She trained with the diocese of Münster in pastoral theology and pastoral psychology and has been serving as a parish pastoral worker since 2010.

Mishal Francis (Pakistan/UK) was born in Pakistan and moved to Scotland at the age of fourteen. She gained an MEng in aeronautical engineering and subsequently an MSc in practical theology. She is currently studying for a doctorate in practical theology while working as a youth development worker for the Diocese of Motherwell. She is also a member of the Board of Trustees of Hope Human Development & Welfare Association, a charitable organization supporting Christians in Pakistan.

Madeleine Fredell, OP (Sweden) entered Saint Dominic's Roman Congregation in 1980 and has held different assignments at the local and international levels. She is presently Prioress of the Swedish vicariate. She has degrees in Latin, French, general linguistics, and teaching from Stockholm University; in biblical studies, Greek, and Hebrew from the *Institut Catholique* in Paris, and an MA in contemporary theology from Heythrop College, University of London. She works as Secretary General of the Swedish Justice and Peace Commission.

Astrid Lobo Gajiwala (India) is Director of the Government of India's Regional Organ and Tissue Transplant Organisation and a consultant at the Tissue Bank of Tata Memorial Hospital. She is a member of several Indian and Asian theological associations, and has been published widely on issues of gender, feminism, and family. She has been a consultant to the Catholic Bishops' Conference of India since 1992 and helped to draft their Gender Policy in 2010 and their Guidelines to Deal with Sexual Harassment at the Workplace in 2017.

Gayatri Lobo Gajiwala (India) is the daughter of a Catholic feminist mother and a Hindu father. Between the ages of thirteen and eighteen, she attended an ashram boarding school that did not encourage religious practice but taught the philosophy of its founder, Shri Aurobindo. At twenty-one, she decided to get baptized. Gaya works as a secondary English teacher at Oberoi High School, Mumbai. She writes and performs poetry.

Giulia Galeotti (Italy) is an historian and journalist. She is head of the cultural section of *L'Osservatore Romano* and the author of several books in Italian, some of which have been translated into Spanish and Portuguese. These include, among others, *Il velo. Significati di un copricapo femminile* (*The Veil: Significance of a Female Headdress*) (Editore EDB, 2016); *Storia del voto alle donne in Italia* (*A History of Women's Suffrage in Italy*) (Editore Biblink, 2006); and *Storia dell'aborto* (*A History of Abortion*) (Editore Il Mulino, 2003).

Cristina Gangemi (UK) holds a master's degree in pastoral theology and lay ministry, with a special focus on disability. She is Director of The Kairos Forum, a consultancy for cognitively and intellectually disabled people. She is currently working alongside disabled people, families, parish communities, and the Livability charity, which connects disabled people with their communities. Recently, she has worked with two pontifical councils on issues relating to disability. During the 2012 Paralympic Games, she was a spokesperson for the Christian community and is a national advisor to the Catholic Bishops' Conference of England and Wales.

Cristina Lledo Gomez (Philippines/Australia) is a research fellow for Charles Sturt University's Public and Contextual Theology Research Centre, Australia. Her main areas of research are ecclesiology, maternal feminism, and language. Her current projects are in ecology, migration, and Asian theologies. Her first monograph, *Church as a Woman and Mother: Historical and Theological Foundations*, is published by Paulist Press (2018).

Jeannine Gramick (USA) is a Sister of Loretto. She received a PhD from the University of Pennsylvania and taught mathematics before engaging in pastoral outreach, education, and advocacy for lesbian, gay, bisexual, and transgender (LGBT) Catholics. In 1977, she cofounded New Ways Ministry, a US organization working for justice and reconciliation of LGBT people and the Catholic Church. Her ministry and dealings with Church authorities are documented in the film *In Good Conscience: Sister Jeannine Gramick's Journey of Faith.*

Johanna Greeve (Netherlands) is forty-four years old and lives in the Netherlands. The Netherlands (and Belgium) are infamous for their relatively loose euthanasia policies, which puts her story into context. She says, "I have no titles; my only title is child of God." (Johanna Greeve is a pseudonym.)

Nontando Hadebe (South Africa) is Senior Lecturer at Saint Augustine College in Johannesburg, South Africa. She is Chairperson of the Southern African Circle for Concerned African Women Theologians, a board member of Catholic Women Preach, and a radio presenter at Radio Veritas, a Catholic radio station in South Africa. Her research interests are primarily related to women and Christianity, particularly the Catholic Church in the African context. Her inclusive focus on all women has extended to sexual minorities, particularly lesbians and their experiences of brutalization that have claimed many lives.

Susan Harford (USA) was the cofounder of Jubilee Faithful, a two-hundred-plus Catholic group convened from 2012 to 2014 to use deep listening skills in sessions "On Being Church," expressly to deal with cognitive dissonance triggered by the Vatican investigation of the Leadership Conference of Women Religious in the United States. She is currently an associate of the Religious of the Sacred Heart of Jesus and lives in Virginia, where she is a mother, grandmother, and marketing consultant.

Alana Harris (UK), a married lay Roman Catholic, is a lecturer in modern British history at King's College London specializing in areas related to the history of gender and sexuality, and "lived religion" (including materiality and popular devotion). Her publications include *Faith in the Family: A Lived Religious History of English Catholicism, 1945–82* (Manchester: Manchester University Press, 2013), and *The Schism of '68: Catholics, Contraception and* Humanae Vitae *in Europe, 1945–75* (London: Palgrave Macmillan, 2018).

Maeve Louise Heaney (Australia) is a consecrated member of the Verbum Dei Community, Director of Theological Formation for Ministry at Australian Catholic University, and a member of the formation staff of Holy Spirit Provincial Seminary, Queensland. A systematic theologian, musician, and composer, she has worked internationally, leading schools of evangelization and spiritual exercises. She writes, composes, teaches, and performs on themes of theological aesthetics, fundamental theology, music, and spirituality.

Colleen Hennessy (Ireland/USA) studied Irish and American social policy for ten years and worked for the Irish government for eight years while living in Galway and Kerry. She has an MA in community development from NUI Galway and a BA from Tufts University. She alternates her time between policy writing and freelance journalism. She is a struggling Catholic.

Katie Humphrey (UK) is currently studying for a PhD in theology at Roehampton University and has a specific interest in women and the family in the Catholic Church. She received her bachelor's and master's degrees in theology from Hull University and has come back into education as a mature student. This follows a number of years working in marketing in the charity, education, and corporate sectors, as well as volunteering and working as the youth coordinator and confirmation catechist at her home church in Bedford. Katie currently carries out administrative tasks for the Catholic Women Speak Network, encouraging and sharing dialogue between Catholic women via social media networks and local groups.

Ruth Hunt (UK) has been Chief Executive of Stonewall, the UK's largest lesbian, gay, bisexual, transgender charity, since 2014. *The Tablet* has named her one of the ten most influential lay Catholics in Britain. She holds an honorary fellowship from Cardiff University and an honorary doctorate from the University of Keele.

Ginny Jordan-Arthur (UK) grew up in south Florida, where the Church played a central part of both her faith formation and her social life. She later moved to England to study photography at university. She has led confirmation classes and youth groups and has been involved in national church youth projects. Since 2001 she has worked on university ecumenical and multifaith chaplaincy teams and has also done postgraduate studies in theology. She is married with two young children and still loves taking photographs.

Colette Joyce (UK) is employed as a pastoral assistant in the Diocese of Westminster (London, UK) and is studying part time for a PhD in theology at Saint Mary's University, Twickenham. She is currently Equalities Officer for the Faith Workers Branch of the trade union Unite.

Gertrude Yema Jusufu (Sierra Leone) is Proprietress of Bysee Preparatory School and Day Care Centre in Freetown, Sierra Leone. Founded by her late mother, Bysee School also caters for orphans and needy children. Gertrude trained as a professional teacher and has worked for three decades in primary and secondary education. Her areas of expertise include English and religious and moral education.

Emily Kahm (USA) is a teaching fellow in religion at Augustana College in Rock Island, Illinois. Her academic research focuses on sexuality education in Catholic and other Christian contexts, especially as it affects young adult women, and the intersection of religious education and video games. She lives in Davenport, Iowa, with her spouse, Chris.

Alison Concannon Kennedy (UK) began serving her parish community at the age of twelve by providing the organ accompaniment at Mass. Her continued vocation to sharing "Music as Prayer" inspired her to compose many hymns and meditative liturgical music, and in 1992, she cofounded the Watermead Music and Publishing Apostolate, which she now runs as CEO alongside her work as a pastoral assistant to a busy city parish in Leicester, England.

Contributors

Clare Keogh (Australia) lives in Melbourne, where she is studying for a master's degree in occupational therapy practice. She is a keen musician and manages the La Trobe University Choral Society in Bundoora, Victoria.

Martha Mapasure (South Africa) was born in Zimbabwe two decades ago. She is currently living in South Africa and doing her PhD in gender studies at the University of KwaZulu Natal. Martha holds a master of theology degree in gender and religion from the University of KwaZulu Natal, an honors degree in religious studies from the University of Johannesburg, and a bachelor of theology from Saint Augustine College of South Africa. Martha is a gender activist and also a member of the Circle of Concerned African Women Theologians. Most of her studies and publications are focused on the correlation of gender and religion.

Mary McAleese (Ireland) was the President of Ireland from 1997 to 2011. She was called to the Northern Ireland Bar in 1974 and, in 1975, was appointed Reid Professor of Criminal Law, Criminology, and Penology at Trinity College Dublin. In 1987, she returned to her alma mater, Queen's University of Belfast, to become Director of the Institute of Professional Legal Studies, and in 1994, she became the University's first female Pro–Vice Chancellor. In 2010, she received a master's degree in canon law from the national University of Ireland and, in 2013, a licentiate from the Gregorian University in Rome.

Kate McElwee (USA/Italy) is Executive Director of the Women's Ordination Conference and serves on the leadership circle of Women's Ordination Worldwide. She is based in Rome, Italy.

Cettina Militello, PhD, STD (Italy) has been associate professor at the Pontifical Institute of Sacred Liturgy in Rome and directs the Constanza Scelfo Institute for problems of the laity and women in the Church (Department of the Italian Society for Theological Research). She holds the Chair of Women and Christianity at the Pontifical Theological Faculty Marianum. Her academic interests include ecclesiology, Mariology, women in the Church, and the relationship between ecclesiology and liturgy.

Marion Morgan, OCV (UK) is a full-time carer, active in a city center parish in Bristol, England, and contributes to various publications. She has a BA in theology from Bristol University and a postgraduate diploma in pastoral theology from Heythrop College, University of London. In 2009, she was consecrated by the bishop as a member of the Order of Consecrated Virgins, for those living a vowed life in the world.

Revai "Elizabeth" Mudzimu (Zimbabwe) is a Catholic nun of the Little Children of Our Blessed Lady (LCBL) order studying for her PhD at the University of Groningen, The Netherlands. Her thesis is on "Violence, the Catholic Church, Culture, and Women's Sexual and Reproductive Health and Rights in Zimbabwe." She holds a honors bachelor's and a master's degree in religious studies and education from the University of Zimbabwe and Zimbabwe Open University, respectively. She has extensive experience in working with Catholic women in pastoral ministry, violence, and human rights in Zimbabwe.

Melanie Newbould (UK) is from Yorkshire. She qualified as a medical doctor in 1979 and has worked as a consultant in pediatric pathology since 1992. She also has an interest in medical law and ethics. She became a Catholic in 2012, deciding after twenty years of marriage to join her husband in the Church.

Jennifer Owens-Jofré (Bolivia/USA) is a PhD candidate at Graduate Theological Union in Berkeley, California. She is completing her dissertation on devotion to Our Lady of Guadalupe at a Latinx Catholic parish in Los Angeles, California, identifying its implications for Mariology and ministry. Jennifer coedited *From the Pews in the Back: Young Women and Catholicism* (Liturgical Press, 2009), and her writing has appeared in scholarly and popular publications, including such websites as *Busted Halo*, *Patheos*, and *Sojourners*.

Sara Parvis (UK) was born in Aberdeen, Scotland, and grew up in Edinburgh. She was educated at the Universities of Oxford and

326

Contributors

Edinburgh, where she wrote a PhD on the trinitarian controversies of the fourth century, published as *Marcellus of Ancyra and the Lost Years of the Arian Controversy 325–345* (Oxford University Press, 2006). She is Senior Lecturer in Early Christian History at the University of Edinburgh and a lifelong Catholic.

Sarah Pearce (UK) has been a volunteer prison chaplain for twenty-one years. Having been raised a reluctant atheist, she became a Quaker at the age of thirty-four and converted to Catholicism in 2010. She has three children and five grandchildren.

Sheila Peiffer (USA) is a retired director of religious education, campus minister, and retreat director with an MA in theology. Her husband, Steven, is a retired Methodist minister, and they have four children and five grandchildren. For the past two decades, Sheila has been active in several Catholic reform organizations, including Voice of the Faithful, the American Catholic Council, and the Women's Ordination Conference. She currently serves as President of the Board of Directors of the Women's Ordination Conference.

Anna Kasafi Perkins (Jamaica) is a Jamaican Roman Catholic lay theologian. She is a former dean of studies/lecturer at Saint Michael's Theological College, an affiliated institution of the University of the West Indies (UWI), Mona, Jamaica, and an institute of the Roman Catholic Archdiocese of Kingston. Currently she is Senior Programme Officer, Quality Assurance, serving the UWI Mona Campus and adjunct faculty at Saint Michael's Theological College. Her research interests include faith and popular culture (especially Jamaican Dancehall), gender and culture, quality assurance and enhancement, and business and professional ethics. She is the author of *Justice as Equality: Michael Manley's Caribbean Vision of Justice* (2010), among numerous other publications, and contributor/coeditor for *Justice and Peace in a Renewed Caribbean: Contemporary Catholic Reflections* (2012).

Jeannine M. Pitas (USA) is a teacher, poet, Spanish-English literary translator, and freelance journalist living in Dubuque, Iowa. Her work has appeared in *US Catholic*, *National Catholic Reporter*, and *Presence: A Journal of Catholic Poetry*, and she also writes regularly for the Catholic blog *Vox Nova*. She teaches at the University of Dubuque.

Martha Pollard (UK) was raised as United Methodist, but in adulthood she was confirmed in the Scottish Episcopal Church (SEC). She has been an associate of the Order of Saint Helena since 2011. Shaped by the history of the Roman Catholic and Protestant traditions, she finds her home in the SEC, in liturgy and sacraments, in contemplative prayer, in mindfulness practice and community, and in Catholic Women Speak, by the grace and love of God, through Christ.

Zuzanna Radzik (Poland) is a Catholic theologian who graduated from the Pontifical Faculty of Theology in Warsaw and the Hebrew University of Jerusalem in Israel. She specializes in Christians' relations with Jews and researches Catholic feminism. Zuzanna regularly contributes to the Polish Catholic Weekly *Tygodnik Powszechny* and, in 2015, published *Kościół kobiet* (*The Church of Women*), which highlights feminist efforts in the Catholic Church from various countries and cultures.

Jennifer Reek (USA) holds a PhD from the Centre for Literature, Theology, and the Arts, University of Glasgow, and an MDiv from Regis College, the Jesuit Faculty of the University of Toronto. She is author of *A Poetics of Church: Reading and Writing Sacred Spaces of Poetic Dwelling*, and coeditor of the forthcoming *Thresholds of Wonder: Poetry, Philosophy and Theology in Conversation*. Currently she teaches seminars in Great Books in the Catholic Intellectual Tradition at Sacred Heart University, Fairfield, Connecticut.

Irim Sarwar (USA/UK) is an American of Indo-Pak ancestry now living in the UK. Irim was born Muslim and became Catholic via teaching at a Modern Orthodox Jewish school. She has an undergraduate degree in biology and a master's in education, but has catalogued books in a Dominican priory and now works in quality assurance at an evangelical mission institution that offers research degrees.

Contributors

Margaret Susan Thompson (USA) is a historian at Syracuse University, New York. She holds an AB from Smith College and a PhD from the University of Wisconsin. Most of her recent work has been on the history of American Catholic sisters, on which she has published extensively, including an eighteen-lecture series available from NowYouKnowMedia. She is an associate member of the Sisters, Servants of the Immaculate Heart of Mary of Monroe, Michigan.

Samantha Tillman (USA) recently graduated from the Franciscan University of Steubenville. She writes bad fiction when she isn't working in mental health with trauma survivors. She lives in Pittsburgh, Pennsylvania and enjoys punk rock too much.

Ursuline High School, Wimbledon (UK) is a voluntary-aided comprehensive school for Catholic girls under the trusteeship of the Archdiocese of Southwark. Part of the worldwide network of Ursuline Schools, the school's mission, sense of community, and identity are based on the charism of Saint Angela Merici and the ethos of SERVIAM. The Ursuline aims to develop kind, confident, ambitious young women committed to their faith, able and willing to use the values of their faith to lead a change for the better. Ten Ursuline students aged fourteen, fifteen, sixteen, and seventeen drafted the letter to Pope Francis included in this volume.

Celia Viggo Wexler (USA) is an award-winning journalist and non-fiction author. She is a cradle Catholic whose second book, *Catholic Women Confront Their Church: Stories of Hurt and Hope*, was published in 2016 (Rowman & Littlefield). Her work has appeared in *The New York Times*, *The Washington Post*, the *San Francisco Chronicle*, *Columbia Journalism Review*, and *The Nation*. She graduated from the University of Toronto, where she received the Governor-General's Medal in English Literature, and earned her graduate degree in journalism from Point Park University, Pittsburgh, Pennsylvania.